European Football's Greatest Grounds

ONE HUNDRED MUST-SEE FOOTBALL VENUES

Pitch Publishing
9 Donnington Park
85 Birdham Road
Chichester
West Sussex
PO20 7AJ

Email: info@pitchpublishing.co.uk
Web: www.pitchpublishing.co.uk

First published by Pitch Publishing 2024. Reprinted 2025.

2

A CIP catalogue record for this book is available from the British Library.

13-digit ISBN: 9781801507516
Design and typesetting by Olner Pro Sport Media. Visit www.olnerpsm.co.uk
Printed in India by Thomson Press

This book is printed on environmentally friendly paper.

European Football's Greatest Grounds

ONE HUNDRED MUST-SEE FOOTBALL VENUES

Leon Gladwell

European Football's Greatest Grounds

ONE HUNDRED MUST-SEE FOOTBALL VENUES

38
31
51
77
80
4
81
22
83
66
90
6
72
99
47
92
71
82
48
74
29
20
25

Foreword

One of the toughest lessons an architectural enthusiast has to learn, and accept with good grace, is the near impossibility of seeing everything, of ticking off all the sites and buildings on one's ever-present and ever-growing wish list. Back in the 1990s I recall waiting at Heathrow Airport's Terminal Two and realising that every single one of the destinations displayed on the flight indicator board was home either to a stadium or stadiums that I had visited, or to stadiums that were already fixed on my travel itinerary.

Dozens of them, from Dublin to Dresden, from Moscow to Málaga. And yet so often all I could think of, with unalloyed frustration, were those towns and cities that I knew I would not be visiting, all the stadiums I would not be able to get to, all the stunning grandstands that I would not see in person, for all the usual reasons; time constraints, budgets, deadlines, family commitments, energy levels and more.

What this book reminds us helpless stadiologists, in words and images, is that it is perfectly possible to celebrate idiosyncrasy and decay as fervently as we admire 21st-century design and engineering at its finest.

Which is why I, and indeed all football ground enthusiasts, should be truly grateful to Leon Gladwell for his herculean efforts to reach those locations that myself and others may have missed out on, for whatever reason.

We can happily debate all day over his choice of icons – the superbowls of Amsterdam, Tottenham, Marseille, Milan and Madrid – and will surely never tire of the curios of Brechin, Great Yarmouth, Braga and my favourite Olympic stadium of all, at Stockholm. But here are venues of which I knew nothing, or only a smidgeon, those I am now delighted to be introduced to on these pages. Is there, in European football, a more absurd vanity project than Hungary's Pancho Aréna? Can anyone name a ground more tightly confined than number 74 on Leon's list, shoehorned into the walls of a Georgian castle? And how come I'd missed the wonderful turf bowl at Tiefenfort (number 35), with its rusting barriers and crumbling concrete?

What this book reminds us helpless stadiologists, in words and images, is that it is perfectly possible to celebrate idiosyncrasy and decay as fervently as we admire 21st-century design and engineering at its finest.

That rectangular patch of turf in the centre is merely the excuse for us all to be critics and adventurers, seeking out the obscure, craving spectacle, but above all, appreciating the universality of our favourite game and, as these pages show so vividly, those palpable aspects of our shared European culture and heritage.

I therefore heartily commend Leon for this hugely entertaining and enlightening collation of riches, but also, quietly curse him for reminding me of just how much there is out there, still to be savoured. The thrill of discovery calls to us all. The quest never ends. The list, your list, my list, will grow with every turn of the page.

Simon Inglis

London-based architectural historian Simon Inglis specialises in the heritage of sport and recreation and is best known as the author of *The Football Grounds of Britain* and *The Football Grounds of Europe*, and as editor of the *Played in Britain* series.

Introduction

For every football ground in this book, there are a hundred more worthy of inclusion. And for every hundred, there are a thousand yet to be discovered. Such is the astonishing enormity of the landscape of European football and its innumerable homes, it would take several lifetimes to unpick each and every one of its multicoloured threads.

From the Azorean island of Flores in the west to Baku in the east, from Svalbard in the north to La Frontera in the south, Europe's bottomless appetite for the game knows no bounds. In Germany alone there are an estimated 31,000 football clubs currently competing while in Spain, a ratio of one club to every 2,270 people illustrates just why they are current European champions. Even in the tiniest of communities football is thriving, whether on the Faroe Islands where 26 fabulous stadiums are shared between a population of just 50,000 or in the sleepy Aragonese hamlet of Embid de la Ribera where just a single pitch is sufficient for its 53 citizens.

Europe's football grounds may come in many different shapes and sizes but as the ultimate playgrounds of human expression, they all serve the same purpose. Each and every one will carry the unique identity of its club and community, some in the form of a club badge embroidered on a corner flag, others through a club name picked out in the colours of 20,000 seats. Many have stood for over a century, floodlights guiding generation after generation to the same green rectangle in an ever-changing world. That they coexist with colossal 21st-century arenas of great innovation and technology, sculpted from glass, steel and even repurposed wooden palettes is all part of the rich tapestry. In eastern Europe and Italy especially, many stadiums will appear almost identical, shaped by the same dictating hand and political climate of the time. Then there are those that have nothing other than a spectacular view of an ocean, mountains, urban high-rises or something altogether wackier, aesthetic elements which again provide that club with its identity. We are spoilt for choice.

Football supporters may be fiercely loyal towards their own club's ground but all will recognise and celebrate a 'great' one. In 30 years spent watching football and photographing grounds on the continent, countless conversations with countless fans were had. One question would invariably crop up, 'What is your favourite football ground?' What may sound puerile to some, this immensely important question gave me the seed of an idea which during the interminable months of pandemic lockdown began to gain momentum. In late 2021, life was beginning to regain a semblance of normality and for myself and many others, the freedom to finally be able to travel again appeared to be within touching distance. I began outlining a project focusing on those stadiums, grounds and pitches that best represented the iconic, historic, innovative, scenic and architecturally appealing grounds in Europe. By early 2022 I had compiled a list of over 600. With the help and guidance of football friends, supporters and fellow stadiologists from across Europe, that list was then pared and pruned down to a final 100, a task that was as difficult as it was emotional. By the summer, I was ready to begin.

Like many others with similarly lifelong interests, I can pinpoint the beginnings of my interest in football grounds beyond that of my own club's Portman Road to a few key moments in my formative years. A replica RC Strasbourg away jersey brought home by my father from an overseas work trip. Summer days spent poring over an enormous Philips World Atlas with my maternal grandfather. More hazy summer memories of the España '82, Mexico '86 and Italia '90 World Cups. And a book called *The Football Grounds of Britain* by a football and architectural historian named Simon Inglis. Although many attractive coffee-table picture books on the subject have since been published, none have managed to combine the warm romance and historical insight of Simon's work with the photographic mastery of Dutch football photographer Hans van der Meer. And while I cannot profess to be at the same level as either, this book does attempt to bring both elements together.

In July 2022 I set off on the inaugural journey to Slovakia's Tatra mountains. The shifting sands of European politics and all-out war in Ukraine had already led to an early reshuffling of the pack and further tweaking of the list was required when both Barcelona and the Latvian national team announced their temporary departures from Camp Nou and Dagauvas Stadion respectively. But after 130,000 miles, in May 2024 in the company of my daughter Elle, I finished at Estadio San Mamés on the

Europe's football grounds may come in many different shapes and sizes but as the ultimate playgrounds of human expression, they all serve the same purpose.

banks of the River Nervion in Bilbao. In total 71 trips across Europe were made using only public transport. Most were undertaken in a whistlestop fashion, out on a Friday evening and back by Sunday. Others provided an excuse for my teenage children to see a little of the world while one even became a family holiday. With the exception of that one, all were done on a shoestring budget.

I had visited places I never thought I would see again, typed 1,000 translations in 100 towns and missed last flights out of Sofia and Copenhagen. In Italy, always in Italy, I put my life in the hands of lunatic Neapolitan taxi drivers while in Basilicata, I was given a lift up a near vertical hill in a battered Piaggio Ape. After a stay in a particularly dubious hotel in Croatia, I returned home and was hospitalised for two weeks with suspected meningitis, thought to have been contracted from the swimming pool. Yet for my poor son Noah, nothing compared to the scene in rural Georgia when faced with the prospect of a friendly match not going ahead after a player no-show – he was thrown a kit and told in no uncertain terms to change. Bearing in mind his deep antipathy to anything football-related let alone playing, he did it with good grace and saved the day. Regarding his penalty in the match, my lips are sealed.

On a final note, it should be stated that many of the grounds in this book will almost certainly generate some debate. Those omitted definitely will and that is a good thing. No volume like this could ever be definitive and each and every reader will have their own ideas of which grounds should or should not have been included. However, should it introduce readers to new places or different football cultures then it will have been worth the effort compiling it. All that remains to be said is I hope you enjoy reading this book as much as I did making it.

Leon Gladwell, July 2024

100

Feldstraße

HAMBURG // GERMANY // FC ST. PAULI & SC HANSA 11

We begin our countdown in shadows cast by the rear end of Millerntor's Nordkurve stand. Beloved home of Europe's original and most recognisable cult football club, FC St. Pauli, Millerntor itself is a delightfully unrefined stadium. Cloaked in the club's iconic brown and white colours, it is patinated by years of peeling fan stickers and murals honouring club legends. Our focus however lies barely two metres away. Next door is Feldstraße, a sports ground used by the club's abundance of amateur teams and Hamburg's historic SC Hansa 11 club. To all intents and purposes it is a largely unremarkable and archetypal inner-city setup with two artificial pitches and a lively clubhouse owned and operated by SC Hansa 11.

By beginning here we not only widen the parameters of this project by looking beyond 'just' the football ground itself, we highlight a key element and recurring theme; the concept of the 'football landscape'. What surrounds, abuts or neighbours a football ground will often define its identity and character. An adjacent church spire or distant mountain will in time become as familiar to the regular supporter as their own front door. As such they become an integral piece of that particular football experience, a focal point to lose oneself during particularly tedious matches perhaps. There are many outstanding footballing landscapes across Europe but none quite as immediately gargantuan as Flakturm IV, the Second World War bunker looming over Feldstraße.

In the early years of Hamburg football there were numerous pitches on the vast Heiligengeistfeld exhibition space next to where Millerntor would be built in 1961. FC St. Pauli themselves trace their origins back to the 'Holy Ghost Field'. On a pitch devoid of grass adjoining the original gymnasium of the St. Pauli Turn-Verein, a club named St. Pauli TV entered competitive football in Hamburg's Kreisliga in 1910. That pitch would become the home of FC St. Pauli upon their formation in 1924 and eventually be laid with a grass surface. Meanwhile, the Hansa 11 club had emerged as far back as May 1911 from the Wandervogel hiking movement popular at the time. They too played on the Heiligengeistfeld which in those early days would have resembled London's Hackney Marshes on matchdays. FC St. Pauli soon began to develop their ground but would not have what could reasonably be described as a stadium on the site until after the Second World War.

In 1940 Adolf Hitler had ordered the construction of three colossal flak towers to defend Berlin from air attack. With Allied bombing intensifying over northern Germany, instructions were then sent to build two similar blockhouse towers in Hamburg. Flakturm IV went up on Heiligengeistfeld in 1942, its muscular design consistingof a large gun tower (G-Tower) and a lead or command tower (L-Tower). The L-Tower was quickly demolished at the end of the war but its counterpart would stand empty for many decades, a troublesome and ominous reminder of the past. In 1961 the entirety of Heiligengeistfeld was appropriated by the Hamburg government for the IGA Expo 1963, an international horticultural exhibition that would be visited by 5.4 million people. This forced St. Pauli into relocating a short distance west to land directly in front of the bunker where they would begin modelling the first Millerntor stadium.

Two secondary pitches were laid out in the arrangement we see today. Until recently both still had the original cinder surfaces, replaced in 2009 by artificial grass. When the Nordtribüne was rebuilt in 2015, it concluded a nine-year project in which Millerntor was entirely rebuilt with a new capacity of 29,546. St. Pauli's amateurs, women's and youth teams were given new changing rooms in the recesses of the Nordkurve and a small bar for supporters was opened on matchdays. The presence of FC St. Pauli next door to such a stark fascistic monument is jarring. But in their continued coexistence and the club's great successes on and off the pitch, there is an irony worth celebrating. St. Pauli are a club that since the 1980s have garnered a reputation as a home for those without a home in football. Drawing fans from alternative subcultures and minority groups, their booming fanbase share ideologies centred on social inclusion and political activism. Matchdays are greeted unanimously with raucous abandon. Flakturm IV has recently served as a live music venue while a project to turn the upper section into a public rooftop garden is nearing completion. For the first time the bunker will also receive a memorial for the victims of the Nazi regime and the Second World War. And as far as footballing backdrops go, there are none quite as astonishing as Feldstraße.

In the early years of Hamburg football there were numerous pitches on the vast Heiligengeistfeld exhibition space next to where Millerntor would be built in 1961. FC St. Pauli themselves trace their origins back to the 'Holy Ghost Field'. On a pitch devoid of grass adjoining the original gymnasium of the St. Pauli Turn-Verein, a club named St. Pauli TV entered competitive football in Hamburg's Kreisliga in 1910.

099

Stadion Hristo Botev

BLAGOEVGRAD // BULGARIA // OFC PIRIN BLAGOEVGRAD

Our next journey takes us to a land that time forgot, a country whose three-decade free-fall from the footballing spotlight has left behind a landscape of creaking concrete bowls, haunted by the ghosts of Asparuhov, Kostadinov and Stoichkov.

Failure to capitalise on 1994's World Cup success, oblique attempts to build stable infrastructures and endless rumblings of corruption have all contributed to leaving Bulgarian football in an apparently permanent state of retrograde. For regular fans, the creeping disillusionment of the early 2000s gave way to a full-blown abandonment of the game, huge numbers opting for the comfort of living rooms and matches broadcast from England, Germany or Spain, countries whose own upsurge in popularity during this time represents the very antithesis of Bulgaria's. Those who remained were often the hooligan elements: tribalistic and intolerant of minorities, tarnishing Bulgaria's footballing reputation yet further. On the field, the football declined to virtually unwatchable levels. Low in quality and tactically primitive, the acquisition of unknown African and Brazilian hopefuls whose poor wages were often matched by their abilities proved a cheaper alternative to investing in youth development programmes.

With the national team now knocking around with Honduras and Gabon in the FIFA rankings, funding for the game is virtually non-existent. Communist-era club stadiums from Pleven to Plovdiv stand at the mercy of nature, permeated by the melancholy of the no longer there. Neglected and dangerous, they are often shorn of their seating as rows of rusted brackets point skywards. Austere and without frills when built, they now make great playgrounds for the urban explorer whose photographs become Instagram hits in the realm of dark tourism. Football nostalgists visit from far and wide, seeking an experience redolent of a simpler time where the most elementary act of standing on a terrace is a given. For the outsider, Bulgarian football has become almost exotic, a budget flight away from stepping through a portal into a lost world.

In Blagoevgrad in the south-western corner of the country, OFC Pirin's Stadion Hristo Botev is tucked between the western foothills of the Rila mountains and grey socialist modernist apartment blocks at the edge of the city. A shamrock-green semi-oval built in 1934, tidy, well-maintained and on matchdays spine-tinglingly atmospheric, it is a stadium which bucks Bulgaria's trend of footballing ruin. With a dash of funding and cooperation from the Blagoevgrad municipality, ongoing improvements have kept one of the country's oldest stadiums looking resplendent as it approaches its 100th anniversary. This is where Dimitar Berbatov first played football and while it may only be half the stadium it once was, the quiet modernisation and considered capacity trimming has led to it becoming a blueprint for how to bring the dilapidated eastern European stadium in line with the requirements of the 21st-century game.

In 2008, the old wraparound southern tribune, whose wooden benches and timber framework shook so violently as 17,000 squeezed in for a match against Slavia in 1973, was demolished and the entire side levelled to become a parking area for visiting team coaches and television crews. Situated in the narrowing back streets of Blagoevgrad, years of matchday congestion were at once eliminated while the magnificent vista over to The Cross on its hillside was opened up further, framed by two sky-tickling floodlights. With the capacity dropped to just 7,500, Pirin's regular fanbase of three or four thousand were forced to group together on the northern tribune creating a togetherness which has gone on to serve the team well. This stand, carved into the forested slopes, was built in 1973 to accommodate Pirin's growing legion of fans as the club reached the top division for the first time. A facelift in 2001 saw the wooden benches replaced with green plastic seating, the name 'Pirin' picked out in Cyrillic in white and the gangways painted yellow, further enhancing the unity with the verdant landscape. To the left of this, a buffer zone and an away section for 500 which remains the only terraced area left, complete with crush barriers and above, a curious enclosed gantry for reporters.

Standing guard at the entrance steps leading up into the arena are a pair of typically bombastic communist-era statues, modelled as muscle-bound footballers, one bearing the faint graffiti of a swastika on his chest that no amount of scrubbing has removed. Such reminders of Bulgaria's social and economic problems are, however, few and far between in Blagoevgrad, a provincial city suffused with the liberal dynamism of its university population. On matchdays this carries to the stadium a respectful boisterousness, deafening when the Sofia teams come to town, but safe and enjoyable, much like Stadion Hristo Botev itself.

098

Sportismuscenter

PFARRWERFEN // AUSTRIA // SC IKARUS PFARRWERFEN

With less focus, the pages of this book could easily have been full of images of players kicking balls beneath snow-capped peaks. During its making, I was regularly asked which country's football grounds I enjoyed visiting most. With little time between trips to consider Europe's enormous variety, I would usually babble on about the atmospheres in Polish and Turkish stadiums or the rich history of those in Scotland and Belgium. Only as the project neared its end did I begin to ask myself the very same question. Of course there were experiences I enjoyed more than others.

The warmth of the Portuguese at matches was without exception and always left a lasting impression. Similarly, Germany's affordable football in an assortment of exceptional new stadiums ranks highly. But ultimately, I found the answer to be the same as it always had been.

For ten years and more, Austria had been providing me with football weekends like no other. The deeper into its amateur game I had gone, the more it would give up its charms. In Vorarlberg, Tyrol and Salzburg, there are communities competing in Alpine wonderlands, in small stadiums occupying positions on sky-high plateaus, thousands of metres up in the mountains. The reverse too, football fields worked into the impossibly green carpeted floors of deep valleys surrounded by slopes of edelweiss. Many are equipped with delightfully eccentric modernist buildings, a clubhouse or grandstand perhaps, sympathetic with the notion of Alpinism and designed to coexist harmoniously with the landscape. For the amateur game's supporters, it is about gathering with friends on sunlit summer evenings, halfway up a hillside, quaffing lager and belting out club songs as if in a demented version of *The Sound of Music*.

In Vorarlberg in the west, football grounds are often visible from roadsides as green rectangles among gently undulating meadows, dotted with the onion domes of village churches and a thousand woodsheds. Meanwhile, in the state of Tyrol, the landscape becomes increasingly dramatic with the explosion of the Bavarian Alps. In Tyrolean mountaineering villages, any flat space for football will have been dug by man. But it is in Salzburg that the best elements of both come together to create a network of idyllic valleys and sleepy dead-end offshoots, many overlooked by spectacular snowcapped peaks. Bisecting the state is the Salzach River,

travelling in a west-east direction from Kitzbuhel to the pretty market town of St. Johann im Pongau. From here, it turns north and winds through a series of small towns and villages which, as a result of their close proximity to Salzburg, have a much younger demographic than those further south. Here football life is positively teeming. Very few communities in the northern stretch of the Salzach Valley are without a team, an area that in old-world football parlance would have been described as a 'hotbed'. About halfway up, a cluster of clubs play within a few miles of one another in the verdant foothills of the Tennengebirge Massif, its rugged Dachstein peaks creating a majestic backdrop to each humble football home.

For the amateur game's supporters, it is about gathering with friends on sunlit summer evenings, halfway up a hillside, quaffing lager and belting out club songs as if in a demented version of *The Sound of Music*.

SC Pfarrwerfen's relatively short football history began on 1 October 1972. A year later the club began competing in the Salzburger 2. Klasse Süd, eight levels below the Austrian Bundesliga in the pyramid on a field which still exists ten miles away in the village of Hüttau. During this time, the first incarnation of Sportismuscenter in the centre of Pfarrwerfen was dug, levelled and developed at a cost of around €100,000. Officially opened on 21 June 1974, here the club competed with little success until two successive championships in the early 1990s. This acted as a catalyst for quadrupled spectator presence at games and the need to accommodate them in an environment more suitable for the higher level of football. While the second version of Sportismuscenter was constructed with a spectator grandstand and two new pitches for the flourishing youth teams, the club decamped down the valley to neighbouring Werfen for what was supposed be a six-month arrangement. The scale of the project, however, which involved creating an artificial plateau using hundreds of tonnes of sand, meant Pfarrwerfen stayed on for almost two years.

On 1 January 1999 they returned home, shortly after adding Ikarus to their name in reference to the eight-person mountain gondola lift of the club sponsors Freienweng Railways. Still under the chairmanship of Alois Lottermoser, the club then began extensive negotiations with the community for a brand new clubhouse. Opened during a ceremony on 9 June 2007 for which most of the villagers were present, Pfarrwerfen's home was finally complete after 33 years. Much like the houses and gardens of villages in the Salzach, Sportismuscenter is an immaculately maintained stadium. Located high above the village centre, the views from here are as astonishing as they are far-reaching; to the north, the medieval rock castle Burg Hohenwerfen stands in spectacular isolation and to the south, the spindly spire of the Pfarrwerfen's 12th-century St. Cyriak church. But of course it is the Tennen Mountains which tower over Sportismuscenter that gives us one of Europe's most stunning footballing landscapes. All over Austria there are a hundred others like it. But only at Pfarrwerfen are the mountains close enough to feel like you can reach out and touch them.

For a million Generation X schoolboys, a rubber-banded stack of sticker swaps depicting footballers with appalling hairstyles was a first introduction to a world beyond their chosen clubs. In 1982 the Panini company released their fourth World Cup collection for the tournament held in Spain. This album had two 'special' sections, one focusing on the extraordinary array of stadiums selected (17 – a record number until 2002's 20) and another on the 14 artworks commissioned to represent each host city. Unwittingly those artworks lured myself and doubtless thousands of other pre-teen collectors into a world of fine art, their 'Spanish-ness' giving that tournament another layer of feeling. Heavyweights such as Joan Miró, Antonio Saura and Antoni Tàpies (an artist who years later I would write my dissertation on) were all commissioned but it was Jiří Kolář's design for Elche that was my favourite and still is.

097

Estadio San Mamés

BILBAO // SPAIN // ATHLETIC BILBAO

To represent Bilbao, Basque artist Eduardo Chillida (record price at auction £4.1m) offered a drawing of a single clenched fist raised to meet a football. Within the ball, the words 'Bilbao 82' are repeated countless times. The starkest of all the images produced, the fist represents the Basque people's struggle, the monochrome colour palette that of the city's history of heavy industry. When I eventually made my first visit to Bilbao's original Estadio San Mamés in 1996, that image was what I mentally carried with me. It wasn't much but in those pre-internet days, Panini had given me something.

On 26 May 2010, a piece of turf from the San Mamés pitch and a brick removed from its facade were handed along a chain of people composed of Athletic Bilbao greats, the club's oldest and youngest supporters and members of the youth and women's teams. At the end they were laid on the adjacent construction site where three years later a very different San Mamés would be opened. This simple symbolic gesture was not only characteristic of the Basque, it defined the people's almost unsurpassable pride in the club. Anyone who has been to Bilbao will tell you that very few window balconies are not strung with red-and-white-striped flags, an image repeated with different colours in San Sebastián and Eibar as we will see later on. Indeed, the original San Mamés didn't get its nickname, La Catedral, by accident but rather from its reputation as Bilbao's centre of sporting worship.

From its beloved original red and white wooden grandstand to the majesty of 1953's arched double-decker main stand, until 2013 the San Mamés was revered across Spain as a traditional, intoxicating nest with an appearance more Goodison than Bernabéu. Knowing its loss would register a devastating blow to its people and send poignant ripples out across the continent, only a world-class, 'Elite category' replacement would suffice. By announcing in 2006 that the new stadium would be built on the site of the old Bilbao International Trade Fair, next door to San Mamés' prominent position at the end of the city's main thoroughfare, the Basques were to some extent placated.

However, as the site became an antecedent of the arrangement at the Tottenham Hotspur Stadium – Athletic playing in a stadium slowly being reduced as its all new partner grew up around – fans remained unconvinced. When the time came to move the 100m or so on 16 September 2013, 102 days after the final game next door, the capacity was still only 35,686 and one end remained completely unbuilt. Whether by design, accident or more likely through necessity, that gap left at the eastern end offered Athletic fans for a season a heart-rendering view on to what remained of their old home. During the following year everything was neatly joined up and the San Mamés was soon being filled to its new capacity of 53,331. The brief but thorny issue of the roof not reaching to cover spectators closest to the pitch was resolved, the extension even winning a structural engineering award in 2017, leaving the San Mamés complete and ready for appraisal.

With a cost of €211m (€57m less than Marseille's similarly sized new Stade Vélodrome constructed at the same time), funding came largely from public institutions including the Basque government, Bilbao City Council and Athletic themselves. Architectural needs were met by IDOM, a Bilbao-based company with a finger on the pulse of what makes the city tick. Such was the success of the new San Mamés, it won the title of 'World's Best Sports Building' at the 2015 World Architecture Festival, and soon afterwards Barcelona integrated IDOM into their own design team for the redevelopment of the Camp Nou. From the wavy, titanium clad façade of Frank Gehry's Guggenheim Museum (one of Europe's most iconic buildings just a few streets away) to Munich's Allianz Arena's night-time illuminations, the San Mamés respectfully borrows but manages complete originality. Hovering above the banks of the steel-grey Nervión, filling the sky at the end of Poza Lizentziaturen or seen up close and personal from the vast eastern concourse, its greatest success lies in its visual connection to the city, something many new stadiums struggle with.

Covering the facade, twisting panels of ETFE plastic creates the impression of rhythm and repetition against the fixed individuality of the old buildings in its shadow. The three giant LED screens, surrounded by chunky red frames, break up the pattern on the exterior and serve those outside without tickets while intensifying the lighting as night falls and the stadium is illuminated. Inside everything is pleasingly steep, the stands tilting towards the pitch creating the feel of the old stadium and the sensation of being 'on top of the pitch'. The new San Mamés is a triumph. Athletic have performed an act of delicate surgery. By carefully evaluating the club's relationship to the city, its people and the landscape, they have taken the heart from their home of 99 years and 11 days and successfully transplanted it into their new one. For most fans, it beats just like the good old days.

Ballstad Stadion

BALSTAD // NORWAY // BALLSTAD UIL

On the ferry from Bodø, the Lofoten Islands loom into view as a dark, menacing wall of geological brutality known as Lofotveggen. Uninviting, it is a landscape straight from Jurassic Park.

096

Anyone voyaging beyond Vestfjorden must eventually reach the wall as it arcs out into the Norwegian Sea like a single demonstrative finger. This first impression of the archipelago, especially on days of squally Arctic rain and low visibility, is however deceptive for beyond the Lofotveggen lies a paradisiacal landscape of golden beaches, jagged mountains and majestic fjords.

Just 100 miles north of the Arctic Circle, one could be forgiven for thinking that this is where football in the Northern Hemisphere ends. But of course football stops for no man. A few hundred miles up the road is Tromsø, city to one of Norway's top clubs; 300 miles north of Tromsø, towns and villages in Finnmark are dotted with football pitches and small stadiums. And even beyond continental Europe, on Svalbard in the Barents Sea there are football pitches: in Ny-Ålesund, a village with a population that fluctuates between 35 and 117, there is a pitch believed to be the most northerly in the world. Further proof then that football is indeed the global game.

In the Lofoten Islands, football has been a mainstay of its fishing communities for over a century, a pastime allowing fishermen to unwind on dry land at weekends with their families watching.

With a population of just 24,500, it is surprising that across its seven main islands there are ten teams playing and that one of them, FK Lofoten, actually competed in Norway's second tier in 1999.

In the Lofoten Islands, football has been a mainstay of its fishing communities for over a century, a pastime allowing fishermen to unwind on dry land at weekends with their families watching. With a population of just 24,500, it is surprising that across its seven main islands there are ten teams playing and that one of them, FK Lofoten, actually competed in Norway's second tier in 1999. Nowadays Lofoten's teams are spread between the regionalised fourth and fifth divisions of the Norwegian football league system where they will often meet their second 11. Ballstad UIL currently play in the fifth division.

In the centre of the archipelago lies the island of Vestvågøya, its landscape strangely prairie-like as the E10 winds through its centre. The village of Ballstad is located on a tiny island off its more mountainous south-western tip. Enveloped by the spectral Skottinden mountain to the west and rolling hills to its east, its mild waters, warmed by the Gulf Stream, have always proved fruitful for its fishermen. In the centre of the village stands the enormous Ballstad Slip, a covered shipyard upon which is painted one of the world's largest murals and appropriately sponsors of the local football team. Since the club's inception in 1923, football has always been played on the same piece of land just to the north of the bridge which links the village. In those early days, the pitch was grass which over time was patched up with gravel. By the end of the 1960s, so much patching had been done that the surface was entirely covered in gravel, a situation which left players and officials with enormous preparatory tasks before each game.

But in the summer of 2008, Ballstad Stadion's pitch was finally replaced with a high-quality artificial surface, similar to the one at Aspmyra Stadion in Bodø back over the water. The relief among the players and supporters was overwhelming as it signalled an end to the pre-match trips to the village shipyards to gather sawdust to mark the lines. No more trench-digging around the pitch to drain surface water. And on icy days, no longer would players need to get their boots spiked at the local car workshop using the same nails used for winter snow tyres. Such scenarios, played out all across the islands, reflect the Nordic spirit, unshakable in the face of extreme weather and hardship.

Across the world, amateur football has always been a community effort, its survival dependent on levels of great will and resource. When over 1,000 people saw the first game on the new pitch, a friendly against professional side Bodø/Glimt, it was a just reward for the people of Ballstad's 85 years of effort. Over the next five years, various buildings were erected: a new kiosk, fencing and changing rooms. In the south-eastern corner of the pitch, a decommissioned lighthouse was placed. It is hard to escape Nordic mythology in Lofoten with its population of fjord trolls and mountain beasts and from the little lighthouse, Ballstad's club mascot Stormåsen emerges from his home on matchday, punching the air to the tune of 'Gje mæ en B!', the club anthem. A row of flares are then lit and the valley fills with orange smoke, the colour of the fishermen's raincoats adopted as the club colours in the 1950s. In this landscape of such staggering beauty, it is a hypnotic scene – all the trimmings of matchday experience at a much larger stadium but in miniature. Ballstad finally has its 21st-century stadium. It may be modest but it will give its people many memorable afternoons for years to come.

096 // Ballstad Stadion

BALLSTAD // NORWAY // BALLSTAD UIL

The Stanks

BERWICK-UPON-TWEED // ENGLAND // BERWICK CHARITIES CUP

095

In 21st-century black American pop culture, the word 'stank' has been appropriated to describe music of a particularly funky nature, a 'stankface' the expression on the face of someone grooving hard on it. In old Scottish and northern English dialects, however, a stank is a pool or a pond. In the old garrison town of Berwick-upon-Tweed there are many of these long-drained moats set below its 16th-century defensive ramparts built to keep out marauding Scots. As football seasons across the continent draw to a close, Berwick's The Stanks becomes home to one of Europe's most idiosyncratic and public-spirited football tournaments.

With the unique status of being a competition that brings teams from England and Scotland together, games in the Berwick Charities Cup are played with an old-world sense of spontaneity. Raffle prizes sit on the embankment, an ice-cream van arrives at half-time and teams with the names of outlying villages and pubs come up against those with the downright preposterous, Murder-On-Zidancefloor a particular favourite. As it has done for over 100 years, everything takes place on a single pitch which justifiably lays claim to being one of the most remarkable in existence.

Berwick's walls were largely rebuilt during the reign of Elizabeth I in a style borrowed from Italy. Bastion towers with walls up to 6ft thick were constructed at regular intervals allowing gunfire between each stretch. It is possible to walk a section of the Lowry Trail along the very top of the walls, a roughly circular route of one and a quarter miles which passes above the four entrance gates into the town. During his stays at the Castle Hotel, L.S. Lowry painted over 30 scenes of Berwick-upon-Tweed. But for an artist synonymous with football scenes of yesteryear, only one known sketch of The Stanks was produced and never developed into a painting. It remains unknown as to whether he sat upon the grassy earthwork on top of Brass Bastion to make his drawing. Certainly it is the preferred spot for younger spectators nowadays. Regardless, watched by a crowd upwards of 500 as most games were back then, it is reasonable to assume Lowry would have been wholly enraptured by the scene in front of him.

In 1915 the *Berwick Advertiser* reported on a tie between Berwick Rovers and a Royal Scots regimental team. Its words evoke not only a sense of the time but the importance of the role the Berwick Charities Cup played in people's lives, 'Without doubt a larger crowd has never gathered at The Stanks.' It continued, 'The excellent sum of £8 10 shillings was raised (for the Berwick Queen's Nurses).' Fundraising for health services continued throughout the 1920s and 30s as teams competed for the Berwick Infirmary Cup, this despite the threat of bans from the Football Association for playing 'unofficial football'. In the North East Film Archive at Teesside University there is grainy footage of the 1929 final being played in front of thousands of spectators. Sat on the embankments and stood along the touchlines, moustachioed men wearing oversized caps play up to the camera as ladies in cloche hats turn away bashfully. Infants in perambulators are lined up on the flat space next to the pitch. The football is largely played in the air, the pitch with enormous grassless areas not conducive to the passing game. It is likely that The Stanks had been recently used to drill Berwick's army reservists or to host an educational travelling show popular at the time.

Although the tournament may have lost much of its appeal in the modern world, it is still organised each year with the same benevolent principles it began with. Clubs from across the border still compete but with the radius for entrants now limited to a maximum of 20 miles, the once thrilling Anglo-Scottish angle has been diluted to become virtually non-existent. As for The Stanks, nothing has changed. Players continue to enter the field through an ancient gateway under the walls, a strong candidate for football's original player tunnel. On the western touchline space between the pitch and 6m-high stone wall is still so tight that even now it poses problems for any player attempting a run-up for a throw-in. Behind the northern goal the Brass Bastion continues as a bulwark against wayward shots in the same way it has for over a century. In a town that is one of the most disputed in Europe, there can be no dispute that The Stanks is one of the strangest and most delightful football fields on the continent.

Only one known (Lowry) sketch of The Stanks was produced and never developed into a painting. It remains unknown as to whether he sat upon the grassy earthwork on top of Brass Bastion to make his drawing.

Arena Garibaldi - Romeo Anconetani

PISA // ITALY // PISA SC

Over 30 years since the circus left the peninsula, shadows cast from the 1990 World Cup continue to darken the corridors and boardrooms of Italian football, haunting its progress. From Palermo to Verona, Italy's football stadiums are lived in and worn out, more decrepit as the seasons roll by and the halcyon days of Maldini and the San Siro, of Gascoigne and *golazzo* recede further into memory. Italia '90's legacy is such that it weaves its way into several stories in this book plus a thousand others that are not. Its persisting weight has both crippled Italian football while simultaneously ushering in a nostalgia for days of untethered Ultras and shoulder-to-shoulder terrace camaraderie. As Italian football flounders and falls behind its peers, its playgrounds have become magnets for visitors from across the world, lured by a grubby glamour lost from the game elsewhere.

With few exceptions, Italian stadiums are municipally owned, built with public money at a time when the fashion was to create simple elliptical stadiums for an assortment of sports. Italia '90's stadium renovation programme may have left us with a handful of the boldest and most iconic stadiums in world football, but it came in 84 per cent over budget in a decade in which Italy had one of the highest levels of public debt in the world. The subsequent salad days of Italian club success only served to mask the impending collapse which in the 21st century is here for all to see: in 2019, the matchday revenue of Spain's big three was 138 per cent greater than that of Juventus, Inter and Milan in Serie A, while England's top trio brought in as much as 114 per cent more. Italian clubs have become suffocated by their stadiums, crying out for help while municipalities, many still burdened by debt, remain fearful of repeating the same mistakes.

Italian clubs have become suffocated by their stadiums, crying out for help while municipalities, many still burdened by debt, remain fearful of repeating the same mistakes.

094 // Arena Garibaldi - Romeo Anconetani

PISA // ITALY // PISA SC

On the face of it, Pisa Sporting Club's Arena Garibaldi is on a different plane altogether to those used for Italia '90, having more in common with the bygone stadiums of fellow drifters Ascoli and Vicenza. Had it been upgraded from its status as 'reserve stadium' for the tournament, we would have been talking about a very different ground today. Instead, it remains unsightly and unkempt having altered little in over 60 years. Its design is as simplistic as its neighbour over the road is ornate. Across Europe, modern arenas dominate skylines yet Pisa's version is lost in the city's backstreets, obscured from view by modest apartments and stone pines. If you weren't looking for it, you'd likely miss it altogether. First-time visitors to the Leaning Tower can often be heard grumbling over its height having believed it to be taller than it is. Those coming for a look at Arena Garibaldi, especially if harbouring memories of Dunga, Vieri, Simeone or Tardelli, are just as likely to be overcome by Paris Syndrome too when faced with its jumble of peeling doorways, liberally stickered by Ultra groups, its damp-streaked concrete and coils of barbed wire.

So just how has Arena Garibaldi found its way into a top 100 of the greatest grounds? It's all about its matchday transformation cooked up by the small provincial cult the club have become. Even the most basic platform can become a theatre in the right hands and when Curva Nord fills, Arena Garibaldi becomes the aural equivalent of pouring popping candy into your ears. Filthy and outmoded maybe but few Italian stadiums carry the noise and colour of the 1990s kicking and screaming into today quite like Arena Garibaldi.

A mere 250m from Piazza dei Miracoli's four UNESCO wonders, the spot which would eventually become Pisa's primary football ground had already been home to a miscellany of Pisani entertainment for over 100 years. A photograph taken from the tower in the early 20th century shows an amphitheatre surrounded by high walls beyond which Tuscan vineyards roll off towards the horizon on as yet undeveloped land. It lays dormant awaiting its next chapter, the grass field within the oval worn bare from a century of horse racing and open-air theatre events. At the same time on the banks of the Arno River, Pisa had been playing matches since their formation in 1909 at Piazza d'Armi, the city's army barracks where a ghostly oval-shaped imprint of the ground still exists to this day, partly covered by military buildings a stone's throw from the Guelph Tower. It is worth mentioning that across the railway line from here, squeezed in between the ancient crenellated walls of Cittadella Vecchia, ASD Freccia Azzurra's fabulously historic Campo Sportivo Abetone represents another branch of Pisa's footballing family tree.

The club purchased the abandoned hippodrome in 1919, playing a test match on 4 May against eternal rivals Livorno where its shortcomings as a football ground were immediately laid bare. Devoid of any spectator facilities, thousands jammed the touchlines, necks craned for the merest glimpse of the action yet it would take a further 12 years before the arena acquired its grandstand. By 1931, Italy was under Mussolini's rule and the stadium, now known as Campo del Littorio in reference to Stile Littorio, an architectural language developed under the fascist regime, had become the property of the municipality. Federigo Severini, dilettantish dabbler of the arts and the architect who would have the single greatest impact on the appearance of modern Pisa, was drafted in to design a simple, single-tier structure with wooden steps which was opened to the public on 8 October 1931. Other than the postwar name reversion back to Arena Garibaldi on 13 July 1947, little changed for almost three decades; the Curva Nord went up in the late 1950s and was soon followed by its opposite number. Then, in keeping with stadium fashions across the country, all existing structures were joined in 1978 to return the stadium to its ovate shape while expanding its capacity to 35,000. Finally, under the ownership of Romeo Anconetani in 1982, Severini's old grandstand was renovated and reroofed as Pisa ushered in another stint in Serie A, one which would begin a golden era of six of the next nine seasons at the top.

Plans to reconstruct Arena Garibaldi have been floated over the years, including one in conjunction with a takeover by an American billionaire. It reimagines the old girl as a clean, white, contemporary cube capable of holding 18,000 in four single-tiered stands. The design cleverly juxtaposes a modernity with Piazza dei Miracoli's white stone and grey marble facades and would undoubtedly suit the club's size and status as yo-yoers between Series A and B. Yet for the thousands who wave their Republic of Pisa flags there is an ambivalence, a deep-rooted loyalty to their threadbare home conflicting with the club's desperate need to update. A familiar story for many fans whose club have moved on to pastures new of course but for the Pisani and their sense of independence, it is felt particularly acutely. Something will have to give in the coming years but before that sorts itself out, Arena Garibaldi still gives us the opportunity to party like it's 1999.

A mere 250m from Piazza dei Miracoli's four UNESCO wonders, the spot which would eventually become Pisa's primary football ground had already been home to a miscellany of Pisani entertainment for over 100 years.

093

Newlandsfield Park

GLASGOW // SCOTLAND // POLLOK

From a pool of over 20 historic Scottish Junior football homes, we arrive at a spot three miles south of Ibrox and four and a half south-west of Celtic Park. Glasgow's Southside swims with footballing history. Nestled in a leafy suburban cul-de-sac less than two miles east is the Hampden Lawn Bowling Club, where Scottish football's original home once stood.

A few streets south of there are the ghostly remains of the Third Lanark club's Cathkin Park and then Hampden, that unsightly cathedral of the Scottish game. Newlandsfield Park was until recently urban Glasgow's greatest surviving bastion of the Junior game, a ground feared by visiting fans and cherished by traditionalists. In over a century of football in the Junior ranks Pollok had developed a reputation as one of its strongest sides, three times holders of the prestigious Scottish Junior Cup and winners of numerous league championships. Through their successes on the pitch the club built an enviable fanbase from the neighbouring suburbs of Pollokshaws and Shawlands, supporters that continue to come despite Pollok's 2020 defection into Scottish football's pyramid system.

As a plethora of Junior parks fall further into decline, Newlandsfield gracefully succeeds in straddling the old world and the new. Quirks are bountiful within its tight confines and you may just spot a palimpsest of a long forgotten advertisement abutting the all-new Lok's Bar. The 21st century catches up with all football grounds eventually, however, and inside the Lok's Bar function room, the picture window overlooking the pitch nowadays has a curtain pulled across it during matches. Sold off and redeveloped as a private concern (a telling reminder of the hardships faced by small football clubs in an era of cheap High Street drinking chains), the owners work with the club on matchdays and help with catering provisions. But the agreement is that curtains remain drawn and no one gets a free view!

Pollok arrived at Newlandsfield having secured a lease for just £10 per year in time for the start of the 1928/29 season. Adjoining the site's western boundary at the time was the Newlands Tram Depot, which had stood since replacing the Newlandsfield Bleach Works in 1910. The tram

Pollok arrived at Newlandsfield having secured a lease for just £10 per year in time for the start of the 1928/29 season. Adjoining the site's western boundary at the time was the Newlands Tram Depot, which had stood since replacing the Newlandsfield Bleach Works in 1910.

depot and subsequent Corporation bus garage would remain the club's closest neighbour until Glasgow's cessation of tramcar operations in the early 1960s led to its closure in 1968. Nowadays the ubiquitous supermarket occupies the site. Before settling into Newlandsfield, however, Pollok had led a somewhat nomadic existence but one always within a stone's throw of their ultimate destiny. From their foundation at a meeting of the Pollokshaws Working Lads Club on 1 July 1908, they began life at a ground named Haggs Park set within the estate of Pollok House. Then the seat of the Stirling-Maxwell family, the football club took not only its name from the house but its black and white colours from its coat of arms.

Sir John Stirling-Maxwell's influence during Pollok's formative years is immeasurable. Gifting the land to the club he then found them a new home when the club were left homeless following the requisition of Haggs Park by the Glasgow Education Authority towards the end of the 1926/27 season. Stirling-Maxwell arranged for use of a pitch in Auldhouse on the proviso that the club take up amateur status. Pollok accepted and while nothing came of it they were able to begin the next season at the Queen Mary Tea Gardens in Spiersbridge. Spending 1927/28 hopping between Spiersbridge and Shawfield Juniors' Rosebery Park, Pollok finally moved in to Newlandsfield on 3 August 1928.

Of all the club's former and temporary homes, only Haggs Park remains in use for football, now under the name Nether Pollok Playing Fields. Such is their spiritual attachment to the place, in 2018 Pollok returned to use the facade of Pollok House as a photographic backdrop for the online unveiling of their new crop of summer signings. The Spiersbridge ground made way for a fitness centre on the edge of Rouken Glen Park while Rosebery Park became another of Glasgow's finest Junior enclosures until Shawfield's demise in 1960. Close to Cathkin Park, Roseberry Park limped on into the 1990s when after the discovery of chrome contamination from nearby factories it was demolished. The site is now covered by the 2011 extension of the M74 motorway.

Pollok took ownership of Newlandsfield in 1946. The Bleachers Association had named a price of £4,850, a cost met through a loan of £4,000 from the Pollokshaws Co-operative and club members paying a £1 levy in addition to their fees. To swell the coffers further, clubs from across the UK were contacted for help. Those who replied include Alloa Athletic, Motherwell, Hibernian and Portsmouth. A donation was even received from the Shawlands branch of the Communist Party. By the end of the 1940s a pavilion had been constructed and in Newlandsfield's north-west corner it still serves as a storage unit for the groundskeeping equipment. The pitch was until 1958 a surface of black ash which according to a report in the *Evening Times* on 12 July 1958 left players looking like 'miners just off a shift'. Behind the terraced enclosure, the notorious and only accessible gents public toilet was until 2020 a brick wall next to where the pie hut queue formed. With no handwashing facilities it was a place of dubious hygiene but good humour.

The wisecracking and witticisms are what make the non-league game in Scotland so special and under Newlandsfield's corrugated iron enclosure there is always an abundance on offer. It is both a time capsule and a home for the future, beautifully maintained and an attractive alternative for those falling out of love with the professional game on their doorstep.

092

Yahya Kemal Spor Kompleksi

ISTANBUL // TURKEY // YAHYA KEMAL 1976 & ÇELIKTEPE ÜMITSPOR

For the fan of the urban football landscape, nowhere offers quite the same scope as Istanbul. As the most-populated city in Europe it has long since exhausted its once plentiful open spaces forcing the northern half especially to expand vertically towards the heavens. So densely packed are ten of Istanbul's 39 districts that their combined population is larger than those of 22 European countries including Denmark, Croatia and Slovakia. Far from the madding crowds of the Blue Mosque and Galata Tower, in northern neighbourhoods minarets scuffle for space with brightly painted mid-rises. Dilapidated *gecekondu* houses sit in shadow beneath new skyscrapers of mirrored glass and steel. Stir into the mix Istanbul's topography of having been built across seven hills, and the crowded up-and-down streets can dizzy the senses to the point where ducking into a coffee shop for some respite is sometimes the only option.

Legacies created by international tournament successes can often be difficult to gauge. Turkey's, however, is a little clearer. From the moment they emerged from the darkness to reach the World Cup semi-finals in 2002, city councils from Çanakkale to Iğdır embarked on an unceasing provision of amateur sports facilities for their communities. Between 2002 and 2010 Istanbul's Special Provincial Administration (now the Governorship of Istanbul) constructed a staggering 72 new sports facilities for its districts. Turkey's relentless building of major stadiums is well-known, but for the 446 Istanbul clubs playing the game below the top four divisions, they are all now able to enjoy the benefits of a multitude of well-equipped new grounds. Aerial imagery of Istanbul is proof of this. Hover your mouse over any neighbourhood and amid a sea of terracotta roofs there will always be an abundance of tiny green squares. In the densely populated district of Kâğıthane at the far northern end of the Golden Horn, no fewer than eight such facilities have been constructed in the past 20 years.

One of those lies a few miles south of Galatasaray's new Ali Sami Yen Stadium in a valley created by a tributary of the Kâğıthane Creek. Although the creek is mostly culverted nowadays, it once fed a nearby paper mill from which Kâğıthane took its name. Land on the valley floor is narrow here and it took a fair amount of shoehorning to squeeze in the Yahya Kemal Spor Kompleksi. The new facility had been commissioned by the Governorship of Istanbul in 2010 and like so many Turkish seats of learning and community buildings across the country, it would be named in honour of poet Yahya Kemal Beyatlı. Built between 2011 and 2013 on land that had lain empty for two decades, its cost was 12 million Turkish lire (approximately €350,000). For this the citizens of Kâğıthane received an Olympic-size indoor swimming pool, a basketball court, two gymnasiums and a football field with a covered grandstand for 1,313 spectators. Not a bad return by anyone's standards.

Although the Nurtepe Stadi two miles south-west remains the preferred stadium for the district's better-supported-clubs, Yahya Kemal 1976 and Çeliktepe Ümitspor both call the Yahya Kemal Spor Kompleksi home. I watch the latter take on a team from the Eyüp neighbourhood in group 11 of the Istanbul first amateur league. The tiny television gantry on the halfway line is locked up and with a 10ft mesh fence between spectators and pitch on the northern aspect, I am invited to take photographs from next to the away side's dugout. Here I discover from the team manager that his youngest is a member of the Sporting Braga squad in Portugal, a club I would visit two weeks later. Not for the first time on my European travels I am struck by the smallness of the football world.

From this side of the stadium, the view beyond the on-field action is unsurpassable. Just as at SüperLig club Fatih Karagümrük's Vefa Stadi 10km south, apartment buildings of every shape and colour are sardined perpendicular above the grandstand. Above the lot, the sparkling domes and twin minarets of the Yahya Kemal Cami, one of three mosque complexes visible from the ground. Around 200 have made their way down the hill from the match from the fetid streets above. Most congregate in the stand, snapping and spitting sunflower seeds, the snack of choice for any supporter watching the game in more favourable climes. Many of Istanbul's inner-city football grounds are comparably confined but here more than at any other, the landscape falls into place that little bit better.

Between 2002 and 2010 Istanbul's Special Provincial Administration (now the Governorship of Istanbul) constructed a staggering 72 new sports facilities for its districts.

Sportpark Strijp

EINDHOVEN // NETHERLANDS // RKVV BRABANTIA

It is wholly fitting that the Netherlands' capital of design should have a football complex as radical in appearance as Sportpark Strijp. Innovation and creativity is ingrained in the spirit of Eindhoveners who live, work and party among the factories and laboratories which changed the face of world technology in the 20th century. The Philips company made superfluous the styptic pencil, banished awkward car journeys and spawned a generation of living room movie buffs with its electric shavers, car audios and videocassette recorders. Unwittingly, Philips even managed to infiltrate early hip-hop culture for what else would LL Cool J have carried on his shoulder if not the cassette tape boombox?

Years before Sportpark Strijp pinged on my radar, I watched a game at PSV's Philips Stadion on a bitterly cold December evening. Jan Vennegoor of Hesselink was playing for the home side, a player who once struck fear into parents from Hull to Glasgow upon hearing their kids' request for the Dutchman's name on the back of replica shirts. Shortly before kick-off, a ring of overhead heat lamps sprung into life and began thawing out supporters below. I had never experienced such luxury at a football stadium before. What I didn't know then was this is just the Eindhoven way: a little sophistication here, a little fun there. Ingredients that would go into the making of the city's most contemporary sporting venues.

Fanning out from the city centre from nine to half past ten, the district of Strijp begins with the steely shimmer of the Philips Stadion and ends just beyond the airport. It incorporates Strijp-S, the former 'Forbidden City', a wedge of industrial buildings once only accessible to Philips employees. Today, the old factories have been repurposed as creative workspaces and its centrepiece Klokgebouw has become the main event space during Dutch Design Week. Further out beyond the ring road is Sportlaan, a green space upon which football has been played for as long as anyone can remember. In its centre stands the candy-striped tubes of Sportpark Strijp, an absolute head-turner set against the sober Dutch-orange brickwork of the surrounding residential streets. Those unaware of its purpose may wonder whether it is an art installation, something in the manner of Gene Davis's Colour Field paintings perhaps. Others have mistaken it for a theme park, a tangle of swimming pool flumes and even a confectionery factory. What influences designers LIAG really absorbed may never be known but the Hague-based group certainly channelled their inner Willy Wonka and delivered on their claim of 'Architects of Happiness'.

In 2006 RKVV Brabantia were in need of a break. A knock-on effect of Strijp's gentrification was that many of its inhabitants had left for the ever-expanding suburbs, leaving club membership at an all-time low. As much a cog in Eindhoven's football machinery as PSV and FC Eindhoven, Brabantia had competed at amateur levels on Sportlaan since 1936. They even played a single season in 1954/55 in the Eerstedivisie, now the Eredivisie and top flight of Dutch football, where a Sportlaan crowd of over 2,000 saw the newly professional side beat Sparta Rotterdam in their opening match. Despite notable victories over Heerenveen and Heracles that season, they would eventually be relegated back into the amateur ranks. Still playing out of the same old wooden pavilion in 2006, heated by a single circular stove around which many tall tales had been told, the situation was such that there was more chance of the club disappearing for good rather than returning to those giddy heights.

A knock-on effect of Strijp's gentrification was that many of its inhabitants had left for the ever-expanding suburbs, leaving club membership at an all-time low.

The lifeline came when Eindhoven's city council announced plans for a new school, the Christiaan Huygens College, to be built on the eastern edge of the sports park. A working group made up of club members was quickly assembled to demonstrate the need for Brabantia to stay put on the land to which their DNA is anchored. A harmonious relationship was forged and over the coming years many potentially thorny issues were successfully resolved including the loss of land for pitches and the local residents' demands to retain the historic 'Tree Lane', an avenue of trees which bisects the site. No fewer than 176 architects submitted designs for the new sports park with six making the final cut. Brabantia and the municipality came together with local residents, the new school and the Rust Roest korfball club, and awarded the contract to LIAG. In 2012 the new Sportpark Strijp was officially opened and the club justifiably purred over their new home, 'It is of unprecedented allure! An architectural triumph that extends far beyond Strijp and appeals to the imagination of many.'

From above, four football pitches are locked in like Tetris blocks around an L-shaped central hub. The upper stem of the L is fashioned as a capsule-shaped grandstand facing out over the show pitch, its curved rear wall striped in Brabantia red and blue. At the intersection, the glass-fronted club bar, restaurant and events rooms lead into the arm of the L, an indoor sports hall with a rounded facade striped in an abstract rainbow of colours. The whole top floor rests upon a base clad in artificial grass from which a curious arrangement of porthole windows peep out. Hidden away inside are the dressing rooms and club offices so that the overall effect is that the colourful tubes are 'floating' above an ocean of green. More than ten years on it is ageing well. Moreover, in a country of lookalike stadiums, it remains one of a kind. The real success, however, is that it has caught the imagination of the young. Kids from far and wide want to play at Strijp and Brabantia's junior numbers are booming. After so many years in the wilderness, Brabantia's future is bright: its future is striped.

Stadion Skala

GARA BOV // BULGARIA // ZENIT TSEREVO

Throughout the pages of this book we will hear of dreams being turned into reality, whether of the grand architectural variety or just those of a few local people dreaming of moving mountains for the sake of football. Often literally. Sheer bloody-mindedness in the face of geographical obstruction just to see football united with nature is another recurring theme. That such dreams are often met with fierce opposition or scoffing disbelief makes their realisation all the more remarkable.

The story of Gara Bov's Stadion Skala (literally Rock Stadium) is one that touches upon elements of all of these. It is one that bears similarities with Stadion Kantrida in Croatia where the unbending vision of a few amateur runners saw an old quarry repurposed as a beautiful football ground. Although 70 years its junior and much less a stadium in the true sense, Stadion Skala was the brainchild of former Gara Bov mayor Grigor Lyubenov. Tasked in 1983 with building a new football ground, Lyubenov made his intentions clear from the outset, 'The football-loving Bovčani people will have a football ground to be proud of. And they will have it within a year.'

As the Iskăr river had risen throughout the 1970s, so had the need for something new. Regularly flooding the club's bare bones village ground (built on the site of a former slaughterhouse 53 years earlier), the Iskăr runs at its wildest here as it makes its way north to meet the Danube. Lyubenov's predecessor had made tentative steps five years earlier, purchasing land in nearby Mezgiovica. But for the mayor this didn't have the required aesthetic appeal and to this day sits

undeveloped under the ownership of FC Minyor Bov. Two further sites were rejected out of hand before he cast his eyes over the old quarry pit on the eastern fringe of Gara Bov.

From the outset, Lyubenov was told the project was doomed to fail. His colleague Milko Stanchev, then the mayor of nearby Svoge, attempted to dissuade him citing the scale of the project as one too great for a village with a population of fewer than 1,000. The villagers too were bemused. Worn down by decades of hardship the collective mindset was one typical of the region, 'We must not build anything new. We cannot just sweep away what we have built in the years before.' Even the Bulgarian Football Association scoffed at the audacity of the idea. But Lyubenov would not be moved. Two years earlier the Ministry of Forestry had corrected the course of the River Selska which flowed alongside the now obsolete quarry and into the Iskăr. This work had included the construction of a huge fortification dyke to prevent the Selska from dragging 1,000 cubic metres of abandoned quarry rock down into the village. In Lyubenov's mind, half the work had already been done for him.

Looking down into the canyon from the small bank of seating, the rapids flow relentlessly. It is impossible to ignore the scale of the challenge which the mayor and his team of villagers undertook. Funds were borrowed, bank balances fudged and favours were called in. Neighbouring settlements became disgruntled at the amount of work going on in Gara Bov. But despite a near-catastrophic episode in late 1983 when the fortification wall partly collapsed and the Selska flooded the newly laid pitch, Stadion Skala was ready for its grand opening in July 1984.

Shortly beforehand, Lyubenov had driven to the headquarters of the Bulgarian FA at Vasil Levski Stadion in Sofia. His news that the stadium was complete was met with ridicule as chairman Lachezar Mihailov admonished him by saying, 'Mayor, I'm too busy to listen to humour!' Lyubenov casually suggested he come and see for himself and the pair were driven back to Gara Bov, a journey of 57km, during which the mayor's enthusiastic tales were met with laughter. When Mihailov saw for the first time Stadion Skala with its goalposts in situ ready for action, he broke into tears, knelt on the grass and humbly apologised to Lyubenov.

Stadion Skala was the brainchild of former Gara Bov mayor Grigor Lyubenov. Tasked in 1983 with building a new football ground, Lyubenov made his intentions clear from the outset, 'The football-loving Bovčani people will have a football ground to be proud of. And they will have it within a year.'

Forty years on it is still easy to see why. Shortly before current tenants Zenit Tserevo are about to kick off in the Bulgarian regional amateur league, a group of hikers arrive at Stadion Skala which doubles as the trailhead for the Pod Kamiko ecotrail. They pass between gathered spectators, all smiles and eyes wide at the sight before them. There is a waterfall a mile or so up the trail and beautiful as it is, it may just pale against this man-made wonder.

Stade Maurice Dufrasne

LIÈGE // BELGIUM // STANDARD LIÈGE

When the local tourist board advertises its city as 'authentic', there is a strong possibility that its football grounds will be too. For anyone seeing the old steel city of Liège for the first time, it is a difficult place to get to grips with, harder still to fall in love with. Just keeping a sense of direction can be tricky among the sprawl of ancient spires, industrial plants and enormous holes of half-forgotten roadworks. What is being built and what is being demolished is often hard to tell. Out in the suburbs, old block stone streets climb the sides of the Meuse valley at improbable angles. Crammed with buildings stained Bible black by a century of grime, ancient viaducts shoot across overhead and dimly lit corner bars plough on. In appearance at least, Liège is every bit Manchester's Walloonian cousin.

From the very beginnings of football, Europe's heavy industrial centres have traditionally punched that bit harder. Like Germany's Ruhr or Bizkaia in Spain, Belgium's *sillon industriel* is a cradle of its country's game. Peppered with historic football clubs, many decorated with low numbers in the matricule system, the majority are nowadays just footnotes in the region's history. Of the many eccentric delights of the Belgian game, matricule numbers are perhaps its most charming. Used to determine the order in which clubs registered with the Royal Belgian FA, they represent the heritage and longevity of that particular club. Even those with numbers in the thousands will weave their prized digits into their identity, on shirts, logos and merchandise.

Forced north by the expansion of the Cockerill-Sambre steelworks, the site of Stade du Pont d'Ougree is now covered by the Liberty Steel coil rolling plant.

During the planning for this book, two clubs with origins separated by just three terraced streets had left me in a quandary. Once owners of matricule number 21, Royal Tilleur had been playing out of their evocative Stade de Buraufosse since 1960 – a stadium with more open terracing you will not find anywhere in Belgium. Until then, Tilleur had played on the banks of the Meuse at Stade du Pont d'Ougree. The ground was virtually next door to Standard's Stade Maurice Dufrasne which for the purposes of local flavour and its preferred name among supporters, we will refer to as Stade de Sclessin. Forced north by the expansion of the Cockerill-Sambre steelworks, the site of Stade du Pont d'Ougree is now covered by the Liberty Steel coil rolling plant. At Buraufosse, Tilleur would quickly develop a ground worthy of inclusion here, one which left me questioning Liège's right to have two stadiums featured. In the end, the decision was made for me when during the summer of 2023, Tilleur joined ranks with FC Ans and departed for the latter's new stadium leaving Buraufosse empty and with a future unknown.

In 1899, students from the Collège Saint-Servais voted for the name Standard Liégeois in tribute to the great Parisian club of the time, five times winners of the French league and fourth-oldest club in France. They took matricule number 16, one ahead of another neighbour, RFC Seraing. A single vote given to the alternative option would have seen the club named 'Skill Club', a missed opportunity one may argue. Beginning high above the city in the hills of Cointe, Standard soon moved to the La Boverie velodrome on the southern tip of the Outremeuse, an island in the Meuse nowadays declared a 'Free Republic' by its working-class residents. La Boverie had also been the home of Standard's great rivals Royal Club Liégeois (matricule number four) who themselves had begun in 1893 on a field within the grounds of Château de Sclessin. Still a focal point for Standard fans walking to the match along the river bank, the 18th-century castle would play a pivotal role in their own history too. From its owners the Sauvage family, Standard acquired their own field for football in 1909. Then under the new chairmanship of Maurice Dufrasne, the club soon set about turning it into their permanent home. On three football grounds within less than a square mile, Liége's three pioneers of the game began their journeys. Only one remains but in European football circles, Sclessin has become synonymous with the fiercest of atmospheres.

From its first year as little more than a meadow where players would change in a nearby cafe, by 1925 Sclessin had grown to become a stadium capable of holding 20,000. Then featuring a single, elegant steel-frame grandstand on the western side, a vast cover was erected opposite in 1940 to accommodate 10,000 standing supporters. In the shadow and smoke of the smelting furnaces, by the 1950s Sclessin began developing a reputation as a place of frightening intensity, a stadium packed with supporters determined to unshackle themselves from the grimness outside. Parallels can be drawn with Liverpool, Dortmund, Lens, Torino and Leipzig, similarly 'authentic' cities where the fervid nature of supporters have carried their teams to untold successes, often against clubs with far greater resources.

For Standard, winners of the Belgian championship six times between 1958 and 1971, on-field success had begun to take its toll on a stadium which by the 1970s was showing its age. For the 1972 edition of the European Championship, Sclessin was selected as host for just a single match, a paltry third-place play-off that the club and city saw as a rebuff. Worse was to follow in the 1980s, years of corruption within the club's core leading to Standard's darkest hour. Infuriated by the affair, fans turned to hooliganism which tore through terraces as lifetime bans and suspensions handed out to high-ranking officials and players alike tore at the club's heart. Eric Gerets, national team captain at Italia '90, was banned for three years (two on appeal) and promptly upped sticks for AC Milan.

Nowadays, Sclessin is virtually unrecognisable from its heyday. With only the long-abandoned steelworks as a reference point, it has emerged from its midlife crisis to become a bright new 21st-century stadium. The arrival of the European Championship in 2000 saw an entire new three-tier stand replace the 1973 tribune at the Quai Vercour end. Next, the main stand and north stand had a third tier added and the two corner voids were linked by the continuation of the top tier. Only the east stand, built to replace 1940's enormous covered terrace which was destroyed by fire in 1992, remains. Such incongruence is what defines Sclessin and gives it a character so often lacking in modern stadia: three stands clad in a cloak of crimson, in places as steep as those at the Mestalla, facing off with a typical concrete Belgian period piece. From whichever direction you approach, it lights up the rust-brown landscape like nothing else. And on matchdays, its fans can be heard singing miles down the valley.

TRIBUNE
3
T
TERRIL
ASSURANCES LIURNO
GILSON
DELFORGE
baloise
0-0

Cappielow Park

GREENOCK // SCOTLAND // GREENOCK MORTON

088

To put Cappielow Park's longevity into perspective, when it was opened to the public in 1879, the town of Greenock was a warren of grimy cobbled streets, shadowy closes and impoverished housing. The 75m-tall Victoria Tower above the town hall was still seven years away from gracing the skyline while the red and white brick warehouses, which appear to have stood since time immemorial alongside the James Watt Dock, had yet to be built. That the dock's giant cantilever crane Titan, a category A-listed structure, did not appear for a further 38 years should come as no surprise.

Although much of central Greenock has undergone urban regeneration in the past 50 years, the majority of its historic 19th-century buildings appear forlorn, unloved and neglected. Not Cappielow Park, however. Its survival among the decline as an immaculately preserved time capsule is one of Scottish football's greatest stories, one that should be seen and heard by any club owner considering radical stadium changes. Generations of shipwrights and stevedores once passed through its turnstiles, then came the sugar boilers and flax spinners from factories and mills long since demolished. Nowadays, it is commuters employed in IT back home from Glasgow who keep its terraces alive. A Scotch pie somehow tastes better at Cappielow, the smell of the rain on the cinder track that bit sweeter.

Morton had been formed in 1874, two years after Rangers and 13 years before Celtic. The club kicked off on a site on Grant Street, close to where the Victoria Bowling Club now stands and where the club's original founders had lived. Almost immediately, the pitch was deemed unsuitable and they soon moved to an extensive area of parkland on the banks of the Clyde called Garvel Park. Although the Garvel Park estate would eventually be swallowed by the Great Harbour Scheme's building of the James Watt and Garvel Dry Docks, the current Garvel Point gives a rough indication of where the ground was located. With the arrival of the shipbuilding and maritime boom time in Greenock, Morton soon upped sticks again and relocated to Sinclair Street, close to a halfway house and toll named the Cappielow Inn on Port Glasgow Road. Originally an oval park, ringed by an athletics and cycling track, it was a rudimentary affair with early crowds watching games from the mounds of earth which ran along the perimeter.

Within a few seasons, the club was attracting the support of those from the rapidly expanding nearby shipyards. A wooden grandstand was assembled along the southern boundary to cater for the growing numbers and it would stand until 1931 when it was replaced by the current main stand. With the field gaining a reputation as one of the finest in the country, Morton became founder members of Scottish Second Division in 1893. Even in the earliest photographs taken over Greenock from the air, the Cappielow pitch always looks flawless. There is a suggestion that Cappielow's unofficial groundskeepers at the time (half a dozen sheep left to graze on the hallowed turf) were responsible. While unlikely, the sheep remained until the 1910/11 season when one, Toby, was deemed surplus to the farmer's requirements and was given the honour of club mascot. Toby became an instant hit with supporters and was given the freedom of Cappielow until he came to a curious and untimely end in the players' bath.

The earthen banking around the ground continued to increase in size and by virtue of its proximity to several cottages that at the time were occupied by Irish immigrants, the western end of the ground became known as the Wee Dublin End. Extended during the 1960s, in the summer of 1981 it was inexplicably fitted with bench seating acquired from the old Centenary Stand at Ibrox. Although planning permission for a roof over the Wee Dublin End was once granted, it was never built, giving rise to the question over why an uncovered terrace in Scotland's often-labelled rainiest town was given seats. Come rain or shine, however, those away supporters standing on the benches will to this day tell you that there are few better places in Scottish football than Cappielow's Wee Dublin End. Indeed, backdropped by the enormity of the 150-tonne Titan, it is a spiritual cousin to Glentoran's beloved City End, itself dominated by the shipbuilding cranes of Harland and Wolff.

In 1958, a roof was erected above the terrace on the northern side of the ground to enclose what became one of football's cosiest 'Cow Sheds'. Opposite the main stand, it remains a place of congregation for the younger supporters where up tight with the Wee Dublin End, they can engage in a verbal stramash with the visitors. The same year, floodlights were installed upon the roofs of the grandstand and Cow Shed in an arrangement both unsophisticated and typical of the era, a style that would be revisited decades later in the trend for roof-mounted lighting. Two new pylons were acquired from St Mirren's Love Street stadium at the turn of the century and installed on either side of the Cow Shed which more recently has had its roof lights removed. Cappielow's centrepiece remains its grandstand, all wooden VIP booths, delightfully archaic signage and the warmth of its people. Its modernisation including new seating and roof has been carried out in a manner befitting of its vintage and as it approaches its centenary, it looks delightful.

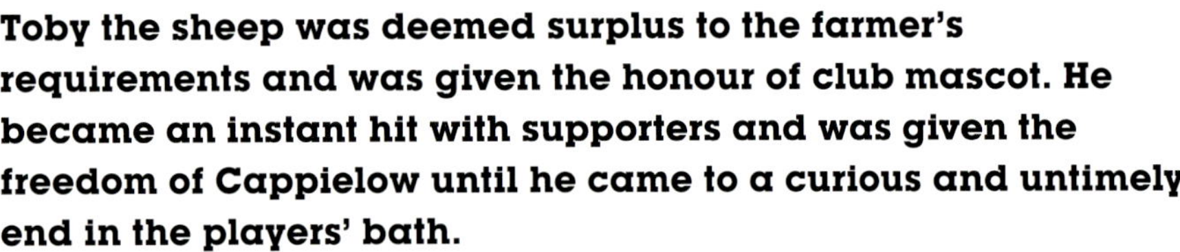
Toby the sheep was deemed surplus to the farmer's requirements and was given the honour of club mascot. He became an instant hit with supporters and was given the freedom of Cappielow until he came to a curious and untimely end in the players' bath.

From a stadium once referred to in a letter to the local paper as a 'bombhole', with terracing like a 'a pile of sticks and dirt' and its grandstand a 'pneumonia conducive, corrugated iron object', Cappielow has come a long way. A very long way. It has outlasted virtually all of its contemporaries to become one of the last traditional football grounds in Scotland. Still capable of performing perfectly in the higher echelons of the game, it is fully deserving of the cult status it has achieved across the continent.

088 // **Cappielow Park**

GREENOCK // SCOTLAND // GREENOCK MORTON

087

Estádio Municipal de Aveiro

AVEIRO // PORTUGAL // SC BEIRA-MAR

Estádio Municipal de Aveiro has in 20 short years gone from one of Euro 2004's headline acts to an unfillable white elephant. From origins in the Kingdom of Siam meaning something highly prized or revered, the term white elephant has over time semantically shifted to denote something burdensome and expensive to maintain. Estádio Municipal is just that, a Portuguese Coney Island, faded and semi-neglected as it stands in psychedelic decline high above the barren terrain.

In recent seasons, Aveiro's senior club Beira-Mar have begrudgingly returned here, their cosy central Estádio Mário Duarte finally falling to the bulldozer's bucket and a new hospital extension in 2020 after 80 years' service. For 1,000 or so loyal Beira-Mar fans, watching mediocre fourth-tier football inside Tomás Taveira's 32,498-seater showpiece can be an anaemic experience despite its splashy primary school colour palette. And with no shuttle buses or public transport out here, it is a surprise so many do.

Taveira had come to prominence in the 1980s when his postmodernist design for Lisbon's Torres das Amoreiras had shaken up Portuguese architecture. Despite being initially met with extreme controversy, the chess piece-themed towers have since become an important and integral feature on the city's skyline. A public scandal not for the pages of this book sent Taveira into retreat before he re-emerged at the turn of the millennium and was selected to design three of Portugal's new Euro 2004 stadiums: Lisbon's José Alvalade, Leiria's Dr. Magalhães Pessoa and Aveiro's Municipal. That Portugal failed to capitalise on the tournament and create a legacy of sustainability should not reflect on the vision of the architects themselves. From Faro to Braga, Portugal ignored the lessons learned from Italia '90 and with wild abandon built ten innovative new stadiums at an estimated cost of €600m. With continuing calls for the demolition of those that have failed most spectacularly (Leiria and Aveiro in particular), they stand as a reminder of the financial ruin suffered by local councils and public bodies alike, those who were drawn into funding the poorest country in western Europe's misjudged attempt at a game-changing tournament.

Through the gloom, however, it is reassuring to note that for Aveiro at least, in the minds of those at the Portuguese FA and city council Estádio Municipal still has a role to play. As I write this, it has just been announced as the venue for Portugal v Ireland where a full house will send *Seleção das Quinas* off to the 2024 European Championship. This is what it was made for, what Taveira envisioned – big games and big nights. And in 2021, Aveiro's city council went some way to appeasing beleaguered Beira-Mar supporters by announcing a €3m investment in a state-of-the-art training complex for the club next door. This fulfils a commitment made to the club many years before the construction of Estádio Municipal and after a decade of financial hardship and demotions, it at last gives Beira-Mar and their many teams a permanent base of their own. I watch a Beira-Mar B game here on the main show pitch and the single concrete tribune is packed. Junior games are taking place on the three adjoining pitches too and it is immediately obvious that with a little more in the way of spectator facilities, this is where the Beira-Mar fan would prefer to watch their team.

Instead, I follow the crowd out and across the road. The elevators up to the stadium concourse are broken so everyone takes the steps onto the

vast wasteland of concrete slabs, weeds poking up through every join. Up ahead, Taveira's toy town, a jumble of giant multicoloured Meccano pieces which, just as intended, will make you smile from ear to ear. Closer up, we see that it is losing its colour, the reds a shade or two lighter than they were in 2004, the yellows streaked with dirt and less vibrant. Here and there, the cladding panels which curve inwards around the stadium's lower half have been lost or removed, the gaps revealing the concrete underbelly of the stands behind. Robbed of the love and care it deserves, transparent mesh balconies have rusted, porthole windows are cracked and startlingly, entrance gates into parts of the stadium not used today left open.

Inside, the theme of spontaneity continues. In the early 2000s, there was a short-lived trend for the random positioning of coloured seats within stadiums, designed to create a more natural appearance than the regimented two-colour arrangements of the 1990s. Estádio Municipal took this idea and ran with it, a haphazard assortment of seats in every colour imaginable running riot around the stadium's two tiers. Above, a roof featuring an enormous red and yellow checkerboard pattern facing out is suspended by a bright crimson rectangular steel truss that in turn is connected to the stadium by 24 steel columns, painted red naturally. For a stadium that is playfully chunky, purposely clumsy even, Taveira's intense tonality gives it the illusion of being in constant motion in much the same way as a Picasso painting does. It is a timely reminder that in an era when the fashion for new football stadiums is for cool, neutral sophistication, there is always room for a little shameless fun. For Aveiro and all those cities living with Euro 2004's legacy of stadiums too big for their clubs and too expensive to maintain, the hope must be that the Portuguese FA roll out their international fixtures and tournaments into the provinces on a more permanent basis. After all, if Coimbra, Guimarães, Leiria, Faro-Loulé and Aveiro were deemed suitable in the first place, they should still be recognised as important football centres.

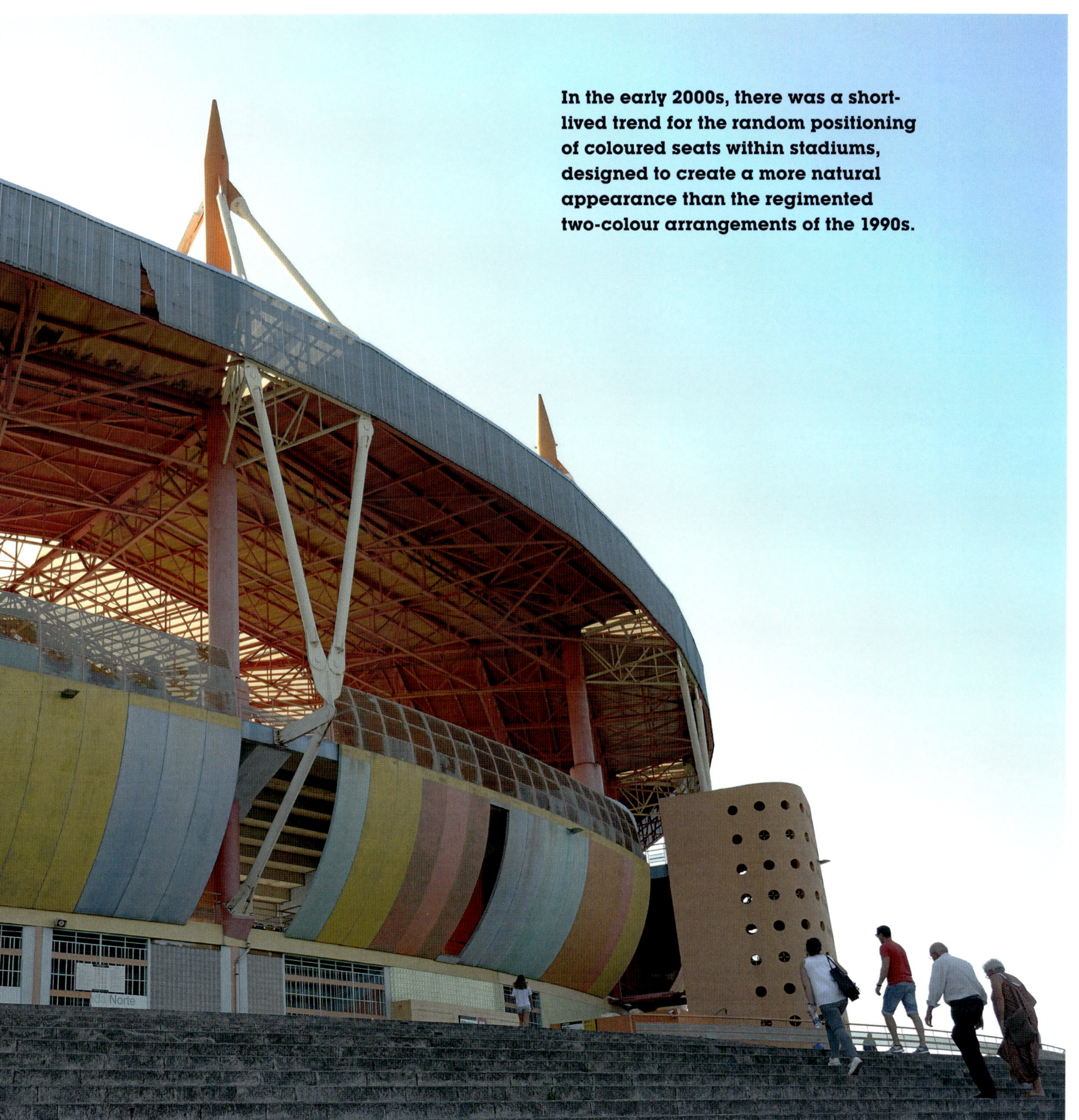

In the early 2000s, there was a short-lived trend for the random positioning of coloured seats within stadiums, designed to create a more natural appearance than the regimented two-colour arrangements of the 1990s.

Stadio Comunale di Sanremo

SANREMO // ITALY // SSD SANREMESE

From Aveiro's kitsch, we travel to the Italian Riviera for something altogether more classical. Once wryly labelled as Stadio dei Milioni – Sanremo is traditionally a casino resort for the wealthy in a similar vein to its near neighbour Monte Carlo – Stadio Comunale is much diminished from its heyday. Its appearance from the roadside may still be one of moneyed grandeur, but inside, it is every bit the home of a team that have existed in middling obscurity, bruised and bedraggled by almost a century in which the football millions at least, have remained just out of reach.

Like numerous stadiums within these pages, it is another built under Mussolini's fascist regime. Far from his empire's remodelling of the Roman Empire at Roma's Stadio Olimpico, however, it carries a faded provincial swagger, its appearance further reduced by the spray-can and footfall of decades of Sanremese Ultras. This visual contradiction is one found in stadiums the length and breadth of Italy and is what makes them so prized among those seeking a more convincing football experience. At Stadio Comunale, you can add the suggestive backdrop of yachts bobbing in the marina and a thousand white stucco villas.

Originally Stadio del Littorio, a name we have already covered in the chapter on Pisa, the stadium was constructed between 1930 and 1932 and inaugurated not by local Sanremese but in a pair of friendly matches involving Imperia, Savona, Genoa and Austrian side Wiener AC. A crowd of 15,000 entered the new stadium that day, those unable to find seats within the stands massing on the athletics track which remained in use until 1970 when the stadium lost its multi functionality. Sanremese were soon welcoming prewar superstars to their home: Juventus in 1935 for a Coppa Italia match in the last 16 and a year later, Internazionale (then known as Ambrosiana-Inter) in the quarter-finals. That season they would be promoted to Serie B where they would play for three seasons but never return. Indeed, Sanremese's history is intrinsically linked with the third tier of Italian football where after the Second World War they played for 16 seasons straight in Serie C including six when the competition operated as a national division, the only club to play in all.

Thereafter, they drifted from Serie D into Ligurian regional football before a return to Serie C for the 1978/79 season which by this point had become a two-division, fully professional league. During this latest nine-year spell, both Roberto Baggio and a teenage Gianfranco Zola played at Stadio Comunale with Vicenza and Sardinia's Torres club respectively while Sanremese even flirted with European football in the Anglo-Italian Cup as Hungerford Town and Bridgend Town both visited. Yet it wouldn't last. Back into non-league they fell and despite a return to Serie C2 around the turn of the millennium, burdened by huge debt the club were liquidated in the summer of 2008. Forced to begin at the very bottom, further periods of mismanagement, crisis and reformation were to follow, leaving Sanremese a shell of the club they once were and one of the many forgotten names in Italian football.

IRRIDUCIBILI·SANREMO
SANREMESE CLUBS
BAR
BARAGALLO STORCHI
IRRIDVCIBILI
CALCIO 1904
FALEGNAMERIA
ARREDI su MISURA
SICA DAVIDE 388.5664952
IORIO SALVATORE 338.4311261
ABBRONZATURA
NA.PA
CENTER
RISTORANTE - PIZZERIA
CLAS
CLAS
CLAS

With so little to cheer, I am stirred by the level of support still committed to the club. I watch a mid-table fifth-tier match devoid of visiting fans yet over 1,000 still pass beneath architect Domenico Parodi's elaborate arched gateway. Comune di San Remo – Campo Sportivo is lettered below a relief of the town's coat of arms, the old non-univerbated spelling of Sanremo a reminder of the fascistic period in which it was built. Inside, we find two stands that could not be less alike. Where until the 1970s there stood a much larger uncovered stand on the northern side, it was replaced by a slender two-tier tribune with six steps of terracing on each. The land behind was backfilled and on top, squeezed between the terraced gardens of properties on Via Val D'Olivi and the tribune's retaining wall, a small training pitch complete with uncovered stand was built in the 1980s.

Opposite, the original 1932 grandstand is an altogether different proposition, a single-tier, rendered concrete structure crammed with as much ornamental classicism as space allowed. Corinthian pilasters, Palladian windows, Roman columns and decorative roof finials, nothing is left out.

To suggest that Stadio Comunale's northern tribune is well-used would be an understatement. While most Italian Ultras will express their deep dissatisfaction with club hierarchies from the grime of the curves, such luxury no longer exists for Sanremese whose own prefabricated curve at the eastern end was removed in 1987 after another period of reformation. The fans therefore have taken to decorating the stand with visual representations of their feelings which, although regularly scrubbed, continue to reappear. Among the art displayed on my visit, a single address to those that brought the club to its knees, 'Ci hai fatto sparire dal calico nazionale e i tifosi vudi denunciare!' which translates as, 'You made us disappear from national football and we the fans want to report it!' Its whitewashed walls, painted over always in the club's sky blue, are peeling, the brickwork crumbling. Framed by manicured gardens which only serve to emphasise its degradation, the northern tribune is a snapshot of Italian football's lower-league climate where once great clubs barely keep their heads above water. It serves to remind us of the suffering endured by loyal fans at the hands of nefarious ownerships.

Opposite, the original 1932 grandstand is an altogether different proposition, a single-tier, rendered concrete structure crammed with as much ornamental classicism as space allowed. Corinthian pilasters, Palladian windows, Roman columns and decorative roof finials, nothing is left out. Domenico Parodi clearly had a lot to get out of his system under Mussolini's instructions. Inside, things become a little more austere, the sky blue and white colour scheme opposite creeping onto pillars and balconies. Two flights of elegant staircases lead down into the club boardrooms but everything is cobwebby and unkempt, corridors used as storage for all manner of sporting detritus. In early 2024 Sanremese presented their plans to the public for a new 13,000-capacity stadium. With a transparent retractable roof guaranteeing complete closure for multiple events including concerts, if realised it will be built on the same site and require the complete demolition of Stadio Comunale. Undoubtedly past its prime, its replacement will come as a much-needed boost for the club and community. However, unlike at Racing Mechelen further on in these pages, nothing of the old ground will be saved and incorporated. If it's football grounds stacked with charm and character that you're after, a visit here is recommended sooner rather than later.

07 VESTUR

Valloyran

SANDAVÁGUR // FAROE ISLANDS // 07 VESTUR

There are moments in history which come to define a nation's football identity. For the self-governing archipelago of the Faroe Islands, 2014's defeat of Greece in Piraeus with the two sides separated by 169 places in the FIFA rankings was one such moment. Many saw it as one of the greatest shocks ever in European international football yet as if to underline it was no fluke, seven months later they did it again.

Another would be KÍ's European campaign in 2023, the Klaksvik club becoming the first Faroese side to reach the group stages of a UEFA competition. But by far the most significant will always be the first visit of the Scottish national team in June 1999. From irregular kick-abouts with the Shetland and Orkney Islands just a few decades earlier to holding the Scots to a draw, the Faroe Islands announced to the footballing world just how far they had come. It remains the single most talked-about game of football on the islands, its enduring legacy such that anyone from Tórshavn to Klaksvík will have their own reminiscences and likely know someone who was there.

In the context of this chapter about a tiny football field in an obscure village, it was the television images beamed back from Toftir that day which began my own love-in with Faroese football. Without Hans Fróði Hansen's last-gasp equaliser, I would likely never have booked that first trip the following summer, the first of three during which I would discover a nation that, per square mile, has the greatest concentration of spectacularly situated football grounds in Europe. Scenes from that rare sunlit afternoon in Toftir are etched in the memory of thousands; the bewildered faces of the Tartan Army who just hours earlier had ran cheering from the ferry's bow door to good-naturedly maraud their way through the village. The packed clifftop Svangaskarð Stadion, the beauty of which had never been seen by most watching on television, its views of the shimmering North Atlantic and grassy slopes dotted with Scottish flags. Over the years I have met a surprising number of intrepid football explorers that cite the game as their first introduction to the Faroe Islands. Similarly, many continue to visit during the summer months after their own clubs' seasons have ended.

You would think that choosing a couple of grounds for this book from a land so rich with possibilities would be a painless task, and yet it took more deliberation than most. Faroese club grounds are unsurprisingly simple affairs and ultimately it came down to which are set in the most spectacular location. EB/Streymur's beautiful new Eiðisvöllur stadium was in the mix, built to replace the village of Eiði's world-famous á Mølini, the loneliest ground of them all. Then there was á Eiðinum on the southern island of Suðuroy, a stadium built in a no man's land between the crystal waters of Vágsvatn Lake and the misty melodrama

07 have blossomed ever since with regular appearances in the Faroese Premier League and multiple First Division championships putting the rural west firmly on the footballing map.

of Vágseiði's cliffs. Víkingur's striking village centre stadium Sarpugerði too had a shout, as did of course the old Svangaskarð, still home to B68 but dislodged as national stadium by Tórshavn's splendid Tórsvøllur. But in the end it was Valloyran's effortless encapsulation of all elements of Faroese life: the fishing harbour, the grass-roofed dwellings, the mountains and the distinctive red-roofed wooden church, the most beautiful on the islands.

Most who come to the Faroe Islands will arrive on the island of Vágar, home of the international airport. And most will make a swift dash off it through the Vágatunnilin to begin their journeys in the capital Tórshavn. True, this green-grey island shaped like a rough diamond is more sedate than those further east, less spiky and less dramatic, but in Sandavágur, it has one of the most pristine fishing villages on the islands. The story of football on Vágar begins in 1900 with the arrival of a character known as the 'football-vicar'. Carl Johason brought with him from Copenhagen a single holdall containing a Bible and a ball and went about dividing his time between the church and the beach in Miðvágur where he would teach local boys the game he had learned in his native Copenhagen. His influence was such that by 1906, three clubs from the neighbouring villages of Miðvágur, Sandavágur and Sørvágur had been established, three of the first seven clubs in the Faroe Islands. It is likely the football-vicar encouraged other roles too, including that of Petur Elias Petersen who, aged just 17, was appointed Sandavágs Bóltfelag's first chairman, possibly the youngest chairman ever in European football.

Fast-forward to 1998 and all three clubs had merged to become FS Vágar, a superclub designed to represent the island as a whole. By 2007, MB from Miðvágur had left the alliance to try their luck back in the lower divisions while the unified club were renamed 07 Vestur in reference to their westerly position within the archipelago. 07 have blossomed ever since with regular appearances in the Faroese Premier League and multiple First Division championships putting the rural west firmly on the footballing map. Although Sørvágur's more developed á Dungasandi stadium has become the club's preferred home, Vestur's second string still use the historic Valloyran which in recent years has become the only stadium where fans can still watch a Vágar derby when Vestur welcome back MB.

As with many small football grounds, the history of Valloyran is peppered with tales of adversity. Until 1938's construction of a wall around the stadium, it stood at the mercy of the Atlantic surf and rainwater spilled from the Stóra river. When not underwater, locals had a habit of popping into the ground to cut lumps of grass from the pitch for shed roof repairs. Then came the occupation by the British forces during the Second World War who between emptying Sandavágur beach of sand for construction, decimated the Valloyran pitch by playing up to three matches a day on it. When British troops challenged the locals to a match, an army of local boys stood up and refused to play unless the military helped with the maintenance of the ground during their stay, which they did. Nowadays, maintaining Valloyran is a little easier. The installation of an artificial pitch has all but eradicated the threat of postponements from the often extreme Faroese weather while Sandavágar's position on the tourist route means the entire village is kept spick and span.

betri
betri

Stadio Comunale Luigi Ferraris

GENOA // ITALY // GENOA & SAMPDORIA

Gauging a football stadium's level of greatness can be a tricky business. A select few have written their own scripts, their association with a particular era, team or tournament enough to elevate them into such spheres with little need for debate. Others may achieve a similar status through architectural innovation or constituent parts, a Kop or a behemothic set of floodlights for example.

Of course all are great in the eyes of their clubs' fans who call them home. But perhaps the ultimate tribute to a ground, one which rubber-stamped an already venerated status, began at a Manchester-based design company in the mid-1990s. So enamoured with Genoa's 1990 World Cup stadium was lifelong Preston North End fan and graphic designer Ben Casey, he sketched out some ideas based on Stadio Luigi Ferraris for his own club. When the time came in 1994 to redevelop Deepdale, Casey's plans were put into action and 850 miles from the sunshine of the Ligurian coast, darkest Lancashire got its own very fine replica.

Italy is featured more than any other country in this book. It is testament not only to the great appeal of the Italian game but to its architects and designers. The fact that many have had to work with pre-existing municipality-owned stadiums and all the financial pitfalls and bureaucracy that brings makes the 20th-century work of Piano, Nervi, Ragazzi and Gregotti all the more remarkable. Faced with a multitude of obstacles, not least the need for a capacity approaching 40,000 in such a tightly restricted space, Vittorio Gregotti built Genoa and its two clubs a ground which almost 40 years on still looks every bit the innovator it was back in 1990.

A prolific designer, thinker and theorist, when Gregotti passed away aged 92 from Covid-19 in 2020 he left behind over 60 uninterrupted years of impeccable work including 1,200 fully developed projects and 30 published books. Within a short period of time towards the end of the 1980s, Gregotti won three stadium commissions. First was the renovation of Barcelona's Estadi Olímpic in readiness for the 1992 Summer Olympics. Then came the complete rebuild of Genoa's crumbling stadium in the Marassi neighbourhood for the 1990 World Cup. And finally, a lesser-known project in the south of France saw Stade des Costières built for Nîmes Olympique as a cut-price, miniature version of Stadio Luigi Ferraris. That stadium lasted until 2022 when it was demolished to make way for the club's new Stade Nemausus, while up on Montjuïc, Estadi Olímpic began a new chapter in 2023 as the temporary home of Barcelona.

When opened on 22 January 1911 for the Genoa Cricket and Football Club, the oldest still in existence in Italian football, Campo Marassi was little more than a horseracing track with a football pitch in its centre. For decades, fields near the Musso Piantelli Mansion had operated as the city's main centre for equestrianism although since 1909, one had been used for football by the Andrea Doria club (named after a 16th-century Genovese admiral). The new stadium pitch had been laid out in an east-west direction (at right angles to what we see today) on the banks of the Bisagno River, the now largely waterless dumping ground fans cross over in front of the main stand. With a single wooden grandstand built in 1915 next to the Marassi Remand prison, it would take the renouncement of the field used by Andrea Doria in 1926 to enable its extension. Between 1929 and 1933, a new seated grandstand and terraces on the north and south aspects were constructed and when the 1934 World Cup rolled into Genoa, the capacity was an estimated 51,000. A year earlier the name of a former Genoa centre-half killed in the First World War was given to the stadium and so it became Stadio Luigi Ferraris.

By 1946 Andrea Doria had merged with a team from the western port district of Sampierdarena, resulting in the portmanteau Sampdoria. The combining of colours from both clubs resulted in the shirt design of red, black and white bands across Andrea Doria's original blue. It would in time become regarded

084

AL TUO FIANCO IO
MOLESTI
CLUB

Its series of ornamental arches that would once have seemed so bold now appear almost twee against the vast cuboid modernism. The entire exterior and much of the inside is brought to life by Gregotti's famous 'Pompeii Red' colouring.

as *La maglia più bella del mondo*, the most beautiful football shirt in the world. Sampdoria moved in with Genoa at Stadio Luigi Ferraris the same year, and as the wooded hills to the east were obliterated by the explosion of postwar housing, they became the more successful of the two. When in 1986 preparations for Italia '90 began it was decided to rebuild the stadium from the ground up. Work began on Gregotti's 40,000 all-seater in July 1987 and after more stumbling blocks than an architect would normally experience in an entire career including a period when the Italian press labelled it as *Stadio per non vedenti* (the Stadium of the Blind), it was completed in time for the tournament. Irish fans in particular will hold a deep affection for the stadium for it was here they beat Romania to reach the quarter-finals, widely regarded as one of the country's greatest ever sporting achievements.

Outside on Via Giovanni de Prà, the original prewar facade integrated during the rebuild joins the dots between the old and the new. Its series of ornamental arches that would once have seemed so bold now appear almost twee against the vast cuboid modernism. The entire exterior and much of the inside is brought to life by Gregotti's famous 'Pompeii Red' colouring. In each corner, a tall block resembling a fire training tower houses ramps up to the second tiers and most importantly, bear the weight of the roofs from the attached white steel girders. It is a theme the architect would revisit in 2011 in his design for Stade de Marrakech in Morocco – another city that wanted a piece of Gregotti originality. Halting the process of Genoa's young spray painters has led to the complete fencing off of the stadium. But conversely, it now means both ends can remain bedecked with their respective fan murals and club colours without any late-night defacements. More than any other Italian football ground, on matchdays Stadio Luigi Ferraris has the unique flavour of an English ground with supporters bunched steeply around the pitch over two tiers. One millennium after the Republic of Genoa and the English both adopted the St George's Cross, this seems entirely fitting.

083

Stadion Bežanija

NOVI BEOGRAD // SERBIA // FK BEŽANIJA

Our first of two visits to Serbia brings us to one of its capital's lesser-known lights, a club whose 15 minutes of fame ended in a hail of bullets. Belgrade's outer districts bristle with footballing talent, the club-to-population ratio similar to that of Prague where seemingly at every turn in the road there is a small club stadium.

Yet for most, the success experienced by FK Bežanija in the mid-2000s, walking out alongside and beating Red Star and Partizan is a dream likely to elude even the very best. Bežanija's story remains inseparable from New Belgrade where, fringed by a panorama comparable with urban Shanghai, they continue to eke out a more honest existence in the fifth tier of Serbian football. There are still big plans for Stadion Bežanija and the club and should they be realised, it will be a chapter without shame this time, one not scrubbed from the history books.

After the Second World War, the ancient swampland across the River Danube from Belgrade's historic centre became the largest construction site in Europe. Only in the last two decades has focus begun to shift from the soaring towers of affordable communal housing to more commercial ventures. New Belgrade's ever-expanding imprint appears to stop for no man and if it's not a new glass and steel business megacentre going up in the distance, it's the building of smart new bus stations and the widening of roads. Indeed, even since Bežanija's stint in the Super Liga, the quiet two-lane residential street from which their stadium is accessed has morphed into a throbbing six-lane highway.

I have a colleague who grew up on the hill above Stadion Bežanija and attended the Milan Rakić primary school next door. He encourages us to seek accommodation in one of the nearby blocks so as to free ourselves of any negative sentiments associated with its communist past. My son Noah and I book an Airbnb on the tenth floor of a decrepit tower in Block 61. A rusted spiral staircase travels up the exterior wall to the 18th floor, noticeably coming away from its fixings. We take the lift up and our host, a young professional estate agent, shows us into her beautiful open-plan apartment. That evening, we are walking back from a restaurant in Block 63. Elderly couples are out taking evening strolls, kids kick footballs around the green spaces and janky Yugoslavia-era trams bisect the grids. In the shadows, artists create their latest graffiti masterpieces; after all, New Belgrade is known worldwide as a living gallery of street art. My colleague once said, '"Commie blocks" make much nicer neighbourhoods compared to newly built places.' Far from the urban hell it is often portrayed as, New Belgrade feels like a good, safe place to live.

Back across the highway, FK Bežanija came into existence in 1921 under the moniker Soko (Falcon) and played at two different fields near Zemun, not far from where Belgrade's Nikola Tesla Airport would be opened in 1962. After liberation, like many clubs at the time they adopted the name Jedinstvo (Unity) and joined the Novi Sad Football Association by virtue of their location west of the Danube. They played briefly without success in the Srem Liga before joining the Belgrade FA in the autumn of 1952, changing their name to Bežanija for the 1955/56 season and moving to a piece of land directly behind the St. George Orthodox Church on Vojvođanska. With their new location a few metres beyond the district boundary and falling within New Belgrade, Bežanija gradually began to attract a small fanbase from the northern blocks and in turn developed a neighbourhood rivalry with FK Sava, a club with a ground in the very heart of Block 45. Towards the end of the century, however, Bežanija, along with several other clubs, began to fall into the hands of a series of shady owners with connections to Serbia's criminal underworld.

While the story of warlord Željko 'Arkan' Ražnatović's association with FK Obilić is well told, an unknown club who leapt from lower-league obscurity to Serbian champions within two years under his ownership, it is still almost impossible to gauge the rampancy and scale of the money-laundering, corruption and match-fixing that went on within football clubs after Yugoslavia's break-up. Stemming from the loss of quality opposition from Croatia and Bosnia, the game was already in a state of decline and clubs became easily obtainable to those with connections. Presenting their plans for huge investment to low-key clubs backed up with promises to help the local community by focusing on sports for children, hardened criminals were soon running the show. For Bežanija and their eyebrow-raising rise to the top, between 1995 and 2006 four club officials were murdered including two presidents. There was even a price put on the head of current president Jovan Rusić who in his two decades at the club has guided them safely out the other side. Amid the chaos, Bežanija finished sixth in the Super Liga and even played one season in the UEFA Cup.

Under Rusić's steadying hand, Bežanija have continued to develop their eccentric but delightful stadium. In the early 2000s, the pitch was rotated by 90 degrees allowing for new stands to be built along each side, one still uncovered, the other a low-slung grandstand with press box and central VIP area. This left little space at either end and forced the club to get creative by squeezing a tall, elevated stand with a 10ft-high retaining wall between the pitch and the hillside. There is an element of fun to the stadium, a juvenile boxiness brought to life by a vivid colour scheme of red and blue stripes covering every inch. It certainly raises a smile in what could be a melancholic place. Images of Bežanija legends adorn the exterior clubhouse walls, a new coffee bar has opened alongside and Rusić has recently announced his plans for a hotel and swimming pool complex on the site. And then there are the views. Whatever your thoughts on the sight of dozens of prefabricated residential towers, it is undeniably breathtaking.

082

Dimotiko Stadion Vasilis Karakitsios

KALABAKA // GREECE // AS METEROA

Travelling by train from Athens to the middle of Greece's in-between, the landscape becomes so utterly uninspiring that the forests of Thrace and beaches of the Cyclades seem like another world. Although distant mountain ranges to the west are occasionally glimpsed, the barren Thessalian plain formed by the lowlands of Trikala and Thessaly stretches endlessly to the horizon. Just north of Trikala, however, as the train rounds a bend and the small town of Kalabaka comes into view, the vista abruptly alters.

Shooting up from the emptiness, a mad composition of immense sandstone rock pillars up to 600m tall stands over the town. Whelked by deep horizontal grooves and slashed with shades of purple and gold, verdant foliage clings to even the most precipitous promontories. These columns of the skies bear an uncanny resemblance to the Hallelujah floating mountains seen in the Avatar movie franchise. This is the Meteora, a geological oddity worn and shaped by millennia of wind and rain. Where once there were 24, there are still six of the world's most vertiginous monasteries upon the summits. A loose translation of Meteora is 'suspended in the air' and when the rainswept murk clears the Monastery of St. Stephen appears as exactly that – hovering between heaven and earth. In the town below looking north down Kalabaka's narrow streets, the sky is blotted out by grey rock at every turn. If Meteora's proximity is enough to bring out pangs of acrophobia, it is likely you won't be climbing the narrow staircases and crossing ravine-spanning bridges anytime soon.

A creaking municipal stadium short on quirks and rarely full is not exactly what I had in mind when I began research for this book. Indeed, Stadion Vasilis Karakitsios would likely be considered thoroughly nondescript if located elsewhere. But sat watching a game from its grandstand looking back out over the town and the Meteora, its backdrop is one to inspire awe in even the most hard-hearted. Moreover, it is as unlike anything else I have discovered at a European ground, a landscape so otherworldly that it barely seems real. Kalabaka's local team is unsurprisingly named AS Meteora and the game I watch is advertised on billboards in the town as the 'derby of rocks'. Visitors Kastraki have travelled from a village on the other side of the rock formation. A good crowd gathers and the grandstand is full, those without a seat scrambling up on to a concrete roof above the turnstiles for an elevated view. The December sun appears briefly but with the winds whipping in across the southern plains it is cold, bracingly so. AS Meteora easily win the match in the Trikala FA regional league, taking them back to the top. In the spring they would aim for a return to the Gamma Ethniki, the regionally divided third tier of Greek football.

AS Meteora's last appearance in the Gamma Ethniki came as recently as 2020/21 and was not without obstacles. During the early days of August and a month away from the season's opener, the Stadion Vasilis Karakitsios pitch was in such poor condition that the club faced the very real possibility of being thrown out and handed an indefinite ban. Factor in Greece's economic climate and the cost of running a club at that level, president Athanasios Thomas appealed publicly to the town mayor and local entrepreneurs who in turn rallied with the financial support needed to carry out the work. For the first time since the 1970s the name of AS Meteora was briefly rekindled across much of northern and central Greece.

Constructed in the early 1970s, the stadium was renamed in 2008 in honour of Vasilis Karakitsios, an everyman who across 30 years involved with the club held the role of kitman, president and everything in between. Without Karakitsios, AS Meteora's stadium would in all likelihood not exist. Between gaining permission for players to play while performing their military service, Karakitsios called on his powers of persuasion to convince the general secretary of sport in Athens to grant funding for Kalabaka's new stadium. On land descending down towards the Pineios River, building began shortly afterwards. In the five decades since the stadium pitch has gone from the original bare earth surface to acquiring natural grass in 2000. Following 2009/10's title-winning campaign during which over 2,000 people saw a game with Farkadona, the stadium's two auxiliary pitches were laid out and the track was given a bright new topping. Support for the team remains unwavering, older generations simply grateful for the sacrifices made to keep the club competitive. From high up in the grandstand they are rewarded with one of the very best views of the rocks.

Stadionul Celuloza

ZÂRNEȘTI // ROMANIA // OLIMPIC ZÂRNEȘTI

081

To the casual spectator, Stadionul Celuloză's 1955 wooden grandstand may appear more suited to stabling a couple of horses rather than offering sanctuary from the heat of the Transylvanian sun. Yet this extraordinary crooked structure is treasured by locals as a symbol of both Zărnești and its football team's tradition, an extension of Brasov County's rich history of peasant architecture and folk art.

Inside the grandstand's gloom, fresh white sneakers rest on oak timber benching, repurposed from a nearby farm all those years ago and slathered in peeling layers of Olimpic's blue and black. Mobile phones rumble and bing, vape fumes curl up around the rafters. Fashions may change but traditions remain an important part of society here, both young and old nurturing a deeply felt respect for their heritage.

Homespun football fields can still be found all over rural Romania, especially in the ancient regions of Bucovina, Transylvania and Moldova. Most were built by local folk with often little or no borrowing of styles from elsewhere, using perishable materials and simple techniques. You would be hard-pressed to find two that are alike, their creation shaped from pride and outlined by individuality. Many club buildings and grandstands are adorned with carved wooded elements; motifs and patterns reflecting the deep connection the village has with nature. Grandstands are slung from adjoining hillsides, propped at the front with intricately carved columns. Others are more conventionally shaped, fashioned entirely from oak or birch, roofs tiled in terracotta, leftovers from village dwellings. Through a fundamental desire to transfer the comfort of home to the playground, very few are without furniture. Even elementary school football pitches are often equipped with small uncovered stands.

In recent years, a group of football tourists from far and wide have made their way to Romania annually for an organised event named Football in Heaven. Brought together by a shared desire to find the lost

spirit of the game in the 21st century, matches are held in both bucolic village and small city industrial settings, in landscapes offering both sides of Romania past and present. With hundreds of options, the tour may find itself at a ground where farmers pass by on horse-drawn carts and primitive haystacks dot the distant meadows before ending up beneath the grimy smokestacks of one of Europe's most polluted towns. Olimpic Zărnești's appearance on the tour came and went leaving an indelible impression on those that visited; in a world more familiar with Higgs boson, this was a throwback to Heath Robinson.

Like many Romanian clubs, Olimpic's history is inseparable from the local industry which in Zărnești's case is the Celuloză pulp and paper mills. Fed by the Bârsa River, the factory still dominates a large area of the town close to the railway station and it was here in 1923 that football began to develop. A small stadium was built alongside the mills and Bârsa Zărnești were founded, playing here until 1936 when the factory's expansion necessitated the move to a new stadium further west. Walking along the Strada Barsei from the mills to the stadium today, it's easy to believe little has changed. The road is still bare earth, dust churned up by passing bicycles as it narrows upon the approach to Stadionul Celuloză where an abandoned car slowly decays beneath the boundary wall. Although the main entrance to the stadium is via a less circuitous route next to an outdoor fruit and veg market, by paying a small entrance fee at this gate beneath the old 'Rooster of the Mountain' club logo, you are immediately enveloped by the Piatra Craiului mountains to the west and the snowcapped Bucego range to the south. A more breathtaking vista in Romania would be hard to find and in Stadionul Celuloză, a more homely football ground unlikely.

Everything here is shaped with love. The pitch, laid by locals in 1950 on a bed of boulders carried to the site by oxen carts, is beautifully maintained. Behind the western goal, the deep-red timber clubhouse constructed in 1973 looks resplendent, its deep terracotta tiled roof all crooked lines and delightful ornamental gables. Opposite the grandstand, the uncovered seated tribune built in 1982 is proudly bedecked in club flags and on matchdays, populated by supporters of a more full-throated nature. The only concessions to modernity are the unavoidable blemishes of new advertising signage for DS Smith, owners of the mills and largest paper manufacturer in Romania.

Aside from two seasons between 1983 and 1985 in the third division and another in 2022, Olimpic have largely operated under the radar.

It is not important. Football in Romania's rural backwaters is a world away from the country's big city clubs and for most supporters, that is how they like it. However, for one afternoon only in the winter of 1983, the people of Zârnesti witnessed the beguiling spectacle of the Romanian national team at Stadionul Celuloză. Playing in the friendly match that day was the seven-title-winning Mircea Lucescu, László Bölöni, Rodion Cămătaru and a 17-year-old Gheorghe Hagi. The crowd of over 1,200 that descended on the stadium that day would only be surpassed in June 2022 when Inter Sibiu visited for a promotion tie. My own visit came in the final days of the 2022/23 season, the game ending beneath a blood-orange sunset that slowly fell away behind the mountains. A crowd of 400 cheered and sang throughout the match and for 90 minutes, I found myself completely spellbound by this little piece of football in heaven.

Jánošovka

ČIERNY BALOG // SLOVAKIA // TJ TATRAN ČIERNY BALOG

In October 2015, a peculiar image appeared on social media depicting a small group of football supporters standing shrouded in thick grey smoke in an uncovered grandstand. This was no ordinary Slovakian pyrotechnic show, however, as through the murk, the source of the fog was revealed to be a small steam engine pulling along a ragtag assortment of carriages.

Beyond, a football match continued with players seemingly unfazed. Within days the story had been picked up by dozens of international media outlets and posted online. With typical hyperbole, Spain's daily sport newspaper *Marca* ran with 'Unbelievable scenes as train passes through a football pitch!' By this point, the slumberous village of Čierny Balog, nestled in the foothills of the Slovenské rudohorie mountain range, had welcomed football tourists and steam enthusiasts from all corners of the globe.

The Čierny Hron railway was built as a logging railway, hauling timber up and down the valley on over 80 miles of narrow gauge track for almost 75 years.

For over 50 years following their inception in 1933, Tatran Čierny Balog played alongside their rivals Partizán in the western end of the village. In 1985 they relocated eastward along the Čierny Hron river valley to the neighbouring settlement of Jánošovka in a bid to expand. Volunteers swiftly enclosed the pitch and built a grandstand on the southern side, sinking steel supports into the wooded slopes and laying a rudimentary framework on top. Seating of various hues has come and gone but the steeply raked rows offer excellent sight lines for all. That is except for a few minutes during the game because when a train trundles into Jánošovka, belching out clouds and passing barely two feet in front of the grandstand, you had best hope there is not a penalty.

It wasn't always this way. The Čierny Hron railway was built as a logging railway, hauling timber up and down the valley on over 80 miles of narrow gauge track for almost 75 years. By the late 1970s, road transportation offered a cost-effective and time-saving alternative and in 1982 the railway finally closed its doors. In 1992, however, the endeavour of local enthusiasts had seen tracks repaired and a small section of the line was reopened as a heritage railway for tourists. It proved extremely popular, shortly afterwards being granted national heritage status, and in 2011 a new stretch of track was inaugurated connecting Čierny Balog to nearby Dobroč.

Following the river valley south-eastward, this new line was routed through narrow land between the foothills and stringy villages huddled on the valley floor. By the time it reached the Jánošovka pitch, there was nowhere else for it to go other than straight through the ground. Hemmed in by steep wooded banks on the grandstand side and the main village road on the other, the topography of the ground dictated that the only solution was to lay the track in the narrow space between the stand and touchline. Rather than face relocation, the Tatran football club and Čierny Hron railway resolved to work together.

Across the world, industry and football are unequivocally bound together. For many seeing that image in 2015 it will have stirred emotions not just of incredulity but of nostalgia, whether lived or learned, of days when football grounds were cast in shadow by chimney stacks and looming foundries in urban settlements across Europe. And of steam train 'specials' to away matches. Far removed from such a setting as Jánošovka is, with it being a simple yet tidy venue for a fifth-tier semi-professional team in a rural backwater, the idea that an operational steam train can co-exist within a football setting in the 21st century is one which piques the excitement of many.

On matchday, the air is fragrant with coniferous forests and venison stew bubbling in the canteen. The acrid tang of smoke lingers above it all. An engine whistle signals the arrival of a train moments before it chugs into the ground at barely four miles per hour, giving spectators the time to pull out smartphones and aim.

On matchday, the air is fragrant with coniferous forests and venison stew bubbling in the canteen. The acrid tang of smoke lingers above it all. An engine whistle signals the arrival of a train moments before it chugs into the ground at barely four miles per hour, giving spectators the time to pull out smartphones and aim. A real sense of amusement then takes hold as those in the stand, with their view of the pitch now hidden, turn their attentions to the train while those in the carriages delight as a throw-in is taken a few feet from them.

The Tatran chairman proudly informs me there have never been any accidents involving trains at the ground, even suggesting that a few of his wingers should hop on and off to get them up the line a bit quicker. Football is always full of surprise and Jánošovka is as surprising as anything in Europe.

079
Estadio Benito Villamarín
SEVILLE // SPAIN // REAL BETIS BALOMPIÉ

In Seville, Spain's hottest city by some distance, the sun shines for an average 274 hours per month, a fact that you might quite reasonably assume would take a little of the heat out of its two major football stadiums. But whether at the home of the traditionally working-class Betis or the historically more socially elite Sevilla, Seville's irrepressible passion for the game is fierce, all consuming and thoroughly intoxicating. Moreover, the levels of rivalry between the pair are unparalleled anywhere on the Iberian peninsula where even the most eagerly anticipated derbies can often be marked by good-natured but largely impassive audiences. We can trace the origins of Seville's 'great divide' back to 1909 when in events similar to those seen on Merseyside in 1892, Betis came into existence as a breakaway club from Sevilla who had, allegedly, refused a player entry to the club because he was 'just a simple worker'.

In 1914 Betis merged with Balompié. Having received their royal patronage the same year, they then renamed themselves as Real Betis Balompié, Balompié a literal translation of the word 'football' rather than the anglicised fútbol. One year later the very first El Gran Derbi ended with fans and players of both clubs coming together in one huge unsightly brawl. So it began and whereas in other Spanish two-club cities there exists a great gulf in the achievements of each (Barcelona and Espanyol or Valencia and Levante for example), Betis and Sevilla have never quite been able to shake one another off. Both have won just a single La Liga championship and although Sevilla outnumber Betis's Copa del Rey titles by five to three, Betis have won seven Segunda División titles to Sevilla's four. This toing and froing of bragging rights is matched by the numbers that turn up to games, a 2022/23 average of 49,740 at Betis's Estadio Benito Villamarín comparing with 35,571 at Sevilla's Estadio Ramón Sánchez Pizjuán. This can swing the other way too if Sevilla are performing better than they have in recent seasons. Fuelled by bad feeling from the off and with so little to separate the two, the ferocity of the rivalry should really come as no surprise.

Three kilometres south of the city centre, Heliópolis is a neighbourhood of striking single-family houses designed by architect Fernando de Escondrillas. Built for Seville's Ibero-American Expo of 1929, Heliópolis means 'City of the Sun' in Greek but it is the nearby River Guadalquivir's Roman name of Betis that gave the club its title. As part of the exhibition, the Estadio de la Exposición had been constructed in the north-eastern corner of Heliópolis a year earlier although it would take until 17 March 1929 for its official inauguration, a Spain versus Portugal international. With its elegant whitewashed walls matching those of the new neighbourhood and a healthy capacity of 18,000, it may seem a little surprising that it took Betis until 1936 to move in. Such was the club's success between 1924 and 1936, however, nothing could have uprooted them from their old Campo del Patronato Obrero home. In 1931 Betis became the first club from the south to reach the final of the Copa del Rey. Better was still to come when under the stewardship of Irishman Patrick O'Connell, they won La Liga in 1934/35 with a squad bolstered by a core of Basque players who had moved to Andalusia.

In the intervening years Betis had occasionally tested the waters at Estadio de la Exposición. Now Spanish champions, they reached an agreement with the municipality to effectively swap their Patronato stadium for Heliópolis, a move that was made easier by virtue of the club's perilous financial situation at the time. In return the city took control of Patronato which continued to operate as a football ground right up until 1974 when it made way for a new bus depot. Here in the El Porvenir neighbourhood the Betis name lives on in the Real Club de Tenis Betis which exists next to where the stadium was. Forty-eight hours after the deal was sealed, the Spanish Civil War broke out and with it, fighting on the streets of Seville. Three years would pass before Betis finally got to use their Heliópolis stadium and when they did, it was something of a damp squib. The impact of the war had taken its toll along with most of Betis's great team from four years earlier. So began a slow and painful spiral of decline. If seven straight seasons in the third tier was bad enough, after the famine came the flood; in February 1948, Heliópolis was submerged under 5ft of rain water, leaving fans rowing to the stadium just to check if the game was on.

By the time the World Cup rolled into Seville in 1982, Estadio Benito Villamarín's whitewash had been complemented with great swathes of Beti green and a new two-tier grandstand on the eastern side. Now minty fresh, it became the stage for Zico, Falcão, Sócrates and the great under-appreciated Brazilian side of the time.

The arrival of Manuel Ruiz Rodríguez as president and subsequent passing of the baton to Benito Villamarín in the 1950s was the catalyst for Betis's first of many great resurgences. Floodlights, each set on towers with necks craned over the pitch, were switched on for the first time on 6 June 1959 and by the early 1960s the stadium had been purchased outright and renamed in honour of Villamarín's achievements. By the time the World Cup rolled into Seville in 1982, Estadio Benito Villamarín's whitewash had been complemented with great swathes of Beti green and a new two-tier grandstand on the eastern side. Now minty fresh, it became the stage for Zico, Falcão, Sócrates and the great under-appreciated Brazilian side of the time.

Sixty years after Betis first moved in, the tenure of one of Spanish football's most celebrated club presidents began in 1996. Manuel Ruiz de Lopera set about convincing the board that the stadium should be completely rebuilt and work began towards the end of the millennium. At the time of his departure in 2006, Estadio Benito Villamarín had a rather hodgepodge appearance, something akin to stands from three different stadiums being haphazardly squished together. For a club that had always defined itself by its self-conscious silliness, typified by the supporter with a birdcage strapped to his head or the deceased father taken to games in a milk carton, it was perfectly Betis.

It would remain this way until June 2016 when the old Gol Sur was demolished and replaced with a new €17m stand that brought with it not only some much needed balance but a new capacity of 60,721. There are many other smarter, more stylish stadiums in Spain. Even 3km across town, their rival's home has recently had a natty new makeover. Estadio Benito Villamarín may now be the fourth-largest club stadium in Spain but when those bonkers Betis fans fill it up, it is with both a cacophonous joy and a uniquely Betis homespun atmosphere.

078

Sportpark Nieuw Zuid

KATWIJK AAN ZEE // NETHERLANDS // QUICK BOYS

From England's east coast we hop across the North Sea to the opposite side where Zuid-Holland's coastal landscape is largely a mirror image of Suffolk's: broad swathes of empty golden-grey beach, chaotic dune systems tufted with tussocky Marram grass and disturbing levels of erosion. Seaside settlements on either side could have been separated at birth, Katwijk aan Zee for example bearing an uncanny resemblance to Southwold right down to the church tower of Andreaskerk mimicking Southwold's lighthouse.

Growing up watching football in Suffolk's coastal towns was often a bracing experience during the winter months. Yet nothing could have prepared me for a February afternoon at Quick Boys. Every football supporter will have a tale to tell about their coldest match experience although I've yet to meet one who saw Rosenborg play Bayer Leverkusen in temperatures below -14°C. For me, standing on a sand dune taking photographs of Stadion Nieuw Zuid as horizontal blasts of sand blitzed my extremities comes mightily close. Quick Boys don't just play near a beach, they play on one in the heart of the Dutch Dunes National Park, a landscape as savage as any.

Amateur football in the Netherlands is a big deal. Below the two fully professional leagues, crowds of two or three thousand are commonplace while the Spakenburg and Katwijk derbies draw in upwards of 8,000.

Rather than attempting to tame nature, the people of Katwijk aan Zee have a history of getting creative with it. In 2015 as part of the Kustwerk Katwijk, a project which seeks to protect the town's coastline, a subterranean parking lot beneath the sand dunes on Boulevard Zeezijde was constructed. As well as giving Katwijk's summer holidaymakers an extra 670 parking spaces, this unique geo-architectural feat garnered praise from across Europe for its ability to double up as a coastal defence system. Quick Boys' history too is intrinsically linked to the dunes for it was on a field laid out among the sand that they began operations in 1920. They would grow to become the most successful amateur club in the Netherlands alongside IJsselmeervogels and, perhaps more satisfyingly, just ahead of neighbours and fierce rivals VV Katwijk with titles won. After leaving the dunes for a new pitch in the Koestal neighbourhood, Quick Boys pitched up in various locations including on Noordwijkerweg, Nieuwe Duinweg and Piet Heinlaan until two titles in three years at the top end of Dutch amateur football necessitated the move to a stadium compatible with the club's on-field success. To the dunes they returned and in the summer of 1955, Sportpark Nieuw Zuid was officially opened.

Amateur football in the Netherlands is a big deal. Below the two fully professional leagues, crowds of two or three thousand are commonplace while the Spakenburg and Katwijk derbies draw in upwards of 8,000. When you consider that the population of the Netherlands is barely a quarter of the United Kingdom's, it gives some idea of just how far-reaching football is here. More impressive is the level of participation, an estimated one in 16 people playing the game across the country. As interest in playing dwindles in the UK leaving historic clubs to fold at an alarming rate, Dutch clubs are regularly faced with the need to add teams to their rosters, some having as many as 300 from junior to senior football.

Since Johan Cruyff, commentators around the world have purred over Ajax's academy and its conveyor belt of talent without really identifying the secret of the country's success. In every small town, children and adults are united through football at facilities capable of hosting multiple matches simultaneously throughout the weekend. While groundhoppers bemoan the slew of dreary doppelgänger stadiums that have swept the nation in modern times, spending government money on an additional pitch for youth teams rather than a fancy new stand has given Dutch clubs the platform for every child to play football for the next 100 years. Quite simply, build it and they will come. Asked what Quick Boys' greatest wish is for, and you won't be surprised to learn it is not a trophy-laden cabinet or a rich new benefactor. Instead, it's the seventh football pitch which financially remains just out of reach. For a club that nurtured the talents of a young Dirk Kuyt, it is a philosophy shared unanimously from the polders to the Vaalserberg.

Once inside Sportpark Nieuw Zuid, any sandstorm that may have been swirling around the beach is quickly forgotten as banked 30ft high in places around three sides, the dunes act as a natural bulwark against the elements. Homely and unpretentious, it's an impressive place even when only half full, crammed with open terracing to delight the more vociferous supporter and plentiful Quick Boys insignia. The centrepiece is a 1,600-seat grandstand built in 2006 to replace the original which had stood on the west side since the 1960s. It cuts a colourful if modest sight against what is often a forbidding backdrop, blue and white seats arranged to highlight the club name. In typical Dutch fashion, Sportpark Nieuw Zuid's clubhouse is cavernous and with 2,200 members, it needs to be. Although the new grandstand was built to accommodate the club's boardroom, multiple offices and sponsors' lounges, it is the clubhouse and 'Youth Base' where identities were formed and civic pride for the town established. More than on the pitch, it is the place lifelong friendships are cultivated, an ingredient which underpins not just the club's prosperity but the unique success of the entire Dutch footballing system.

From the grey, weather-whipped coast of the Netherlands we head to Špis in north-eastern Slovakia where in comparison, the Carpathian landscape of wide basins and hilly ranges appears impossibly green. Many grounds across Europe find themselves spectacularly cosied up to castles or ancient fortifications.

This coupling of two well-loved themes provokes a sense of romanticism in many, a convergence of the ancient and modern world. ASD Bacoli's uncomplicated Stadio Tony Chiovato lies beneath the walls of Castello Aragonese in the Gulf of Naples while FK Budětice's home in south-western Bohemia is nestled in shadows cast by the ominous ruins of Rabí Castle. Similarly, Richmond Castle in North Yorkshire rises majestically behind Richmond Town's beloved Earls Orchard ground long after the first team departed for pastures new. And as we will soon discover, there is a team in Georgia actually playing within the walls of a 16th-century fortress.

This side-by-side existence of castle and football ground reaches its zenith in Spišské Podhradie, a sleepy town of 3,775 some 60km south of the Polish border. Built in the 12th century to guard Hungarian royals from flying Tartar arrows before being consumed by flames in 1780, the ruined Spišský hrad is one of Europe's largest castles and since 1993 a UNESCO-listed building. Crowning a travertine hill above the town, from the air its ghostly footprints of long lost structures resemble patterns from the Peruvian plains of Nazca. Seen from the town and especially from Štadión Spišské Podhradie which doubles as a perfect viewing point, Spiš Castle appears half-sketched, its stone walls bleached almost white from the sun giving it an almost ethereal presence. Many of the original towers became material for manor houses constructed alongside and it is this expansion spread across the summit of the hill that gives Spiš Castle its enormous scale.

Beginning in 1927 on a field in the neighbouring ecclesiastical town of Spišská Kapitula, like many Slovak clubs Spišské Podhradie would change their name many times in keeping with the ever-changing political climate. As ŠK Spišské Podhradie they quickly established a home on the road to Košice, a bumpy pitch that still exists for training and which locals refer to as the 'old field'. After a spell representing the railway workers as Lokomotiva, Spišské Podhradie's on-field successes in the Prešov regional leagues led them to searching for a more suitable base. Just off the Štefánikova road behind an old branch line railway terminus, the club identified a field with nothing between it and the foot of the hill up to the castle. Its aesthetic appeal was instant and obvious. Then renamed Pokrok (Progress) to reflect the communist era of the time, the club moved there in 1952 and quickly began to construct facilities on the western aspect of the ground.

Even with 200 noisy fans from professional club Tatran Liptovský Mikuláš inside for a Slovakian Cup match, Štadión Spišské Podhradie is a remarkably tranquil spot. A greener vista would be hard to find even in Austria and Switzerland and the stadium's carefully maintained plant borders only serve to enhance its verdant appeal. The 1970s grandstand straddles the halfway line on a bank flanked by weeping silver birch, its steep rake offering unencumbered views out over the pitch and castle beyond. Behind the southern goal the new changing rooms have replaced the club's old outdoor swimming pool and sauna added in the 1960s. Everything is delightfully rustic, a little shabby even in the case of the clubhouse where through the smoke of barbecuing *klobása* on the verandah, the club president tells me the story of his son's high-profile career at FK Senica. Everyone wants to talk to one another; it's that kind of club.

In 1998 the football department severed ties with ŠK Slovan with whom they had affiliated 16 years earlier. With a fresh committee and a new name, MŠK Spišské Podhradie won promotion twice to reach the third level of Slovakian football. More important was a new focus on youth football. Two decades on and those efforts are being rewarded as Spišské Podhradie's youth teams rank among the most successful associated with non-professional clubs in Slovakia. Like tens of thousands of clubs across the continent, Spišské Podhradie's story is all fairly unremarkable: ups and downs, fleeting successes and decades of typical camaraderie keeping things going. But in their beloved patch of grass beneath the castle, they have a home with a view that on sunny days is virtually unsurpassable.

077
Štadión Spišské Podhradie
SPIŠSKÉ PODHRADIE // SLOVAKIA // MŠK SPIŠSKÉ PODHRADIE
STAVEBNINY
PNEUSERVIS
SLOVNORMAL
PEKÁREŇ
KOLKÁREŇ
STUDENEC

Stade de Frontenex

GENEVA // SWITZERLAND // URANIA GENÈVE SPORT

To begin to understand how a sporting venue as elaborate as Stade de Frontenex came into existence, we need to travel back to Geneva at the turn of the 20th century. Between the founding of the Red Cross in 1863 and the headquartering of the League of Nations in 1920, Geneva was a city thriving both socially and politically. For the hosting of the Swiss National Exhibition in 1896, an entire village with 56 houses and an artificial mountain were built in Parc de Plaisance, a rural idyll designed to wow the 2.3 million visitors from across the world.

For the majority, the star of the show would remain tantalisingly out of reach, tethered high above the city for four months. Whisking only a select few away at sunset, Urania was a yellow silk hydrogen-powered balloon from which its owner Eduard Spelterini would embark upon some of the most important adventures in early aerial photography. The Genevois were captivated; a local football team even adopted the name Urania for itself.

With the Knie Brothers Circus a regular fixture in town and the Geneva International Motor Show arriving in 1905, those with the means embraced the limitless possibilities of science, entertainment and creativity on their doorstep. With Switzerland spared the direct impact of the First World War, Geneva waltzed into the roaring twenties as a burgeoning global centre of peace where anything and everything seemed possible. The feeling of the time went a long way to informing the appearance of Switzerland's most unusual football ground and although its shortcomings in the modern game are undeniable, it stands as a lasting expression of the period. Stade de Frontenex's pomp and show are a reminder that when it comes to buildings dedicated to entertainment, there is always room for a little of that pioneering spirit.

A stone's throw from Lake Geneva, Stade de Frontenex has now served the 1931 Swiss Cup champions Urania Genève Sport for over a century. That they languish in the Swiss regional divisions is neither here nor there – their home, their violet colours said to have been inspired by the wines of a local merchant, are as synonymous with Genevois football as any. Under instruction from administrative advisor and football fan Jules Peney, on 20 March 1920 two plots of land known as La Giroflée in neighbouring Cologny were purchased for the new stadium. Peney's vision had been to give the community of Eaux-Vives a stadium they could call their own, where from dawn to dusk footballers both young and old from the district could play. Rather than the rudimentary wooden grandstands seen at Geneva's other football grounds, his would be constructed from concrete, its design so ambitious that it would inspire sporting greatness for decades to come.

A stone's throw from Lake Geneva, Stade de Frontenex has now served the 1931 Swiss Cup champions Urania Genève Sport for over a century.

Financed in part by William Favre, a Geneva politician who two years earlier had bequeathed nearby Parc la Grange to the city, the cost of Stade de Frontenex was a little under half a million francs. In comparison with other enclosures in the city, it represented a tidy

076 // Stade de Frontenex

GENEVA // SWITZERLAND // URANIA GENÈVE SPORT

076

sum but with labour provided by the area's unemployed, it was completed within a year. At the time, FC Genève and FC Urania had been wandering nomadically from ground to ground, hampered by the costs of paying rent to private owners. FC Genève had played within the racecourse at Hippodrome des Charmilles, adjacent to where Servette's old Stade de Charmilles would be built in 1930. Meanwhile, Urania were based within the boundary of Eaux-Vives at Pré-l'Evêque, a field which for centuries had been used for archery. Stade de Frontenex represented an opportunity for both to create something great together, a team to challenge Servette and Lausanne. The pair merged in 1922 and took up residence at the stadium where within ten years, they would finish runners-up to Grasshopper Club and win a Swiss Cup.

In the UGS clubhouse, photos of Stade de Frontenex from the period illustrate just how

Financed in part by William Favre, a Geneva politician who two years earlier had bequeathed nearby Parc la Grange to the city, the cost of Stade de Frontenex was a little under half a million francs.

popular the club were, thousands crammed on wooden terraces in front of the grandstand. Such was the demand for tickets, in the early 1930s plans were drafted for three new stands to enlarge the capacity. Coinciding with the city's proposed road crossing over (or under) Geneva harbour, fears that the stadium would need to be completely dismantled to make way for access ramps meant the idea was soon dropped. Instead, Frontenex became the city's premier athletics stadium until the construction in 1948 of Stade Richemont virtually next door. With the track abandoned and faced with the possibility of losing its status in the city, in the early 1960s a cycling track was laid in its place. Today it has evolved into a municipality-approved horizontal canvas for Geneva's street artists and been renamed as the Urban Art Velodrome. Set against the backdrop of the ornate 400-seat grandstand, adjoining porticos and decadent trimmings, this improbable melding of two worlds is what keeps Stade de Frontenex going. That and the continued presence of a great old football team.

Bruno-Plache-Stadion

LEIPZIG // GERMANY // 1. LOKOMOTIVE LEIPZIG

Leipzig's pioneering role in the history of the German game remains undisputed. It was in the city's Zum Mariengarten restaurant (now Büttnerstraße 11) on 28 January 1900 that representatives of 86 German football clubs gathered to establish the German Football Association (DFB). Although the groundwork had begun 25 years earlier when footballs were kicked in Dresden's Großer Garten and at Braunschweig's Martino-Katherineum school, the DFB quickly shaped the game's rules and became an umbrella beneath which all German clubs and regional associations were united. Leipzig's own four clubs at the time were among the first to register, including VfB Leipzig who within three years would become the first champions of Germany and with whom the current 1. Lokomotive Leipzig share their DNA.

As Germany's eighth-largest city and one with such an illustrious past, it begs the question how, by 2009, Leipzig had become a football power vacuum, a city so devoid of anything approaching first-class football that it piqued the interest of the Red Bull corporation over nearby Dresden. With multifarious threads involving political shifts, bankruptcies, name changes and more, the story of domestic football in Leipzig is a convoluted one. To even begin to scratch the surface would require many more pages than I am given here. But with the city's two main clubs, Lokomotive and Chemie, locked in a century-old battle of provincial hatred for one another and operating as mere shadows of their former selves, Leipzig represented a blank canvas for Red Bull to add to their portfolio a prized German branch.

Buying up the playing rights of fifth-tier Markranstädt and promptly swerving DFB policies on advertising by naming the club RasenBallsport Leipzig, in 2016/17 Red Bull gave the city Bundesliga football for the first time since 1994. Leipzig simply represented a gap in the market, a corporate opportunity taken and with oodles of cash splashed, taken well. For a new generation of fans the club has been a gift, an introduction into a bright new world of Champions League football and all the talent and prestige it brings. More importantly, RB have offered family units in particular the opportunity to put some distance between themselves and the extremist factions which gather on the terraces of Lokomotive and Chemie. Red Bull will have known from the outset that their wealth-fuelled fast-tracking would be met by a nationwide contempt for the club, one which shows no signs of abating as it follows the team around the country on their away journeys. But for the city of Leipzig, the project has been an enormous success.

With RB installed at the rebuilt Zentralstadion which when opened in 1956 was one of largest in Europe with a capacity of 100,000, Leipzig's original pair plough on at their own traditional stadiums. Chemie's charming 1915 Alfred-Kunze-Sportpark may have had its capacity chopped to just 5,000 but it evokes the early spirit of the German game more than most. Meanwhile, 13km across town in Probstheida, Lokomotive's Bruno-Plache-Stadion is an altogether different period piece, vast and timeworn but so earnestly cared for. It is one of just a handful of Germany's last truly special prewar stadiums. I watch the team take on Eintracht Frankfurt in the German Cup, yet another detested rival by virtue of their friendship with Chemie. Bruno-Plache-Stadion is imbued with the feel of the 1970s and 80s, a time when the original Lokomotive were in their prime and reaching the business

end of European cup competitions. It's the kind of place where you still expect the Scorpions' 'Wind of Change' to blare from the PA as fans tip up in kuttes, the cut-off denim battle vests so favoured of the time. Instead it is Kraftwerk, bucket hats and an almost tangible sense of imminent disorder which hangs over the stadium as 11,100 make their way in.

Opened as the Probstheidaer Stadion in August 1922, it was at the time the largest club-owned stadium in Germany with an estimated capacity of 40,000. The opening celebrations lasted for a whole week and culminated with a replay of the German football championship final between Hamburg and Nürnberg. It was a match that has the dubious honour of being the only one which failed to produce a champion when after 105 minutes, it was abandoned with Nürnberg reduced to seven players.

The grandstand on the western side has stood since the very beginning and although extended in 1932, the listed central section represents one of Europe's oldest surviving wooden stands. Today it offers sanctuary from the palpable tension out on the terraces. Craning my neck around a wooden support column, I catch Randal Kolo Muani score for Frankfurt. Three weeks later the striker moved to PSG for €90m, a pointed reminder of the abyss between the haves and the have-nots. After the visitors' seventh goal the crowd quickly lose interest and make for the exits. Only then does the grandstand reveal its true splendour, a tangle of century-old whitewashed crossbeams and wooden A-frame trusses above, while below is bench seating patinated by decades of wear. In the last few years, countless fans have given up their own time to help with the renovations and to layer on the club's yellow and blue colours. Should Lokomotive one day stumble across the millions needed for a move away, it has been made clear that the stand would be integrated into any new stadium.

RB's arrival on the scene led to a re-evaluation of Bruno-Plache-Stadion's merits which in turn developed into a concerted effort to conserve their home and embrace it for what it is rather than what it is not. Many Lokomotive fans share the typical 'against modern football' mindset which fits the old stadium well. Here they can hang off the fences, bounce unhindered on the terraces and plaster every inch of the ground with flags and banners. Maybe even sneak in a little pyro. For anyone averse to the corporate experience across town and looking for something more authentic, Bruno-Plache-Stadion is the genuine article.

Kvarlis Tsentraluri Stadioni KVARELI // GEORGIA // FC KVARELI

074

In 2020, a rumour among football groundspotters began circulating on social media. It was said that in the ancient viticulture region of Kakheti in north-eastern Georgia, a team had begun regularly training and playing friendly matches on a pitch inside the walls of a 17th-century fortress.

News spread quickly among enthusiasts and soon after photos began appearing online from the few who had travelled to see for themselves such a unique situation. Within the pages of this book we will look at other castle-themed grounds, whether it's castles forming stunning backdrops or architectural elements incorporated in stadium designs as seen at Stockholms Stadion. But Kvarlis Tsentraluri Stadioni remains the only known modern day example of football actually being played within a castle.

We can be forgiven for assuming that any level of football played here would be of a very low-key variety. Such an outlandish setting would surely be a novelty, serving an amateur team with little in the way of support and infrastructure. Yet long before the advent of the internet, this peasant fortress known as a *galavani* had been home to one of Kakheti's most successful teams in Duruji Kvareli. Perhaps the most remarkable aspect of this story is that as recently as 1996, Duruji hosted top-division Georgian football here playing in front of four-figure crowds against teams well-known across Europe such as Dinamo Tbilisi and Torpedo

Kutaisi. The history of football in the former states of the Soviet Union remains notoriously undocumented and as such, only a handful of blurry photos from Duruji's halcyon years exist. They show thousands of supporters gathered in the fortress, many sardined on wooden balconies affixed to its walls and accessed by narrow stone staircases within the semi-cylindrical central towers. Huddled up hard against the western wall, a rudimentary 2,500-seat wooden grandstand stood packed to the gunwales while Duruji's flag flew atop the towers alongside the five-cross flag of independent Georgia. For a club from a provincial town of barely 8,000, those few years of shoulder-rubbing with Dinamo Batumi et al was no mean feat. The fact they did it all within a castle is mind-boggling.

Duruji Kvareli were dissolved in 2000, the football furniture cleared away shortly after. Except for a handful of those wooden balconies still clinging precariously to the stone walls, little trace of Duruji's 53 years of tenure is left and the scenes that took place here seem almost incomprehensible to the outsider. However, a few tantalising secrets are given up within the very fabric of the place. In one half of the freshly marked pitch, a small area of stone is visible through the grass which from above appears as a ghostly rectangular shape. This was the scene of an infamous sinkhole, now filled and bricked over, which opened up during a match in the 1978 season. Unbeknown at the time, a series of 17th-century tunnels and rooms ran under the pitch, built to store *kvevries* (huge earthenware vessels used for the fermentation and ageing of Khakhetian wine). When the pitch suddenly gave way, a Duruji player went down with it and head first into a *kvevri* full of ancient wine. Within an alcove level with the halfway line, an old wooden scoreboard from the Duruji period is tucked away among mowers and line markers while the stone base upon which the grandstand was erected is still there, overgrown with vegetation and saplings. It is also worth noting that on the eastern fringe of Kvareli, on a road leading out to Lake Kvareli, there exists the remnants of another much larger stadium which was built for Duruji in the 1980s. Based on the original architectural drawings of the Valeriy Lobanovskyi Stadium in Kiev, this stadium was used briefly by the team but abandoned in 1998 in favour of keeping supporters happy at the more central fortress, the team's spiritual home.

The fact that a pitch is still marked out and goalposts remain in situ at the fortress is testament to one man's devotion to bringing football back to Kvareli for future generations. Enter Jano Zatiashvili, a native of the town who in 2020, on trips home from studies in Tbilisi would sow the first seeds of FC Kvareli. Gathering friends and players from the town and neighbouring villages, Zatiashvili worked his players hard in training sessions, designed a new club badge for the team and gained permission from the town council to use the Kvareli Fortress to which he was handed keys to the iron-studded entrance gate. Shortly after, FC Kvareli joined the Georgian league system at the eighth and bottom tier. Zatiashvili's aim is to turn the fortress into a fortress for his team.

Aware that I was interested in documenting this most idiosyncratic stadium, he arranged a friendly match for our visit. The warmth and gratitude expressed by those involved on that humid September afternoon in 2022 was extraordinary. The players looked resplendent in new kits and the football was of a surprisingly excellent standard. Numerous photographs were taken and appeared online soon after, greeted by supportive comments from people from all over Georgia backing the new project. Much like a four-sided stadium, the 400-year-old walls shield the world from view during the game, the only hint of modernity being Kvareli's futuristic House of Justice building ballooning up incongruously just beyond the northern wall. For 90 minutes, we are locked away in a time capsule, the strangeness of the scene accentuated by Kakheti's otherworldly light, brought about by the proximity of the Caucasus mountains and broad flat plains where unclouded skies can look dark and thunderous yet simultaneously lit by sunshine.

With the fingers of modernity reaching out into all the old corners of Europe nowadays, it is unlikely that Kvareli Fortress will ever see top-flight football again. But that's OK; for a town with a rapidly decreasing population, the very fact that football is back in town is enough.

Huddled up hard against the western wall, a rudimentary 2,500-seat wooden grandstand stood packed to the gunwales while Duruji's flag flew atop the towers alongside the five-cross flag of independent Georgia.

ESTRELLA DAMM
DIEM NO
TOLDOSARIS
www.solfinc.com

Estadio Nou Sardenya

BARCELONA // SPAIN // CE EUROPA

There are a million stories within Barcelona's rich tapestry of footballing history. Some are well-told, the weft of the weave, others are hidden behind the picture we all know so well and the characters who populate it.

073

These stories represent the warp, vibrant yet little-known threads of history running deep through the city's barrios. Just below La Liga's radar, a host of backstreet clubs have been quietly keeping Barcelona's football machine well oiled for over 100 years. Names such as Sant Andreu, Sants, Júpiter and Europa may be met with blank expressions elsewhere but for the football-loving Catalan of a certain age, they will be as familiar as Barcelona and Espanyol themselves.

The charming, faintly bohemian neighbourhood of Gràcia lies to the north of the city beginning just beyond Antoni Gaudí's La Pedrera-Casa Milà and La Sagrada Familia. A few boulevards south of Carmel Hill upon which Parque Güell reflects the architect's naturalist phase sits a small football stadium, obscured by elegant balconied apartments and modern high-rises. This is Estadio Nou Sardenya, home since 1 December 1940 to one of the ten original La Liga clubs, Club Esportiu Europa. Although we will delve deeper into the importance of the neighbourhood football club further on, Nou Sardenya has in recent seasons joined the likes of Clapton's Old Spotted Dog in London and Paris's Stade Bauer in becoming a polestar for younger supporters of a more left-wing mindset. When in 2021 Europa declared itself formally against racism, fascism, sexism and homophobia, the first club in Catalonia to do so, a surge of new blood descended upon Nou Sardenya. That they mingle and fraternise so effortlessly with sometimes three generations of Europa supporters is testament to the warmth and inclusivity of the club.

There is an image of Barcelona taken from the cockpit of a biplane in the mid-1910s. In it, the earliest towers of Sagrada Familia rise majestically from the then undeveloped grid system of the city. Visible directly in front of the cathedral and one block north are two football pitches, both belonging to Europa who had been founded in 1907 from the merging of the Provençal and Madrid de Barcelona clubs. Club legend has it that while working on his masterpiece, Gaudí would often take breaks from his work to watch Europa train. Although there is no supporting evidence, it is tempting to imagine what Europa's next home would have looked like had Gaudí become involved with the club. Instead Campo del Guinardó, located in Gràcia between Carrer de Lepant and Carrer de Sardenya, a few blocks from the current Estadio Nou Sardenya, was developed in a more traditional style with a capacity of 19,000. Meanwhile, 2km south-west on the corner of Carrer de París and Comte d'Urgell, Barcelona were beginning to attract crowds far larger than their 6,000-capacity Camp de la Indústria could contain. The thousands who would sit upon the surrounding walls during matches became known as *cules*, an informal Spanish term for the buttocks, a nickname Barca fans proudly carried with them on to the terraces of their new Camp de Les Corts in May 1922.

Opened on 1 December 1940, decades of urban sprawl has greatly altered the appearance of the stadium from one with spacious terraces and a grandstand for 1,000 (built in 1944 with the proceeds from Antoni Ramallets' transfer to Barcelona), to one which has fended off the inner-city strangulation through a series of remarkable architectural accomplishments.

Barcelona's move west across the city proved a blessing for Europa. Arriving at Campo del Guinardó on 8 December 1923, they quickly became an alluring prospect for football fans in the northern neighbourhoods. Within a few short years, Europa were going toe-to-toe with Barça in one of the earliest Catalan rivalries. They won the 1922/23 Campionat de Catalunya with Barcelona runners-up and Espanyol in fourth and as champions, qualified for the Copa del Rey. Having defeated Sevilla and Gijón, the *escapulats* (so named after their distinctive chevron jerseys) reached the final where despite hitting the woodwork ten times, they lost to a single Athletic Bilbao goal. Europa's loss of the so-called 'unlucky final' delighted the 30,000 inside the Les Corts crowd. Largely composed of overzealous Barcelona fans still sore from losing the title to Europa, they cheered every Athletic kick.

Back at Campo del Guinardó, Europa's heyday was short-lived. After joining the inaugural La Liga competition in 1929 and finishing eighth behind teams which, with the exception of Arenas from Getxo, are the same as we see today at the top end of the table, they lasted four seasons before the high costs of participation and the rise of professionalism led to the folding of the club. Disgruntled supporters soon formed a new Europa which to this day aims to carry the spirit of those early years. Although they would never again reach the dizzy heights of La Liga, five seasons in the second tier representing their greatest postwar success, Europa have modestly gone about their football ever since. After Europa left Campo del Guinardó in 1932, the stadium gained a cycling track and until its definite

closure in 1964 it was known as Mostajo Velodrome. No trace of the historic stadium exists today, the site having been covered by the Baix Guinardó gardens in 1995. A few seasons in Vilapicina followed before Europa returned to Gràcia in 1935 where after four seasons at a primitive arena known as Camp del Carrer de la Providència, club members volunteered to take down the forest next door to begin construction of Camp Sardenya.

Opened on 1 December 1940, decades of urban sprawl has greatly altered the appearance of the stadium from one with spacious terraces and a grandstand for 1,000 (built in 1944 with the proceeds from Antoni Ramallets' transfer to Barcelona), to one which has fended off the inner-city strangulation through a series of remarkable architectural accomplishments. Between 1993 and 1994, Europa moved out and Sardenya was rebuilt in its entirety at the behest of the municipality. Raising the height of the pitch four metres above the original stadium, a sports centre and underground car park were constructed below giving Nou Sardenya the character and feel of a mini-Monaco albeit one resplendent in blue and white chevrons. A smart new 1,144-seat cantilever grandstand was erected at street level alongside Carrer de les Carmèlies while on the three remaining sides, not an inch of space was wasted as narrow terracing was tucked in high above the sloping streets. On matchdays the noise from the disparate new fanbase gathered behind the goals ricochets off the looming blocks all around. At tables overlooking the pitch outside the bar, octogenarians leisurely kick back with friends and coffee. And in the grandstand, kids of all ages from Europa's multiple youth teams belt out the club anthem which crescendoes with the line, 'We can retrieve our great history!' In a way, they already have.

072

Stadion pod Bijelim Brijegom

MOSTAR // BOSNIA & HERZEGOVINA // HŠK ZRINJSKI MOSTAR

In December 2023, the English media were united in their indignation over what they perceived to be the primitive containment of 490 Aston Villa fans at Mostar's Stadion Bijelim Brijegom. Certainly, the pre-emptive measures taken by herding fans into an old terrace 'cage' was a huge failure on the part of those responsible for the game's risk assessment. Many went so far as to suggest that Bijelim Brijegom was not fit for staging European football but of course UEFA's stadium inspection team had green-lighted the venue as one up to the task. While it didn't look good in the eyes of both sets of supporters and left Villa fans departing Herzegovina an aggrieved bunch (not least because they were held to a draw), the hosting of such a prestigious match in the city was something many never imagined they would see again.

Nowadays, Mostar is a generally peaceful place to which two million tourists flock each year. Most will watch svelte young divers leap from the Old Town's Stari Most bridge. Others will pose for photos in front of bullet-riddled buildings, left as painful but important reminders of the city's troubled past. And most will leave without noticing the dividing line which keeps Muslim Bosnians and their minarets separate from the ethnic Croats with their steepled church. Although everyone is of course free to roam where they please, each side of the Neretva River has a distinctly different flavour, pork *ćevapi* on the west and beef *ćevapi* on the east. This divide informs the history of the city's two clubs, Zrinjski and Velež, and moreover, the unending debate involving which have the rights to Stadion pod Bijelim Brijegom.

Since the beginning of the Bosnian War and subsequent incitement of Croat-Bosnian hostilities, Zrinjski (a club founded by young Croats in 1905) have held the keys. But that the 1992 war forced eviction of Velež from their spiritual home, one they had played at since its inception in 1958, remains the source of great anger among not just supporters but the wider public in general. Now playing miles from the city in the hills of Vrapčići, Velež's Stadion Rođeni has been developed at a painfully slow speed through a combination of lack of funds and a continued municipal antipathy towards the club. Many public figures including Croatian intellectuals have advocated for Velež's return to Bijelim Brijegom but after Rođeni was in 2022 fitted with a new hybrid pitch funded by the club, the Bosnian FA and UEFA, it seems more unlikely than ever. Most looking in would agree that the whole affair seems more than a little unjust.

Researching Bijelim Brijegom's history in Mostar's city library, I am told by an elderly librarian in no uncertain terms that it is, was and always will be Velež's stadium. And yet I discover that it was Zrinjski who before the Second World War had initiated plans for the building of a new, larger stadium for Mostar, one with an athletics track, bowling alley and tennis courts. By 1939 Zrinjski had even found a suitable location in the western neighbourhood of Bijeli Brijeg. Designs were drawn up and approximately half the funds needed for construction had been raised. Yet they would never see their project realised. Immediately after the Communist Party of Yugoslavia was installed at the end of the war, Zrinjski was banned from all further activities.

In 1947 the People's Republic of Bosnia and Herzegovina, an integral part of Yugoslavia at the time, launched an action for the construction of sports facilities across the region. Sarajevo opened the doors to its enormous Koševo Olympic Stadion and shortly afterwards, work on Željezničar's Stadion Grbavica began. Left out, Mostar began its own campaign to raise 500,000 dinars which eventually was donated by the government. Although construction began in 1947, Mostar lacked the mechanisation and large machines at Sarajevo's disposal needed to carve into the Bijelim Brijegom hillside and so work on the project quickly ground to a halt. By the mid-1950s, large state-owned enterprises had moved into the city bringing with them the tools to finish the job. Work intensified throughout 1957 and by 1958 Stadion pod Bijelim Brijegom was completed under the ownership of the City of Mostar who in turn permitted Velež to use the stadium. At the time, what would eventually become the gargantuan double-decker western stand, there stood just a single tier able to accommodate 5,000. Favoured by the more vociferous fans, opposite was a small uncovered terrace which although demolished when the stadium gave in to its future as a single-sided ground, can still be spotted in the long grass of the banking.

Between 1958 and 1992, Velež played 1,167 matches at Bijelim Brijegom. Three times Yugoslav First League runners-up (to Red Star Belgrade, Hajduk Split and Partizan Belgrade) and twice winners of the Yugoslav Cup, Velež were until 1992 Mostar's only major football club and as such, supported by all people from the city. So good were they on the pitch that in 1989 they positioned higher in UEFA's Team Ranking List than Manchester United, AC Milan and Paris Saint-Germain. Crowds upwards of 20,000 would regularly gather on Bijelim Brijegom's unique single side and on 1 August 1979, an estimated 30,000 turned up for the game against Hajduk Split. But despite everything Velež had done for Mostar and its people, at the fall of communism in 1992 the city authorities promptly ushered them out the door and welcomed back the newly resurrected Zrinjski club after 47 years of dormancy.

Zrinjski have never quite reached the heights of their rivals. A crowd of 15,000 gathered under new floodlights on 19 September 1999 for a match against Sloboda and four years later supporters were thrilled by a young Luka Modrić's eight goals while on loan from Hajduk. But those days of city unity, of one-club support were long gone. Stadion pod Bijelim Brijegom's reappearance in European club competitions has been as remarkable as it has strange, not least because its unwieldy lopsidedness seems so out of place among all the bright new identikits. It is however a welcome return for one of the Balkans' more historic stadiums and should it get past the ham-fisted handling of its visiting supporters, it will hopefully go on for a long time yet.

Stadiumi Gjirokastra

GJIROKASTËR // ALBANIA // AS LUFTËTARI

Albanians are the masters of arriving late to the party. As their neighbours eagerly shook off the communist shackles, Albania was caught blinking nervously at the thousands of shiny new possibilities laid out at its feet. Such dilly-dallying put the country on the back foot and in many ways, it has never recovered. It remains one of the poorest countries in Europe, its commerce tangled in a permanent game of catch-up and the infrastructure for mainstream tourism still very much in its infancy.

071

Albanian football, however, would appear to be in rude health, at least from the outside looking in. The ripple effect of the mass exodus of players to Europe's monied leagues at the fall of the Iron Curtain, players who had until then been forbidden to leave, is now being felt a generation on. Finally delivering on a century of player promise, Albania have reached two European Championship finals tournaments in the first quarter of the 21st century albeit with squads composed almost exclusively of players based anywhere other than their homeland. Lorik Cana and Altin Lala have achieved the status of Black Eagles legends through glittering careers at Marseille and Hannover respectively and the national stadium, Tirana's unlovely Qemal Stafa, has made way for the state-of-the-art new Arena Kombëtare.

This upwards trajectory of international football, however, only serves to mask the startling reality of Albania's domestic game which remains very much a secondary government concern. With each passing season it falls further into qualitative decline, its infrastructure fractured from the top down. Stadiums once unfailingly packed during the Stalinist era lie virtually empty on matchdays, the camaraderie and communal banter born from a mutual suffering replaced by thin crowds of Italian-influenced Ultras inclined towards violence. In back streets from Shkodër to Sarandë, Futboll Lagjesh (street football) has all but disappeared too. Once a rich seam for sourcing talent for the big clubs, young entrepreneurs now favour new avenues in which to accrue their fortune.

Beyond the messy new town, Gjirokastër is a UNESCO World Heritage city of narrow cobbles winding up to its Ottoman fortress. Views from up here are astounding, taking in everything from the Mali i Gjerë mountains to green plains which appear endless.

At Tirana bus station it is a chaos of maddening proportions. Minibuses departing for distant towns are loaded with everything from sacks of potatoes to old fridge freezers, drivers taking a few extra Lek to transport unofficial extra loads. People rush from bay to bay wearing dazed expressions, information on which bus goes where apparently a game of chance. Although I am very fond of the Albanian capital, my heart rate slows as we leave the noise and confusion behind and head south towards Tosk country. After two hours we reach the Drinos Valley where each new vista at the bend of the road becomes more spectacular than the last. Lord Byron wrote of the landscape around his beloved Gjirokastër, 'Ev'n on a plain no humble beauties lie'; 200 years on from Byron's Grand Tour and virtually unaltered by man, it is here that Albania's mysteries run deepest.

Beyond the messy new town, Gjirokastër is a UNESCO World Heritage city of narrow cobbles winding up to its Ottoman fortress. Views from up here are astounding, taking in everything from the Mali i Gjerë mountains to green plains which appear endless. Stadiumi Gjirokastra is easily spotted from this altitude too, the only curved structure in a sea of blocks laid out below. Similarly, from the stadium the scene is just as spectacular, a panorama of shabby but brightly coloured apartments, mountains, distant woodlands and atop the lot, the castle. Such a dizzying overabundance of variety is the reason for Stadiumi Gjirokastra's inclusion here. Without the uniquely Albanian backdrops offered from every angle, it would be much the same as every other communist-era stadium in the country; a low, squat bowl with a central seated tribune, pint-sized copies of those in Bulgaria reflecting Albania's much smaller population.

As in Italy, football success is rare in Albania's south. Only Flamurtari from Vlorë and Skënderbeu from Korçe have broken the northern stronghold in almost 100 years of competition. Skënderbeu's period of dominance between 2010 and 2019 in which they won seven Kategoria Superiore titles, six on the bounce, is particularly significant. Initially it signalled a changing of the guard, derailing the Tirana juggernaut, but what followed was altogether more symbolic of the Albanian game. Barely had the confetti stopped falling when allegations of match-fixing during Ardjan Tekaj's presidency were directed at the club and it was followed by UEFA handing out a whopping ten-year ban from European competitions.

Scandal is never far away in the Albanian domestic game and for Luftëtari Gjirokastër, it came in 2020 as the club collapsed as a result of financial mismanagement. Until then, Luftëtari had briefly threatened Skënderbeu, finishing fourth upon their return to the top flight in 2016 and third a year later. They even ventured out into Europe for the first time in their history. For a few short years football fever gripped the city in scenes reminiscent of the late 1970s when Luftëtari ran Vllaznia Shkodër mighty close in finishing runners-up. In preparation for life

Scandal is never far away in the Albanian domestic game and for Luftëtari Gjirokastër, it came in 2020 as the club collapsed as a result of financial mismanagement. Until then, Luftëtari had briefly threatened Skënderbeu, finishing fourth upon their return to the top flight in 2016 and third a year later.

back in the big time the old stadium, once known as Stadiumi Subi Bakiri after a war hero of the Stalinist regime, underwent important alterations including a new playing surface, 300 plastic seats, the installation of CCTV and a complete overhaul of the changing rooms. Costing 15 million Lek (around €110,000), the work was funded by the municipality, the Albanian FA and club owner Grigor Tavo. Luftëtari were rewarded with crowds upwards of 2,000 and as many as 3,000 for games against Partizani and Tirana.

Nowadays, a reformed Luftëtari are competing in the regional third division. Despite no entrance fee, barely 100 turn up to the match I see against a side from nearby Tepelenë. Washing is put out and washing is taken in on balconies around the stadium yet no one pays much attention to the football below. With little maintenance, it is surprising to see just how quickly the place has fallen into disrepair and the overall sight is indicative of Albanian football as a whole. However, unlike at many other stadiums, Stadiumi Gjirokastra's fabulous views serve to drive away any feelings of melancholy.

071 // Stadiumi Gjirokastra

GJIROKASTËR // ALBANIA // AS LUFTËTARI

070

Batarija

TROGIR // CROATIA // HNK SLAVEN TROGIR

070 // Batarija

TROGIR // CROATIA // HNK SLAVEN TROGIR

Rarely does a month pass without an image of Trogir's Batarija stadium initiating a new surge of infatuation on social media, its topographical splendour depicted in yet another shot taken from a drone camera. Such images lend themselves perfectly to glossy travel brochures and the imagination of those in need of a little escape. The islet barely 500m long, separated from the mainland by a narrow sea passage of turquoise water, the handsome UNESCO walled town, a tight tangle of towers and terracotta roofs.

On its southern tip sits Batarija, home to Slaven Trogir, squeezed by a Venetian fortress and a circular fortification tower at either end and by moored yachts along one touchline. There is no question that from up in the air this little ground ticked all the boxes for entry into the 100.

However, it was with some trepidation that I approached Batarija. For the football supporter attending games on two feet, aerial photography can often be misleading. Spectacular images shot from high above had in previous years led me to Portorož Piran in Slovenia and SV Hielpen in the Netherlands. Framed by the defensive Walls of Piran and loftily positioned on a plateau above the old town, Stadion Pod Obzidjem represented a flawless football landscape. Likewise in the ancient Dutch trading port of Hindeloopen, a vista of striking Hanseatic townhouses and the ocean formed a spectacular backdrop to Hielpen's Sportpark De Meenskar. Although both venues were tidy enough, the reality was disappointingly unremarkable with only a fraction of what was suggested visible from on the ground.

I previously visited Trogir in the summer of 2009. Seeing Batarija from the top of Kamerlengo fortress back then, it appeared as little more than an unenclosed field, marked out for football but worn and lumpy from years of unofficial kick-abouts. More interesting was the Glorijet Marsala Marmonta, an 18th-century Napoleonic gazebo of hexagonal design between the pitch and the water. When the English navy first introduced football to Trogir in 1896, the stone structure stood in the very centre of pitch. During the earliest games played at Batarija, players had to actively avoid colliding into the base such was its presence in the midfield. By 1910 football fever held the town in its grip. Vast groups of young people were suddenly chasing improvised balls through the narrow streets, fresh from watching the latest impromptu match between sailors docked in the port and in Saldun Bay. The arrival on the scene of a young doctor named Ante Madirazza would give the town its first team and identity. Between his studies in Vienna, Madirazza would return home with footballs and eventually an Austria Vienna kit for the team he founded in 1912: Sport Club Trogir.

By 1910 football fever held the town in its grip. Vast groups of young people were suddenly chasing improvised balls through the narrow streets, fresh from watching the latest impromptu match between sailors docked in the port and in Saldun Bay.

But finding a home became an ongoing problem for the club. Scouting parties were sent to identify possible land for a pitch as far as Solin on the outskirts of Split before the club returned to their only real option at Batarija. However, the town's authorities remained staunchly opposed to the idea and a long and inconclusive tug-of-war between the two ensued. Itching to get going, the frustrated players took matters into their own hands. Under the cover of darkness on a rainy night in 1913, a group entered Batarija and chopped down several 'superfluous' trees. At once it opened up access to the field and ultimately forced the authorities to concede use of the land. A fabulous if slightly dubious result. Sport Club Trogir played for many seasons with the spectre of the Glorijet monument on the pitch. Eventually it was dismantled and rebuilt on the water's edge but not before the team had developed some excellent wingers.

Sport Club Trogir played for many seasons with the spectre of the Glorijet monument on the pitch. Eventually it was dismantled and rebuilt on the water's edge but not before the team had developed some excellent wingers.

Trogir have existed largely under the radar in the fifth, sixth and seventh levels of the Croatian league system but for two seasons between 2007 and 2009, they rose to the second division. The adventure may have been short-lived and the subsequent bankruptcy a difficult pill for fans to swallow but it proved to be the catalyst for a complete overhaul of the Batarija field. The old wooden bleachers were swept away and a new uncovered stand with smart blue and white seating erected in its place. Next came the mesh fencing and artificial pitch, at once banishing late-night loiterers and those terrible pitches of yesteryear. Finally the clubhouse and changing rooms were given a thorough makeover and even an electronic scoreboard was fixed to the side of the 15th-century St. Mark's Tower. Not only does the new Batarija unite the ancient and the modern, it has proved itself worthy of the love it receives – from the air or on the ground.

Stade Émile Anthoine

PARIS // FRANCE // ESPA PARIS

At Campo Pio XI in Rome, home of Vatican City's football activities, Michelangelo's dome of Saint Peter's Basilica rises just beyond the football field's northern touchline. Meanwhile, up the coast in Pisa the Leaning Tower can be spotted in a crooked silhouette behind Arena Garibaldi's Curva Sud. As we have already seen in Barcelona, Gaudi's Sagrada Familia cathedral was once a 20th-century neighbour of CE Europa's first football ground while in a later chapter we will discover how Bologna's world-famous porticos form an actual part of Stadio Renato Dall'Ara. Although there is no evidence of contemporary football taking place within eyeshot of Moscow's St Basil's Cathedral, Berlin's Brandenburg Gate or the Acropolis of Athens, there is a small ground on Boechoutlaan in Brussels sat in the shadow of the 102m-high Atomium.

069

But at Stade Émile Anthoine in Paris, football's geographical connection with Europe's most famous landmarks reaches its zenith. Separated only by the elegance of Avenue de Suffren's neo-renaissance apartment blocks, the Eiffel Tower's latticework girders rise majestically above the action on the pitch. As the ultimate man-made object of desire and fascination, every year millions of photographic souvenirs with little variation are taken from the landscaped picnic spots of Champs de Mars or from the Jardins du Trocadéro across the Seine. But from inside Stade Émile Anthoine, the ordinariness of keep-fit routines and low-level football casts the Eiffel Tower in a very different light, one in which its colossal presence barely registers with amateur urban athletes.

Opened in 1979, Center Sportive Émile Anthoine was designed by Anthony Béchu, a Parisian architecture group whose 21st-century eco-friendly designs especially have become celebrated worldwide. A vast complex of sports facilities including swimming pools, indoor halls and Stade Émile Anthoine, in 1979 it was chosen by the French Ministry of Youth and Sports as the headquarters of the CIDJ, a national youth information centre focussed on all aspects of daily life from employment to health and leisure. Various regional football tournaments had taken place at the stadium throughout the 1980s but until 1990, its role had been primarily as an athletics venue.

All over Europe there are bottom-rung clubs leading an often transient existence. Most will have been established in a spirit of great ambition and after the paperwork is signed off, they will kick off amid the great excitement of players, members, families and friends. Nearly all will represent the fulfilment of their founders' dreams. While some go on to great longevity, many quickly disappear in a muddle of financial instability and lack of commitment. The stories of those that survive their first few years are testament to the resilience and perseverance of their people.

In 1990, a brand new football club with enough players for two teams set up base at Stade Émile Anthoine. Named Entente Sportive des Petits Anges Paris (Little Angels Paris), by 2024 ESPA had grown to become one of the largest clubs in the city with upwards of 1,050 members and over 50 teams. In 2018 a women's section was added to the roster which already has 130 players.

With so many teams, therefore, from dawn until dusk Stade Émile Anthoine's football pitch is in constant use. Youth matches especially will often see a few hundred spectators gather on the small terrace while for men's first-team games, it's a quarter of that if they're lucky. But in the depths of the Paris Île-de-France district league, where hundreds of teams from Poissy to Meaux are competing for the public's attention, any support is welcomed. A few curious tourists wander in, having veered off the unending stream headed for the tower from Bir Hakeim metro station. Some will watch the action while taking a breather from their track exercises; one young supporter is draped in a blue and white ESPA flag. It's not much but with a view like this, does it really matter?

Separated only by the elegance of Avenue de Suffren's neo-renaissance apartment blocks, the Eiffel Tower's latticework girders rise majestically above the action on the pitch.

Verlengde Sportlaan

ALMELO // THE NETHERLANDS // AVC HERACLES

I watch the 2023 edition of the Almeloos Feestje in the company of the estimable Herma Hinnen. The annual party in which Almelo's professional Heracles club return to their original home and take on the town's amateur players is, as always, a sell-out. A fresh coat of paint had given the interior of the historic 1924 wooden grandstand a pleasing aroma and from one of its period wooden booths, Herma reminisces enthusiastically about 1999's campaign to rescue it from a future of being turned into firewood. With her husband and a few like-minded volunteers, Herma is secretary, treasurer and the driving force behind Stichting tot behoud Monumentale Tribune Heracles 1924, a group dedicated to the ongoing preservation of the grandstand.

Through the foundation's intensive lobbying to the municipality and fund-raising through subsidies and donations, in 2000 it was dismantled in its entirety and painstakingly reconstructed 150m alongside what would become AVC's new Verlende Sportlaan stadium on the site of the old training pitch. Although a few rotten timbers may have been sacrificed and replaced, M. Krabhuis's English-influenced grandstand looks a picture, so good in fact that in 2011 it was granted National Monument status, one of only two pre-1940s Dutch sporting

In nearby Hengelo, the HVV club have held on to their delightfully ornate brick and wood grandstand of a similar vintage while up in Friesland, at Sneek's LSC 1890 club, Jan de Kok's 1928 Amsterdam School-inspired grandstand was masterfully renovated in 1999.

buildings to be given the title along with Amsterdam's Olympisch Stadion.

As touched upon in the Brabantia and Quick Boys chapters, Dutch amateur football's proclivity towards function over form has seen much of its tangible sporting history erased from the map. Very few period football buildings remain and those that do are often a result of a similar level of devotion as Herma's. In nearby Hengelo, the HVV club have held on to their delightfully ornate brick and wood grandstand of a similar vintage while up in Friesland, at Sneek's LSC 1890 club, Jan de Kok's 1928 Amsterdam School-inspired grandstand was masterfully renovated in 1999. A fabulous 1939 wooden stand reminiscent of those that graced the prewar grounds of London amateur clubs remains in use at VVO in Pinkenberg and there are other comparably fine examples at AGOVV in Apeldoorn and Den Haag's VUC club. In the town of Rijssen, the narrowest of wooden grandstands, again influenced by 1920s English design, had stood in yellow and black glory at the Vooruit club since 1928. When Vooruit merged with RKSV in 2019 to form SV Rijssen, it was decided to bring the old stand to the new stadium in another faithfully executed reconstruction. Thirty kilos of nails which held the stand together were removed by hand and, now repainted in blue and black, it occupies pride of place in the most modern of settings.

As the wave of postwar industrialisation swept across Europe, Dutch football clubs began replacing tired old wooden grandstands with something altogether more futuristic. Enter Elascon, a design and engineering company founded in Leiden in 1953 who had initially spotted a gap in the market for car garages and cold-war storage facilities. Elascon's designers imagined a steel-framed, U-shaped aerodynamic technology which was soon outsourced to steel companies for manufacturing. Such was the success of this unique, wind tunnel-tested design the company tapped into the next logical market with a need for shelter from the elements; the sports stadium. In doing so, they unwittingly became the forefathers of the 21st-century modular kit stand but while those bland but affordable edifices have become the scourge of the traditionalist, especially in the UK, the elegant curvature and slimline frames of Elascon structures were always inherently more seductive. Much like a classic car, over the years they become increasingly venerated, those clubs lucky or smart enough to still have a functioning model finding themselves on growing lists of must-see stadiums. For the very best examples, SC Gramsbergen's circular economy version was saved from demolition in 2011 and now stands resplendent in green and white, one of the most prized around. DHC Delft's 1959 grandstand is among the largest made while in Amsterdam, VV Zeeburgia's more tubular model is straight out of the Race for Space. Elascon stands exist in Luxembourg, Germany and Belgium too where at RVC Hoboken's Stadion de Visputten one of the most attractive survives.

Back at AVC, Herma's husband shows me inside the wooden underbelly of the grandstand. The communal baths have long gone but everything below is surprisingly light and airy, the unpainted trusses and rear windows as meticulously maintained as above. In a documentary made by the club, third-generation AVC player Tom Egbers recalls events witnessed from the grandstand which have shaped his own life; as a child glimpsing a marriage proposal through a gap between the seats, Heracles defeating Ajax in the cup, a supporter falling dead and the uniquely English atmosphere which permeates the place, felt particularly keenly by Tom with his own English ancestry. Another visitor tells the story of how he would sit with his back to the action in petulant protestation at being dragged to watch the football by his father and how he would take solace in losing himself in the pastoral vista of cows and meadows espied through cracks in the floorboards. He now brings his own son to football practice here despite still never having found a love for the game himself. In protecting AVC's grandstand, Herma's foundation has protected the stories and memories from a century of football to live on in the very fabric of the place. On my phone, I show her a photo of Great Yarmouth Town's grandstand, England's oldest and most celebrated outside the professional game. She beams from ear to ear, beckoning over her husband. Aside from the obvious similarities in the elegance of both, they immediately recognise a kinship with the people behind its preservation. To Herma's foundation and the countless others across Europe who devote their time and resources to keeping alive local sporting heritage, we should be thankful. These are the people who allow us to be part of football as it used to be.

Stadio San Filippo – Franco Scoglio

MESSINA // ITALY // ACR MESSINA

Splayed out across the valley floor like an enormous spatchcock chicken, Stadio San Filippo – Franco Scoglio's red rooster colour scheme is slowly fading to fleshy pinks and washed-out yellows. The second of two great stadiums to have played home to Messina's premier football club, it may be ageing quickly under the Sicilian sun but it remains a triumph of early 21st-century stadium design.

Should plans announced in May 2024 for a €2.6m upgrade come to fruition, it would propel San Filippo back to its rightful place at the top table alongside Italy's very finest stadiums. Thereafter the question will be whether its club can find a prolonged period of stability in which to fill it and moreover, keep the municipality interested enough in maintaining it.

In comparison with Sicily's big hitters, Palermo and Catania, Messina have led an unexceptional existence. Five seasons in Serie A, a sole Serie B title and in between, multiple downward spirals concluding in all-out collapse. For this reason Stadio San Filippo remains largely unknown beyond the peninsula. It is not steeped in history in the way Florence's Stadio Artemio Franchi is nor has it witnessed the glories seen at Milan's San Siro. Indeed, since its inauguration on 17 August 2004, it has hosted a paltry three seasons in Serie A. But with its delightful modern twist on the horseshoe stadiums of ancient Athens and the modern United States, it is a thoroughly unique arena. In the same way Trieste's Stadio Nereo Rocco deserves better, it must be hoped that both club and city can start to fall in love with it again.

Under various guises, Messina had played since 1932 at Stadio Giovanni Celeste in the airless backstreets of the Mangialupi neighbourhood. If ever there was a more archetypal Sicilian stadium I have yet to see it. Located on a single block, Celeste appears to have been forcibly crushed into an area half its size, two corners sheared off completely by the surrounding road layout. Uniformly filthy, it stands in semi-dereliction, hidden behind grubby shop fronts on the SS114 highway to Catania. Until 2018 it played host to a club called SSD FC Messina, a direct descendant of the city's historic Camaro club. Following that club's move out to a striking new stadium in Rione Bisconte however, football has yet to return.

In comparison with Sicily's big hitters, Palermo and Catania, Messina have led an unexceptional existence. Five seasons in Serie A, a sole Serie B title and in between, multiple downward spirals concluding in all-out collapse.

During the late 1980s Messina had become mainstays in Serie B, the second tier of Italian football. With a capacity of just 11,900 Stadio Celeste was regularly sold out for matches and so in 1988 the municipality began drafting plans for a 'modern, comfortable, great new theatre' in the valleys of San Filippo. Announced during a press conference on 29 March of that year, the *Giallorossi* would have their new stadium within three years. Yet as is the way in Sicilian life, promises are often made to be broken. After Messina's financial meltdown in 1993 and subsequent demotion to the seventh tier, all parties including the fans quickly lost interest in the new stadium. It would take the arrival in 1994 of a club named US Peloro to resurrect the project. A lightning-quick climb up the divisions took them into Serie C within four years and Serie B three years later. Changing their name to FC Messina and under the ownership of local entrepreneur Pietro Franza, they then sent shockwaves through the country by reaching Serie A, 40 years on from the original club's last dalliance with the big boys.

Opened for a friendly against Fabio Capello's Juventus, it had taken 16 years for the project to be realised. Such was the esteem in which the new stadium was held, however, the Italian national team under Marcello Lippi soon arrived for a match against Finland. Then 40,000 turned up for a Serie A game between Messina and Juventus as remarkably the *Giallorossi* ended their first season in seventh place. Everything appeared rosy in Messina and through its footballing exploits, the city began to shake off its reputation of 'just a crossing point'. Messina would survive one more year in Serie A before yet again it all began to come apart at the seams. In July 2008 Franza announced his decision to withdraw his support. With no new investors forthcoming, Messina gave up their Serie B status and were admitted into Serie D. For fans of the Red Roosters already incandescent with rage, things got a whole lot worse in November when the Court of Messina declared the club bankrupt.

Made up of three tribunes arranged in a horseshoe shape, the seating capacity for each is strangely irregular with 9,569 on the eastern side, 9,263 on the western and 8,692 on the Curva Nord. Opposite, the Curva Sud is detached and flanked by a pair of L-shaped buildings into which a steep seating sector for 8,791 is recessed. With a central VIP area in the western stand for 2,407, the current capacity of San Filippo is 38,722. Numerous services are housed beneath Curva Sud and within the adjoining blocks including the council of Messina's second district. The overall appearance is of a smaller, budget variation on Ohio Stadium in Columbus, the third-largest on-campus stadium in the United States. This is not intended as a criticism as San Filippo was created at a fraction of the price that stadium would cost to build in the 21st century. Moreover, it simply doesn't require the frills or internal space of that stadium. What it does need is a steady football club, one that can bring a modicum of pride back to Sicily's third-largest city. When they get there, Stadio San Filippo can finally achieve what it was made for.

Stadionul Mircea Chivu

REŞIŢA // ROMANIA // CSM REŞIŢA

Some 375km west of Bucharest, the historical region of Banat is widely acknowledged as the cradle of Romanian football. Decades before Steaua and Dinamo were founded and even earlier than Bucharest's Venus and Rapid clubs emerged as contenders in national competitions, Banat was producing Divizia A (now Liga I) champions left, right and centre. In the centre was the city of Timişoară and a pair of clubs that, as a result of Banat's geographical spanning of the Austro-Hungarian Empire, had been given something of a head start over their Romanian contemporaries.

Achieving great things in the Hungarian league before Timişoară officially came under the administration of Romania at the end of the First World War, Chinezul Timişoară's kicked off 1921/22 in Divizia A's first season as a fully nationwide competition. They won it and the next five on the spin, a record only matched by Steaua Bucureşti some 71 years later.

Next to enter the picture in 1928 were Ripensia Timişoară (a brand new club founded by Chinezul's recently departed president) who promptly took over from their city rivals to claim four titles themselves. However, between the passing of that particular Banat baton, there was for a solitary season another champion from the region. UD Reşiţa emerged like a cannonball to win the 1930/31 championship and in doing so were embellished with the epithet 'Milan from Banat'. Almost a century later and the club now known as CSM Reşiţa still cling to their title dearly. Moreover, they continue to play at their home since 1926 which despite its shaky structure remains one of the finest in Romania's plethora of football grounds set within the natural environment.

Consistent with the fluctuating population and fortunes of a city once described as Romania's most important industrial centre after Bucharest, Stadionul Mircea Chivu has spent its existence see-sawing between the downright decrepit and the refreshingly radiant. In the same way an artist will rework a painting when new inspiration arrives or if an aspect of it isn't working, Reşiţa's only large stadium has been scrubbed back, reworked and varnished umpteen times over the decades. Since I took these photographs on a visit in 2022, CSM Reşiţa have won promotion back into Liga II after an absence of 11 years; 8,000 new bucket seats have also replaced those flaked with decades-old paint, instantly breathing new life back into the stadium. But behind this colourful new veneer, so striking against the viridescent backdrop of the Valea Domanului (Doman Valley), tell-tale reminders of its age are plentiful.

066
GUARDIA
ULTRA
GAZON ARTIFICIAL
JAKO
SPALATORIE COVOARE
MARKET
GRADIMEX
BANAT | TV
FM | BANAT

Unlike nearby Timișoară's Stadionul Dan Păltinișanu or Craiova's Stadionul Ion Oblemenco, funding to extend Stadionul Mircea Chivu around the site's oval footprint never materialised. The distinctiveness of the ground centres around its two wildly disparate grandstands, on the eastern aspect the especially fragile central tribune constructed in 1926 and opposite, a stand shaped like an inverted isosceles triangle, hewn from the Bârzăviți Hills in 1928. With an overhang supported by a series of slender pillars beneath which fans take refuge from the elements, this stand is abruptly interrupted by a boxy stone building operating as a car workshop. A wide flight of steps leads up on to its roof from where the Guardia Ultra 1995 group make their way down to their favoured spot on the upper tier. Peculiar doesn't quite do it; only Croatian club Imotski's grandstand (as we will later see) is scooped and crafted from similar terrain.

As the last building of any significance on the road leading out from Reşiţa's southern end, the whole stadium is hugged tightly by the forested slopes of the Valea Domanului. Just beyond Dealul Golului hill, the rusting steel mills of the Reşiţa Works occupy an area 20 times larger than the stadium, dominating the skyline as it has done the lives of Banat Romanians for centuries.

A teenage member of the Guardia Ultras takes time out from duties selling club merchandise to show me around the club's museum, tucked away beneath the eastern stand. Walls are adorned with photos of players past, most notably from Reșița's Romanian Cup-winning side of 1954, and those who graduated from the club to achieve international success. Romania's most-capped player, Dorinel Munteanu, played here as did Basarab Panduru, Dudu Georgescu and Cristian Chivu, whose father Mircea was honoured in the naming of the stadium after a career as player and coach of Reșița and captain of the national team.

As the last building of any significance on the road leading out from Reșița's southern end, the whole stadium is hugged tightly by the forested slopes of the Valea Domanului. Just beyond Dealul Golului hill, the rusting steel mills of the Reșița Works occupy an area 20 times larger than the stadium, dominating the skyline as it has done the lives of Banat Romanians for centuries. During more prosperous times and especially if Metalul were playing well, fans would finish shifts and in their thousands make their way to the stadium through a network of ginnels between the colossal sheds and blast furnaces. Stopping only to buy sunflower seeds wrapped in newspaper cones, if Stadionul Mircea Chivu was sold out (and it often was), many would find a window through the forest vegetation high above the triangular stand from which to watch. Such levels of fervour have of course waned but there is still a tangible sense of pride which permeates Stadionul Mircea Chivu, something absent from so many Romanian stadiums in an era of televised football. In 2026 it will reach its centenary, structurally altered little from when it was opened. It may be a relic but it is Romanian Banat's final link to the region's footballing greatness.

065

Ellenfeldstadion

NEUNKIRCHEN // GERMANY // BORUSSIA NEUNKIRCHEN

Towards the end of 2023 with just a handful of journeys left to make and months of writing ahead of me, only one ground in south-west Germany was on the list of 100: Kaiserslautern's monolithic Fritz-Walter-Stadion. The inclusion of Neunkirchen's historic Ellenfeldstadion, a veritable repository of German football past, under normal circumstances would have been a shoo-in but since the previous spring its gates had been bolted shut.

Ongoing structural concerns centred around the formidable Speiser Curve and the installation of a new playing surface had left tenants Borussia decamped at Ellenfeld's artificial surface to play their sixth-tier matches, usually in front of fewer than 500 supporters. However, in early 2024 an email dropped into my inbox, a club newsletter from Borussia with tentative details of their return home. By March, the club had announced the date and the opposition and the following month, I reshuffled the pack and headed for the Saarland rust-belt.

What we have lost from the game in western Europe can never accurately be replaced. Younger generations of supporters yearn for the revitalisation of stadiums, a desire usually centred on being able to stand on terraces. Those who have watched football for long enough are just as likely to tell you that certain aspects of the 20th-century game are best left there, that terrace culture has no place in an era when football is more popular and inclusive than ever. In recent years, multiple clubs have bowed to the demand with the slow introduction of small safe-standing areas, heavily patrolled by security and requiring intrusive body searches to enter. However, football and nostalgia are largely inseparable and a supporter's radar for authenticity is finely tuned. Accusations of tokenism have been levelled at clubs, measures such as safe standing merely hollow gestures aimed at keeping revenue from fans rolling in. In club shops, retro-themed shirts hang unsold on sale racks in favour of the real thing bought from online auctions, graphics teams' attempts at retro match programme designs roundly mocked. More and more, fans want something real.

My visit to Neunkirchen therefore turned out to be in every sense as though the modern era of the game had been merely a dream. Six hours before kick-off, train after train departed Saarbrücken hauptbahnhof, sardined without exception with supporters bound for a long-overdue Saarland derby. On my own train rumbling alongside the grimy River Saar, through rain-lashed windows I glimpsed mountains of rusted scrap metal, burning flare towers and long-disused blast furnaces. Most Saarbrücken fans I shared the carriage with were in full singing voice. To a man, everyone drank. At Neunkirchen station football specials were laid on to bus supporters across the old steel city to Ellenfeldstadion where in the small parking lot on Mantes-le-Ville-Platz, thousands thronged in the rain in a smog of grilling bratwurst, cigarette smoke and steaming piss puddles. Others huddled for shelter beneath the creaking ribs of Ellenfeldstadion's curious corner tribune, held aloft by its few spindly concrete pillars. Still the rain found them, through holes and cracks in the terrace above. My 12-year old daughter Elle, who had spent the previous Sunday largely disinterested at Berlin's Olympiastadion, looked on wide-eyed.

In terms of appearance, Ellenfeldstadion hasn't come very far in its 113 years of service. It looks very much the product of a town in decline in the same way that football grounds in the north of England did before redevelopment or demolition. It is a living, breathing, creaking relic of a place, patinated by the footfall of a million souls who have stood upon its terraces. Opened in 1912 on land leased by local brewer Otto Schmidt, Ellenfeldstadion has served its city and its people unfailingly through the trials and tribulations of life in a heavy industrial town. In 1933, a charity match against Admira Vienna was played for the benefit of the relatives of the 65 victims killed after a gasometer explosion at the nearby ironworks, a disaster which reduced much of Neunkirchen to rubble. On 12 March 1995, Saarland miners fresh from the pit and blackened by coal stood in unison on the terraces with 6,000 Borussia fans to protest against regional pit closures.

Beneath the main stand is a bygone world of dimly lit corridors, old power distribution boxes and liminal spaces. In the old changing rooms where once Kaiserslautern's Fritz and Ottmar Walter prepared, a hole in the wall indicates the spot where the stove pipe used to heat the rooms led outside.

Conversely, many of Neunkirchen's happier times are inexorably linked to the stadium, not least Borussia's promotion into the Bundesliga for the 1964/65 season. For the opening match against Borussia Dortmund 25,000 descended upon Ellenfeldstadion, an attendance that would regularly be bettered over the next few seasons. It is worth noting that despite Saarland's population boom during the 1960s, the city of Neunkirchen's estimated population was still fewer than 60,000, suggesting that Borussia were very much a team of the labouring classes in the mould of a Burnley, Bolton or Blackburn.

Beneath the main stand is a bygone world of dimly lit corridors, old power distribution boxes and liminal spaces. In the old changing rooms where once Kaiserslautern's Fritz and Ottmar Walter prepared, a hole in the wall indicates the spot where the stove pipe used to heat the rooms led outside. In 1921 a grandstand company independent of the club was founded and through finances raised by the sale of shares and entrance fees, a large wooden grandstand was built. It stood until December 1928 when a fire ripped through its timbers and a more substantial reinforced concrete structure with function rooms and office space was erected in its place.

Opened in 1930, the ground level remains unspoiled to this day. Following the purchase of the stadium site from from Schmidt brewing family in 1949 and with Borussia becoming a force in the Oberliga Südwest alongside Kaiserslautern, Pirmasens, Saarbrücken and Wormatia Worms, architect Felix Schaan was brought in to design the expansion of the stadium. However, with Saarland's government financially committed to Saarbrücken's Ludwigparkstadion, only the construction of the standing terrace cut into the Spieser hill and the base of a new sports hall at the western end took place. For the club's 50th anniversary, the Schloss Brewery donated to the club a larger-than-life statue of a footballer sculpted by Karl Hock which nowadays stands guard in front of the corner tribune.

Ellenfeldstadion finally got its expansion during the 1964/65 season at a time when it was needed most. Saarland government contributed 50 per cent of the cost and Borussia were able to begin their Bundesliga odyssey. With 28,000 seats and a capacity tested to the limit when 33,000 saw Borussia beat Bayern Hof 4-0 in 1967, winning promotion back to the Bundesliga for one final season, it has altered little since those halcyon days. The partial closure of the grandstand's standing paddock in 2007 and the padlocking shut of the wonderful Spieser Curve in 2011 has reduced its capacity to under 12,000. Borussia's freefall into the lower echelons of German football has been stark; indeed they are currently the lowest-ranked former Bundesliga club still in existence. But on days like today, a Saarland Cup quarter-final against their old foes of 100 years and more, Ellenfeldstadion offers the most genuine football experience around.

Ipurua

EIBAR // SPAIN // SD EIBAR

064

It is often said that men from the Basque Country are either noticeably very tall or very short. Another stereotype is that they speak louder and more animatedly than the rest of Spain, a trait that likely derives from the area's ancient *irrintzi* shepherding traditions. Such characteristics can reasonably be applied to the region's three most senior football clubs where between the giants of Athletic Bilbao and Real Sociedad, diminutive Eibar continue to weave their story of the ultimate underdogs long after any logical conclusion.

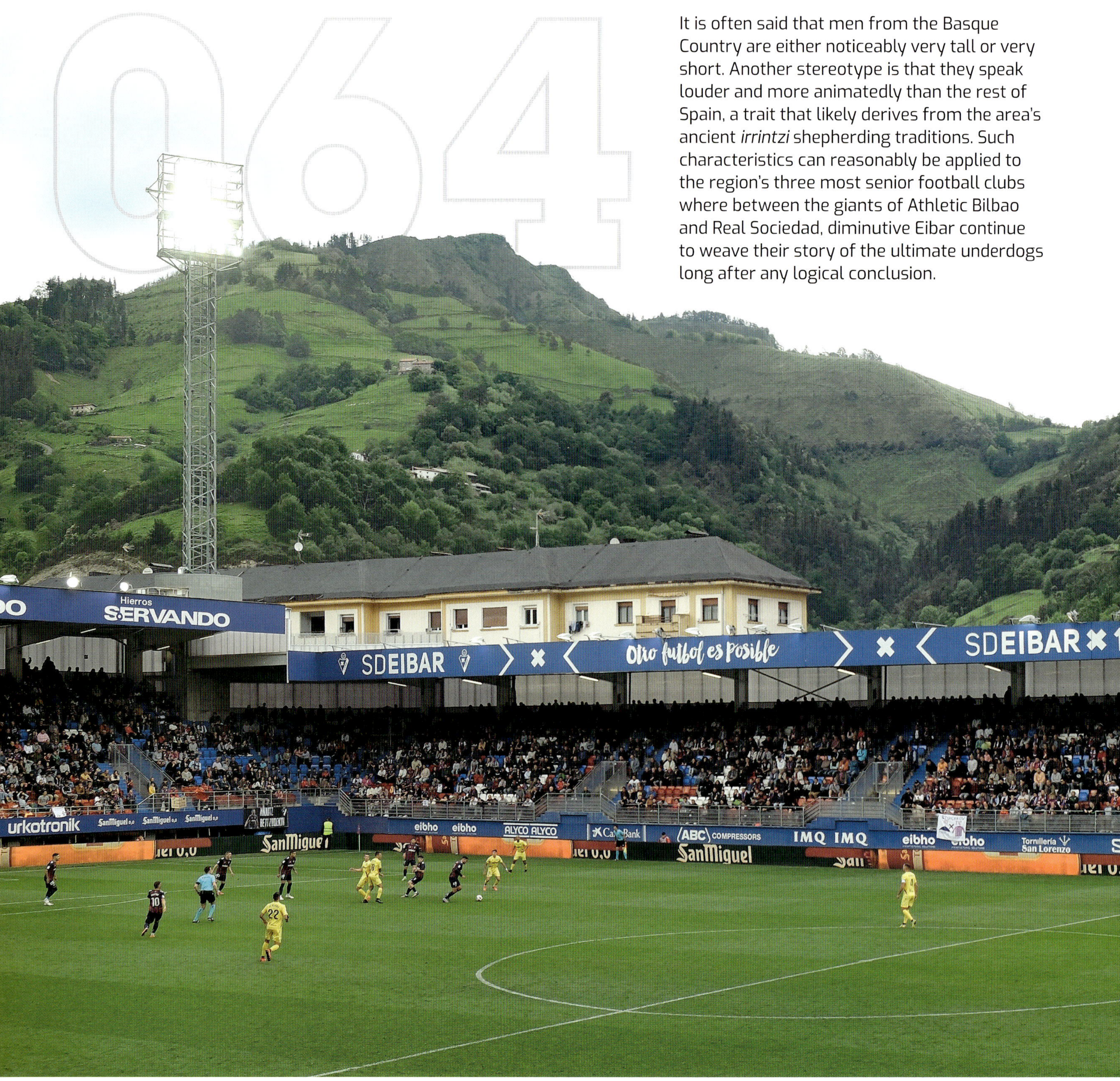

Located in a valley traditionally associated with its finery forges and arms manufacturing, Eibar is a town both fanatical and fervid about its sport. In the 1990s, the club's Eskosia La Brava fan group was founded through a mutual love of Scotland's rousing rugby displays both on and off the pitch. Recognising similarities in their geographical isolation and in their strong regional identities, it is a kinship that still brings an abundance of tartan to matches and the occasional belting out of 'Scotland the Brave'.

To put the scale of Eibar's 21st-century achievements into perspective, during the 2019/20 La Liga season, their sixth in a run of seven, the average Ipurua attendance was 6,059 – 34,921 fewer than Athletic Club 48km away and 24,931 fewer than Real Sociedad. The first El Clásico of the season at Camp Nou drew a crowd of 93,426, almost 15,000 more than Eibar's

Eibar's origins can be traced back to 1911 and the arrival of Pedro Mandiola, the first man from the town upon whom the footballing spotlight fell. Frustrated by his beloved hometown's lack of interest in the game, Mandiola would return from Athletic Bilbao with a football and a bag of tricks to impress the local townsfolk.

combined attendances for the entire season. While this may suggest a poorly supported club, the opposite is in fact true. From a pocket of just 27,000, Eibar attracts around 25 per cent of the town's population to matches at Ipurua while an estimated 45 per cent follow *Los Armeros'* (the Gunsmiths) games on television. Eibar is to all intents and purposes one of European football's greatest anomalies. And Ipurua is not just one of the smallest grounds to ever host football in Europe's top five leagues, it is the bedrock from which miracles are born.

Eibar's origins can be traced back to 1911 and the arrival of Pedro Mandiola, the first man from the town upon whom the footballing spotlight fell. Frustrated by his beloved hometown's lack of interest in the game, Mandiola would return from Athletic Bilbao with a football and a bag of tricks to impress the local townsfolk. In response, the Izarra football club was born and although short-lived, their small stadium in the nearby hamlet of Otolaerdikua would

SDEIBAR

become the home of several of Eibar's clubs and ultimately, SD Eibar themselves. No trace of the original stadium remains, the abandoned Norica airgun workshops standing roughly where it was located. At the end of the Spanish Civil War and with Eibar laying in ruins, the town's council encouraged Unión Deportiva Eibarresa and Deportiva Gallo to fuse together to create a single entity for the town to get behind. Sociedad Deportiva Eibar were founded in 1940, playing firstly 7km away at Campo de Lerún in Elgoibar before setting up at Otolaerdikua between 1943 to 1947. But as the 1944/45 campaign drew to a close, a site for a new custom-built football stadium was identified up on the hill of Ipurua, land that had since the end of the war been used as a waste dump for rubble and timber.

Meaning 'land unplowed', Ipurua opened its doors on14 September 1947. Fringed by a thousand black umbrellas, neighbours Elgoibar came, scored twice and took away local bragging rights on an afternoon remembered as much for the torrential conditions as the football. The following year construction began on Ipurua's grandstand, a simple, narrow concrete building which would stand for 50 years on the southern side offering panoramic views over the town and Cross of Arrate beyond. Images of the ground from the time illustrate just how limited space was even before the arrival of the neighbouring high rise apartment blocks. Squeezed between the hill and Santainés Kalea, room for just six steps of terracing on the northern side and a few more on Ipurua Kalea street existed. On 14 October 1970, the first edition of the Trofeo Amistad, a summer tournament organised by SD Eibar to celebrate the shared pride of the Basque clubs, was held at Ipurua and won by Athletic Bilbao. Other than the extension of the grandstand and new floodlighting in the mid-1970s, little changed at Eibar. But as the 1990s swung into view, so did the potential of the club who had evolved into serious contenders in the second tier of Spanish football.

Through financial contributions from the Higher Sports Council and the Professional Football League, Eibar set about remodelling their wearied home in the summer of 1998. Firstly, a new central grandstand was constructed with a row of balconied VIP lounges set above 11 rows of seating. Next, the 'English' and 'La Bombonera' stands at either end were built and by 2000/01, a brand new north stand was operational albeit with just three rows of seating following two years of construction work from the challenging confines of Santainés Kalea. Under normal circumstances, the remodelled Ipurua should have seen the club through the next 50 years but normal is not a word in Eibar's vocabulary. By 2014/15 they had in two seasons bounced from the third level into La Liga, a feat that to this day leaves supporters of the underdog pinching themselves. With the exception of the grandstand, Ipurua was quickly demolished. Three unfussy new stands went up and corners were joined for a fully enclosed feel. The exterior was aptly clad in a gunmetal transparent mesh with liberal crosses of Saint Andrew punched into the metalwork. Inside, Eibar's *blaugrana* colours (adopted from Barcelona in 1943) run riot throughout the seating arrangements.

By 2014/15 they had in two seasons bounced from the third level into La Liga, a feat that to this day leaves supporters of the underdog pinching themselves.

Taking the series of steep street escalators up to Ipurua, I find myself among a group of older supporters dressed in Bearnais berets and *blaugrana* neckerchiefs. Outside the club's small museum, kids are draped in flags, the narrow streets swarming with replica shirts. Everyone is smiling because yet again, Eibar are again on the cusp of something special. They say good things come in small packages. And with a capacity of 8,164, Ipurua is proof of that: a beautifully engineered stadium of tiny but perfect proportions where great things happen.

On the day in 2022 that Campo Gerini celebrated its 70th anniversary, the past generations of players, coaches and volunteers in attendance were reminded of the field's motto, 'If children do not return to play here, in the streets, squares and oratories, this sport of ours will disappear.' This time, however, it was communicated more as a rallying cry, a plea to all it has served to do their bit to help save one of the last remaining bare-earth fields in Rome. Three years earlier, concerns had been raised that property vultures had been spotted circling overhead, eyeing the thin green wedge of the Appia Antica Park which enfolds Campo Gerini and runs from near the Colosseum out to Castelli Romani and the distant hills.

063

Campo Gerini

ROME // ITALY // PROCALCIO

The second-largest urban park in Europe, this is a protected landscape of exceptional importance and Arcadian beauty where Roman treasures jostle with riding stables and rehabilitation centres among flower-filled meadows. Four year later, the concerns were justified.

Eleven kilometres south-east of the Colosseum, the importance of the role Campo Gerini has played in the lives of the people of Cinecitta and Quadraro cannot be accurately measured. It is, however, safe to say it is huge. Since 1952 tens of thousands have passed through its unassuming entrance gates with its little mailbox and dazzling flower pot displays. No fewer than 38 clubs have called it home, the list of those reading like a paean to the imagination of their creators. From 1952's first occupants, Tarcisius, in their cheap amaranth-coloured jerseys, teams with such exotic monikers as Cavalieri del Sud, Rimet '70, The Fourth Mile and Roma Cappanelle, a footballing branch of Italy's oldest cricket club, have all played here. And this because Campo Gerini is not a club football ground in the true sense. Long before the 'community hubs' of the 21st century, with their caged artificial surfaces and ever-rolling roster of matches, Gerini existed as a kind of archaic prototype serving its community's various football factions seven days a week from junior football right through to senior.

With the need for such quick-fix stadiums increasing across Europe, the 20th-century ground with its problematic pitches and high maintenance levels disappearing one by one, one can be forgiven for assuming that Campo Gerini is perfectly positioned for an overhaul. After all, this is land bequeathed to the city for the purpose of social inclusion, sport and culture by Marquis Alessandro Gerini, the 'Builder of the Gods' who made his billions through property speculation in Rome during the postwar period. Yet in the summer of 2023, old worries were amplified when newspapers ran the story that 40 hectares of the land (the equivalent of 60 football pitches) had been sold to private individuals including a supermarket entrepreneur. Those responsible for the conservation and management of the land, the Fondazione Gerini and the Salesians were the very same people who had sold it, land including a non-profit sports rehabilitation centre for people with disabilities. People tore at their clothes, the anger among the people of Rome very real not least because the Lazio government failed to exercise the right of pre-emption to stop it. The waters are muddy, the future uncertain.

Standing watching current tenants Procalcio play in the dark basement of the Lazio football pyramid, my mind inevitably wanders towards Emperor Claudius and what he would have made of the scene played out in 2023. There is a lot of effort, a lot of hopeful swinging, petty squabbles and dust being wiped from eyes, something Claudius would no doubt have approved of himself, being a great advocate and competitor of gladiatorial sport at the Colosseum. His aqueduct stands in sun-blessed decay a few feet beyond its boundary, its own birthday recently passed although when you reach the grand old age of 1,970, no one takes much notice anymore. Tempus Fugit. He would surely have raised a smile at his empire's building techniques being so much more advanced than today's. Coexisting alongside the Aquedotto Claudius as it does, Campo Gerini rubs shoulders with history like no other football ground in Europe. It may only be approved for hosting senior matches in the Terza Categoria, the ninth level of Italian football, and its place in the great pantheon of Roman sport may only be a minor one. But for the sake of its unique place in the landscape and the people who will continue to enjoy it, we must hope common sense prevails.

Standing watching current tenants Procalcio play in the dark basement of the Lazio football pyramid, my mind inevitably wanders towards Emperor Claudius and what he would have made of the scene played out in 2023.

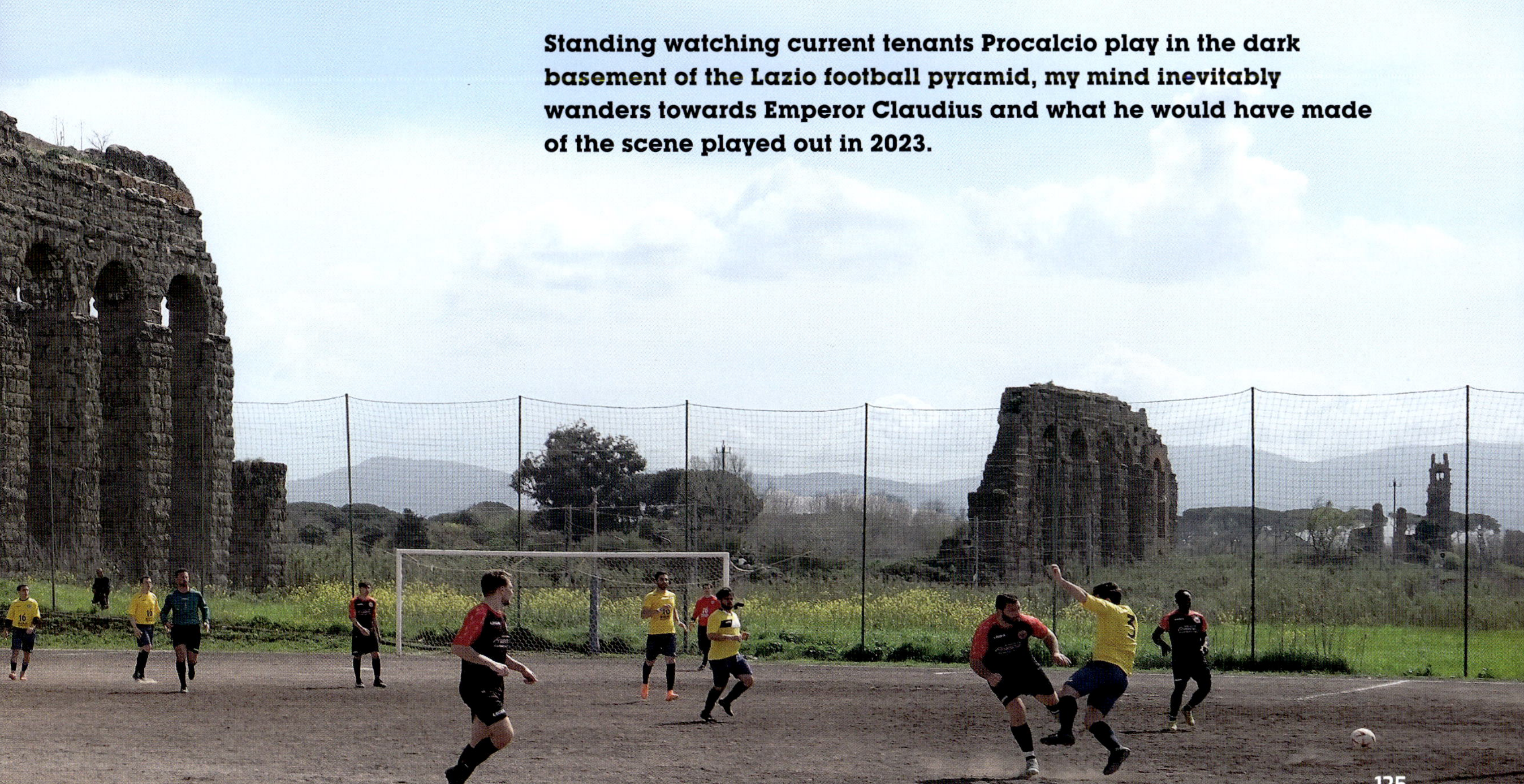

062

Campo de Fútbol San Miguel

EMBID DE LA RIBERA // SPAIN // EMBID CF

When we think of Spain, we picture its historic cities, its arts, beaches, holidays and sun. It is unlikely we focus on its immense emptiness or gargantuan mountain chains which lacerate its interior creating vast uninhabitable regions. Spain is second only to Switzerland as Europe's most mountainous country. Yet this explains only part of why areas within Spain's doughnut-shaped population void are as empty as Lapland.

During the Francoist dictatorship, mass emigration from a stagnant economy emptied much of impoverished rural Spain in the postwar years. And when in 1959 Spain's economy was turned on its head with the introduction of free markets and industrial reforms, further plummeting of the rural population occurred as huge foreign investment in the coastal metropolises saw one in four from the interior relocate to places such as Gijón, Bilbao, Barcelona and Málaga.

Nowadays, the doughnut with the anomaly of Madrid in its hole represents 70 per cent of Spain's landmass and yet only ten per cent of its population live here. That translates as 18 people per square kilometre, a statistic unparalleled anywhere else within western Europe. More staggering is that within the doughnut an area roughly the size of Ireland known as the Serrania Celtiberica, that number drops to just eight people per square kilometre, making it the second most sparsely populated area in Europe behind Lapland. No wonder they call it Laponia del Sur: South Lapland.

Here the very existence of Sunday afternoon football is as much about avoiding becoming the dreaded 'village without a team' and there is an unspoken understanding that each club must continue for the sake of its neighbours.

So, can football at amateur level survive here in the Serrania Celtiberica, in a landscape of ghost villages where griffon vultures circle overhead? The answer is unequivocal for more than just survival, there is a 19km ribbon of villages with football teams strung along the Rio Jalón in Aragon defying odds and indeed logic. Here the very existence of Sunday afternoon football is as much about avoiding becoming the dreaded 'village without a team' and there is an unspoken understanding that each club must continue for the sake of its neighbours.

Downstream from Calatayud, the Rio Jalón is enclosed in a valley of steep fluvial gorges of quartzite, slate and limestone. A single-track road and railway line follow it for a while through seemingly impassable mountains, the road hairpinning around seven tiny communities nestling in the plains which all have football fields and teams. From the hamlet of Embid de la Ribera, its population just 47, the next

three villages of Sabiñan, Morés and Sestrica have a combined population of barely 1,000. As the Jalón then sweeps eastwards to meet the Ebro in Zaragoza, the road continues north to Brea, Gotor and Illueca, whose Copa del Rey run in 2019 culminated in bringing Deportivo de La Coruña to their bare-bones village ground and in doing briefly shone a spotlight on this most unlikely of footballing hotbeds.

It is Embid de la Ribera that we return to, however, for the barren splendour of its tiny Campo San Miguel. There are football fields in the Arabian peninsula that look a little like this, one or two in the Moroccan Sahara, but nothing like it in Europe. All around, a natural amphitheatre of steep shady slopes, tawny in colour, squeeze the valley, the sumac, broom and wild jasmine growing on the lower slopes muted in the March cool. In the plains on the valley floor, neat grids of traditional orchards and a one-train-per-day railway line, the only evidence that man has tampered with the landscape. The people of Embid carved the pitch into the top of an old conical earthwork a mile or so east of the village in 1967, clearing away abandoned single-storey farm buildings and levelling the land. Initially used for kick-abouts, a football club was formed in 1970 and joined the regional Aragon leagues where they played for four seasons before disbanding, unsurprisingly being unable to attract players. Embid went into a prolonged period of abeyance as the village population further dwindled and football seemingly became just a minor footnote in its history. In 1982, however, Embid CF tentatively returned to action with a new generation in the bottom tier of the regional league and keen to keep up with the Joneses up the valley, set about constructing a small kiosk and covered area upon the raised bank.

Players drive away back to Calatayud or Illueca after matches, bandages hiding cuts and grazes of all shapes and sizes on knees, elbows and shins.

Little has changed at Campo San Miguel in the 40 years since, on and off the pitch. A finish near the bottom of the lowest division for Embid CF is as likely as the sun rising while a crowd of over 50 gathers just once a season when neighbours Sabiñan visit. The bare-earth pitch, one of very few left in Spain, looks like remaining ad infinitum as any form of funding from the landowners to this the village of 47 people is unlikely and government sports grants for communities of this size are virtually non-existent. And so games continue to be halted for the arrival of the wet towel, to mop dust and grit from eyes. Players drive away back to Calatayud or Illueca after matches, bandages hiding cuts and grazes of all shapes and sizes on knees, elbows and shins.

When club secretary David unlocks the kiosk to serve coffee laced with rum to the few who have come to watch, it opens on to a pocket-sized club museum where old photographs, club scarves and tarnished trophies from forgotten games sit on dusty shelves among liquors of all variety. This humble display represents Embid's history; small, lean, inadequate for most but for Embid, proof of their existence in such isolation and therefore worth showing off. He takes me out on to the pitch, gestures with a broad sweep of his arms towards the mountains and says with a grin, 'Camp Nou. Bernabéu.' His pride is unmistakable, his meaning clear; this is Embid's Camp Nou and who could wish for anything more?

While visiting the football grounds in this book, no place gave me the sense that I had reached the end of the world quite like Basilicata. Squeezed between Puglia, Campania and Calabria, and seemingly unknown by the rest of Italy, Basilicata is a forgotten world of quietude and stillness where everything seems hazy and undefined. It is a place where time drips like rivulets of water, where people live slowly in ancient hill towns much like they have done for centuries before.

061

Stadio Paolo Carbone

TRICARICO // ITALY // TRICARICO POZZO DI SICAR

The small town of Tricarico sits atop its narrow hill, melancholy and gloomy, bleached a ghostly shade of ochre from too much light from the scorching sun. Pete Seeger's social satire spoke of little boxes on the hillside but Tricarico's are not of the ticky-tacky variety, rather ancient brick and mortar that appear to have stood since time immemorial. Two hours before the local football team kick off their game in the Eccellenza, the fifth tier of Italian football, the only sounds are the church bells on the quarter-hour and the occasional roar of an old Piaggio Ape three-wheeler climbing the narrow streets at speed.

In a country permanently gripped by *calcio*, some regions more than others have had to fight that little bit harder for their game. It could even be suggested that football in these parts means that little bit more, *calcio* historically being a tool used to improve the family name and a player's status in the towns of the region. The Basilicatese people are fighters, toughened by their circumstances and hardened by life's hardships, the bloody spirit of brigandage running deep through generations. Giuseppe Selvaggi's history of Tricarico's football team reads like a boxing gym injury log, marked by numerous incidents of scrapping and violence. In one particular chapter, in a game against rivals Melfi in 1972 Tricarico came up against the feared Mossucca brothers who, in response to a goal from Ricotta, beat the referee senseless and forced the home side to lock themselves in the changing rooms. Supporters then took to the field, brawling in the dirt of the old pitch on Via Lucana. In church the following morning, players and supporters hugged and congratulated themselves on restoring Tricarico's pride.

As in much of southern Italy, in Basilicata the church is still intertwined with all aspects of life

061 // Stadio Paolo Carbone
TRICARICO // ITALY // TRICARICO POZZO DI SICAR

In a country permanently gripped by *calcio*, some regions more than others have had to fight that little bit harder for their game. It could even be suggested that football in these parts means that little bit more ...

including football. The football club's current guise of Tricarico Pozzo di Sicar is a reference to the Roman Catholic Diocese of Tricarico who work in collaboration with the current team in the fight against social exclusion and deviation among its players. Isolation, economic struggle and injustice are ingrained in the Basilicatese's make-up and after five minutes in one's company, you will know about it. On street corners in every town old men regale one another with tales of woe and misfortune while in a bar in Tricarico's central square I overhear a man in his 60s bemoaning the fact that Tricarico players don't try like they used to. This despite winning 5-0 a few hours earlier. Even my guesthouse host complains for half an hour about how no tourists come to Tricarico, preferring the UNESCO city of Matera 50km away. Moaning is a pastime in these parts, a way to get through the day.

Founded in 1950, Tricarico originally played on a bare earth field high up in the old town where the elementary school now stands. Here, for 20 to 25 days each season, football

would be put on hold as wheat carried up from the sloping fields below was laid out around the goalposts for threshing. In 1962, the town's first purpose-built football ground was opened a little further east along Via Lucana on land owned by the church, only to be commandeered a few years later for the same purpose. This ground remains in the shadow of the Norman Tower; gloomy and bolted shut, a reminder just how far football has come in this town. Season 1988/89 was played away from home while their new stadium was constructed on a raised plateau in the river valley between the old and new towns. Officially opened in September 1989, it would be known as Stadio Paolo Carbone in tribute to Tricarico's greatest ever striker, known affectionately as 'Bomber'. Although the ground is unremarkable in its simplicity, its backdrop evokes the Italian south like no other. When standing on the 14 rows of crumbling terracing, the ground acts as a viewing platform with the whole town of Tricarico laid out on its hillside a few hundred yards away. Other similar footballing backdrops can be found at Campo Sportivo Gaetano Scorza in Morano Calabria and Stadio Dante Popolla in Ceccano, but none quite as vast or evocative as in Tricarico. Like a Cubist painting, every building appears stacked on top of another, Tricarico's cathedral and medieval Norman tower at the very top, reaching for the heavens.

Although Potenza and Matera have scuffed around in Serie B in the past, Potenza last spotted there in 1968 and Matera in 1980, no other clubs from Basilicata have reached that level of football since let alone Serie A. In fact, Basilicata remains one of only four regions of Italy to share the dubious distinction of never having had a team in the top division alongside Molise, Trentino and the Aosta Valley. Remarkable when you consider its relative proximity to both Naples and Bari. However, in the dying weeks of the 2022/23 season, Tricarico and its surrounds were gripped with the unfamiliar feeling of impending success after the team won the Basilicata Eccellenza Coppa Italia. This earned Tricarico a shot at Serie D through a complicated sequence of group and knockout games. Tricarico lost to eventual runners-up San Marzano from Campania but the excitement levels among the younger supporters and Ultras were such that a trip to Salerno was arranged for the sole purpose of buying red and blue flares and smoke bombs for the games. For just a few short weeks, football had brought a feelgood factor back to the town not witnessed since the late 1980s. Fast-forward one year and Tricarico are mid-table and playing poorly. The natives are moaning again. Normality has firmly been restored.

Tottenham Hotspur Stadium

LONDON // ENGLAND // TOTTENHAM HOTSPUR

After the preternatural stillness of Tricarico, we turn to the reassuring bustle of Tottenham High Road. Since 2019, the grimy shopfronts, tatty old pubs and run-down terraces have taken on an almost preposterous appearance set against the colossal sculpted curves of the new Tottenham Hotspur Stadium. On the ground they appear incongruous, lost in time. Seen from the stadium by those 48.6m up on the glass walkway of the 'Dare Skywalk' or forward descending down its side from 'The Edge', the entire neighbourhood must seem infinitesimal. The whole skyline has been shaken up by the arrival of the stadium. It has brought with it great hope and a fresh new identity for North Tottenham. When on 11 February 2011 Tottenham Hotspur finally lost their bitter battle with West Ham United for the rights to the Olympic Stadium, few could have realised just what a blessing in disguise it would turn out to be.

While the glorious Olympic summer of 2012 lives on in the collective consciousness of the British public, the Olympic Stadium in the hands of the Hammers quickly became a noose around the club's neck. Already deeply unhappy at having to give up their beloved Boleyn Ground in 2016, after just a handful of games at the renamed London Stadium fans were up in arms over the perceived unsuitability of the stadium as a football ground and moreover, its distinctly chilly atmosphere. On the pitch, West Ham struggled to find any form let alone home comforts. Despite an upturn in fortunes under David Moyes, including a first major European trophy in 60 years, a 2023 survey taken of 11,000 Hammers fans revealed that 67 per cent are still firmly against the London Stadium.

The afternoon of 6 August 2011 will be remembered as the start of the most severe civil unrest the UK had seen for a generation. But it is also the moment when unbeknownst at the time, Tottenham Hotspur's destiny was decided. Outside Tottenham police station 300 people had arrived seeking justice and answers over the killing by police of local man Mark Duggan. Five hours later, riots were breaking out across the capital and later, in cities across the country. When the dust settled, Haringey Council and Tottenham Hotspur quickly set to work and announced plans for the Northumberland Development Project, a scheme that would bring rejuvenation to the beleaguered area with the football club in the centre. Having by this point shaken off the disappointment of missing out on the Olympic Stadium, Spurs returned to their earlier idea of completely rebuilding White Hart Lane.

By October 2013 they had revealed plans for a multi-use stadium to host, among other large-scale events, American football. An agreement was then reached with the NFL to host a minimum of two games per season over a ten-year partnership beginning in 2019. With this, a new design team was assembled and the revised plans were signed off by Haringey Council, allowing work to officially begin in early 2016. Rather like at Athletic Bilbao's San Mamés stadium six years earlier, Spurs stayed put during that first season while White Hart Lane was dismantled before supporters' eyes. But for the 2017/18 campaign and all but five games in 2018/19, Spurs relocated to Wembley Stadium as their old home was completely demolished and their new one took shape.

White Hart Lane by the turn of the millennium had become tired and outmoded, its capacity of 36,000 too small for the modern game and the direction the club were headed. It echoed the club's position a century earlier when in 1898 they had found themselves hamstrung by their pitch on Northumberland Park. The final straw came when, during a match against (not yet local) rivals Woolwich Arsenal, the refreshment stand had collapsed under the weight of the supporters who had climbed on its roof for a better view. A new facility was needed and

Since 2019, the grimy shopfronts, tatty old pubs and run-down terraces have taken on an almost preposterous appearance set against the colossal sculpted curves of the new Tottenham Hotspur Stadium.

HARRY KANE
HE'S ONE OF OUR OWN
SPURS' ALL-TIME RECORD GOAL SCORER!
SPURS
CRYSTAL PALACE

0
0
46:23+3
AIA

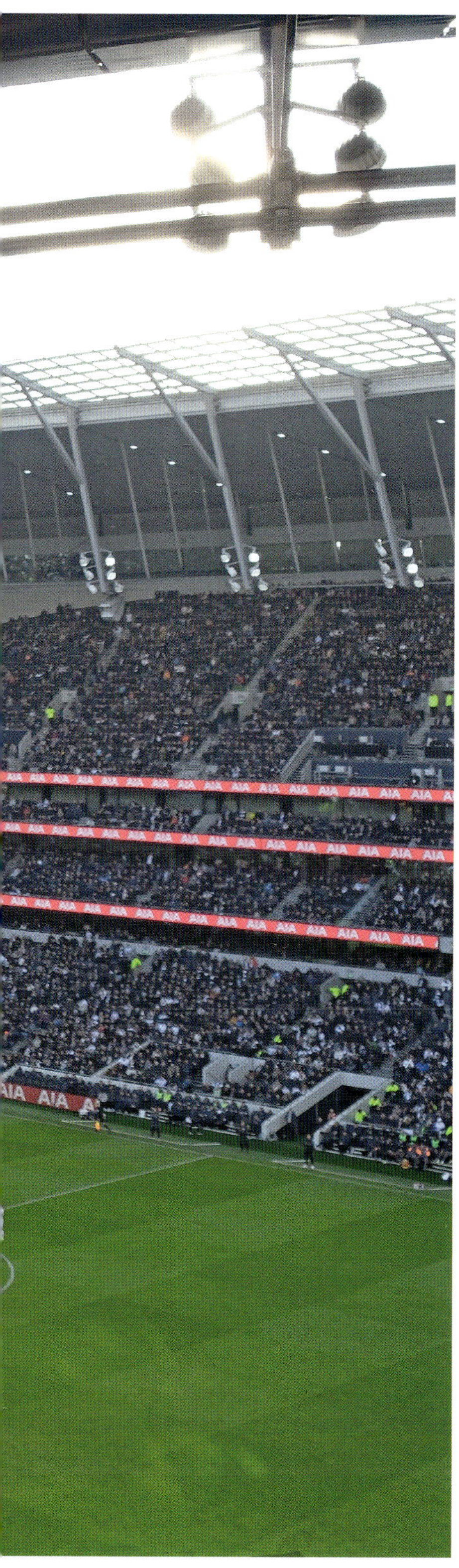

With a capacity of 62,850, the Tottenham Hotspur Stadium was officially opened on 3 April 2019 for a game against Crystal Palace.

on a piece of land behind the White Hart pub, owned by brewers Charringtons and previously used as a plant nursery, Spurs moved to White Hart Lane on 4 September 1899. Under the auspices of Archibald Leitch, the ground was developed into one of Britain's finest prewar stadiums and although altered significantly during the 1960s and 1980s, it remained a firm favourite of travelling fans.

Having changed the face of the USA's baseball parks during the 1990s, the architectural practice Populous were tasked with the design of the Tottenham Hotspur Stadium. With a capacity of 62,850, it was officially opened on 3 April 2019 for a game against Crystal Palace. Covering an area almost twice the size of the old stadium, the asymmetrical bowl was an instant hit not least because the four distinct stands, each set at angles of up to 35 degrees (the maximum permitted in British stadiums), brought fans in close to the pitch. Journalists were quick to lavish praise, from its 'feeling of intimacy' to its ability to 'retain the feel of the old White Hart Lane'. Supporters too were thrilled, a survey of 4,302 fans revealing that 84 per cent were satisfied with the atmosphere for league games, rising to 98 per cent for European ties in which Spurs were beginning to excel. Across Europe and beyond, plaudits were coming in thick and fast, as were the awards for structural engineering and architecture.

Down in the concourses, over 60 food outlets were opened to serve gourmet variations of humble football scran while 'the Market Place' boasted Europe's longest bar. Even the local craft brewers moved in with the Beavertown Tap Room. This was football colliding with the great American shopping mall, fine-tuned for the British game in an arena at the very apex of contemporary stadium design.

Of course the Tottenham Hotspur experience is not for everyone. Above all, it is prohibitively expensive. For the 2023/24 season, season tickets were priced second only to the country's most expensive in Fulham, a far more affluent part of London. It has led to some turning their backs on the stadium completely with a few now regulars at Coles Park at the other end of the Lane. Here, non-league Haringey Borough play a good standard of football and charge buttons in comparison. The modern game's great divide is nowhere more apparent than in Tottenham. But if you can afford it, it's the best high-end football (and NFL) experience in the country.

Between 4 and 6 July 1997, over half the Czech Republic's annual rainfall fell across large swathes of Moravia and Silesia. Riverside cities and villages were decimated as rivers burst their banks and almost one-third of the country's landmass was impacted. It is estimated that more than 10,000 people lost their homes while Olomouc's handsome city centre, crammed with historic Baroque and Romanesque architecture, found itself completely under water. Nearby, mud-brown water from the Morava River lapped at the crossbars of the city's Andrův Stadion.

When the waters receded to reveal the true extent of the destruction, the approximated cost of the damage to Olomouc came in at over €2.5bn in today's money. For SK Sigma, proud owners of the Andrův Stadion but averaging crowds of just 5,588 during the 1996/97 season, the bill for repairs totalling €120,000 came as an absolute hammer blow.

Yet it would take the devastation of the Czech Republic's 'Flood of the Century' along with the lottery of a UEFA Cup first round draw in 1998 to inform the fresh appearance of one of European football's most idiosyncratic stadiums. With a dash of respectful plagiarism from the south of France, Sigma's board of directors chose to ignore the late-90s rulebook of stadium design and with wild abandon, began to sculpt a new Andrův Stadion. Had it not been for the club's remarkable rise in the early 1990s to become genuine challengers to Prague's big two, it is likely the stadium would have been patched up in an altogether more mundane fashion. Instead, Sigma Olomouc decided to build something which embodied their newfound successes: a UEFA Cup quarter-final with Real Madrid, European ties against Hamburg, Fenerbahçe and Juventus and less than 12 months before the flood, breaking Prague's grip on the league for the first time in three seasons by finishing runners-up to Slavia.

With the exception of its floodlights, perhaps the most unique in all of Europe, Andrův Stadion looked much like any other provincial Czech stadium before the floods. An oval-shaped arena with curved terracing at either end, two low stands occupied each side of the pitch. On the western side 1977's main stand had been built to replace a wooden tribune, hastily erected at the end of the Second World War following the Wehrmacht's destruction of the original 1938 reinforced concrete grandstand. Intended only as a temporary solution, it would serve the club for over 30 years and in its time achieve a symbolic status among older supporters for whom it represented freedom from oppression. During 1985's winter break, the eastern stand was constructed in record time with room for 6,000 standing spectators and opened in the spring of 1986. Andrův Stadion's fabulous lollipop floodlights, two cylindrical barrels housing the lamps atop each pole like illuminated Venn diagrams, were financed by Sigma's then record transfer of Pavel Hapal to Bayer Leverkusen in 1992.

During 1985's winter break, the eastern stand was constructed in record time with room for 6,000 standing spectators and opened in the spring of 1986.

With the ground still swampy and strewn with debris, supporters and committeemen alike gathered to straighten up the stadium in the summer of 1997. Considering the damage, it is remarkable to note that only the opening game of the season was postponed. Sigma went on to finish third and qualify for the 1998/99 UEFA Cup where after despatching Kilmarnock, they drew Marseille. Returning from a then roofless Stade Vélodrome a well-beaten team, the party that travelled to France that day were so enamoured with the French side's stadium that they resolved to pay homage to the steep, arcing stands back home. Firstly came the reconstruction of the main stand, its extension to both goal lines mirroring its counterpart opposite. Next, the terracing at either end was dismantled and the curved aspect of the stadium squared off. The southern end briefly gained a prefabricated structure while opposite, construction began on what was then Andrův Stadion's crowning glory.

While most clubs hang a club pennant above the bar to remember their European adventures, Sigma built their own little piece of the French Riviera as a memento, complete with striking blue, white and red tricolour seating pattern. Premiered on 8 August 2000 for Sigma's Intertoto Cup Final against Udinese, the curvaceous lines and pleasing gradient were an instant hit with fans and the city itself. With three sides of the stadium complete, Sigma set about finishing the job in 2009. The prefabricated stand at the southern end was dismantled and in its place, a spectacular new building began to take shape. Architecturally, its design mimics its opposite number until halfway up, above the 2,534 seats, a series of 'skyboxes' for 460 VIPs with seated balconies rise to an equal height. At the rear, 30 adjoining residential apartments were constructed, a groundbreaking arrangement which preceded the fashion for hotels and living accommodation with stadiums by a good few years. It was a brave decision to build two entirely uncovered stands for purely aesthetic reasons so soon after the floods. But Sigma have always been ahead of the curve. Finally finished and now in the hands of the city, their beautiful Andrův Stadion will continue to buck trends for decades to come.

Andrův Stadion

OLOMOUC // CZECH REPUBLIC // SK SIGMA OLOMOUC

058

Stadion Feyenoord

ROTTERDAM // THE NETHERLANDS // FEYENOORD

Of the thousands of fan club stickers seen on my journeys, one kept turning up more than others. Plastered on crush barriers in Warsaw, metro stations in Paris and lamp-posts as far away as Shkodër in Albania, the fans that had left behind a cartoon drawing of De Kuip seemed to have been everywhere.

Feyenoord's aptly nicknamed De Kuip ('the Tub') has since 1937 been a place of gathering for Rotterdam's less affluent. Between Feyenoord and cross-city rivals Sparta Rotterdam there has always been a clear disparity. Sparta's origins lie in the student-led Rotterdamsche Cricket Club while Feyenoord's originate from the poverty-stricken shipbuilding neighbourhood of Feijenoord on the muddy banks of the Nieue Maas river. Another traditional, well-supported working-class club then, adding to the many represented in this book whose grounds are always that little bit more cherished.

When Feyenoord's then chairman, Leen van Zandvliet, woke from a dream shouting 'I got it, I got it!' one winter's morning in 1931, he quickly set about sketching out his vision on a notepad. Three years earlier Amsterdam had its elegant Olympisch Stadion built for the 1928 Summer Olympics and van Zandvliet reasoned with some justification that Rotterdam should too be represented with a stadium of similar impact. He imagined it big, very big. Able to accommodate 60,000 to 75,000 spectators, it would be home to both his Feyenoord and ultimately the Dutch national team.

While van Zandvliet's grand vision was adopted in a members' meeting on 21 March 1934, many still expressed doubts over its feasibility, not least because the Dutch economy at the time was being bashed by the Great Depression. Indeed, many of the club's 600 members had found themselves unemployed while the municipality was unable to lend any financial support. Nevertheless, the headstrong van Zandvliet pushed ahead and succeeded in gathering signatures from local businessmen for a petition that would lead to the procurement of land adjacent to the Varkenoord shipyards. With several deep-pocketed merchants on board, architects Johannes Brinkman and Leendert van der Vlugt were then hired. Fresh from their commission to design the Van Nelle tobacco factory, the city's beloved triumph of modernist architecture just over the train tracks from Sparta's Stadion Het Kasteel, the pair were sent on study trips to various stadiums abroad.

Arsenal's Highbury made a deep impression on the party that travelled to London. This was two years before the famous East Stand was built, the pinnacle of football's brief but fruitful dalliance with the art deco movement. Highbury was still relatively primitive with huge swathes of banked, uncovered terracing, desperate for a little of Villa Park's grandeur but still a few years away from it. However, Ferrier and Bennie's West Stand had been erected in 1932 and from its two-tiered construction, the

With several deep-pocketed merchants on board, architects Johannes Brinkman and Leendert van der Vlugt were then hired. Fresh from their commission to design the Van Nelle tobacco factory, the city's beloved triumph of modernist architecture just over the train tracks from Sparta's Stadion Het Kasteel, the pair were sent on study trips to various stadiums abroad.

Feyenoord group went home with a seed that would become a key component of their new stadium. Influenced too by the Eiffel Tower's majestic rise from similarly flat land, work began in July 1935 with club captain Puck van Heel laying down the first stone. Throughout its construction van Zandvliet, always conscious of the precarious financial balancing act, would regularly take a new construction drawing hot off the drawing board and order its building. In this way Stadion Feyenoord rose quickly and without frills, an ad-hoc temple of the game whose final appearance would not be designed until work was well under way.

The result was a stadium lauded as a hugely influential example of the functionalist style, its appearance of cold bare steel the very antithesis of Amsterdam's 'Brick Expressionism' with its decorative window boxes and classical statues. And unlike Olympisch Stadion, two tiers swept around Stadion Feyenoord giving it more in common with Lisbon's Estádio Nacional, which was designed around this time (but not built until 1939). From their humble 12,000-capacity Kromme Zandweg home, Feyenoord moved into their new 64,000-capacity stadium on 27 March 1937 where a then Dutch record crowd of 38,000 saw them beat Beerschot of Antwerp. The crowds came and the years rolled by as Feyenoord swapped Sparta for Ajax and PSV as their main rivals by becoming one of Dutch football's big three. Superseding its Amsterdam counterpart decades earlier, De Kuip would go on to host over 150 Netherlands internationals and European finals were regularly awarded as the stadium became synonymous with the *totaalvoetbal* of the Dutch. Throughout it all, De Kuip altered little, its skimpy minimalism more unsightly with each passing season and in desperate need of complete renovation.

It came in late 1993 when plans were presented to tackle the full gamut of De Kuip's innumerable problems. Reopened by Prince Willem Alexander on 6 November 1994 before the Netherlands' international against the Czech Republic, from the outside at least De Kuip did not appear greatly changed. Still vaguely Pompidou with its mass of exposed stairwells, slim steel columns and of course, the four isolated floodlight pylons, the real work had been carried out inside. On the eastern side a new grandstand with luxury seating and skyboxes had been fitted into but built separately from the existing stands. Crowning De Kuip, there was finally a roof, supported on columns outside the stadium so as not to impede spectators' views. Constructed of materials including aluminium plates (pitch side) and transparent plastic (outer side), it 'floats' above the stadium while allowing natural light to creep in, much needed in a stadium that can often feel shadowy. The capacity had dropped to 51,117 but it was now an all-seater.

Plans for a brand new stadium have regularly been put in motion only to be promptly shelved. It is likely Feyenoord will stay put for some time, something that suits their diehard *Het Legioen* (the Legion, the club's supporters) just fine. De Kuip is a rarity, a stadium sacrosanct to its people but often regarded as unsightly by outsiders. What cannot be argued is that by retaining its 1930s intricacies and shaping them to suit the 21st-century game, it is a football stadium like no other in existence and for that we should be grateful.

n feyenoord

Campo di Calcio Zuel

CORTINA D'AMPEZZO // ITALY // ZUEL

Four kilometres south of its final destination, the bus from Belluno reaches Zuel, a sparse Alpine hamlet nestled in a Dolomite wonderland. In the distance, Cortina d'Ampezzo's Trampolino Olimpico appears in a clearing between the verdant forest canopy and flower-filled meadows below. Stark and slender, it stands as a symbol of Cortina's great sporting heritage which in 2026 will be reaffirmed when the city hosts the Winter Olympic Games for the first time in over half a century. Yet lit by dazzling mountain sun and with no trace of snow on the ground, for some its purpose may at first be indeterminate. Those too young to remember Roger Moore as James Bond taking his jump in *For Your Eyes Only*, all while being shot at by an East German biathlete, perhaps.

As we pull level, however, the structure reveals itself for what it is: the most architecturally exquisite ski jump still in existence. It may have been abandoned three decades ago when the venue lost its International Ski Federation certificate, but despite the obvious ruin, its rural solemnity is captivating. The 49m-high launch ramp constructed of pre-stressed reinforced concrete for the 1956 Winter Olympics has a weatherbeaten elegance, the faded Olympic Rings painted on the frontage a reminder of its once important status. Flanking the slope, the peculiar pair of 5,000-capacity wooden grandstands and judges' towers are slowly collapsing in on themselves yet they still retain a tangible air of Alpine grandeur.

In Chapter 38 we will visit Finland's Lahden Stadion where both winter and summer sports take place in seamless concinnity. The Trampolino Olimpico may nowadays be surplus to requirements but down in the bowl of the outrun, the remarkable Campo Sportivo di Zuel has been saved from complete abandonment by a group of local football clubs and curiously, AC Milan. Since 1971, for five weeks between July and August each summer, six often hurriedly assembled teams representing each of the six districts compete here in the Torneo di Calcio dei Sestieri d'Ampezzo. Having been played on various pitches in Cortina including the town's main Stadio Antonella de Rigo, the tournament moved to Zuel in 2003 following AC Milan's installation of a football pitch for the club's junior summer camps.

Flanking the slope, the peculiar pair of 5,000-capacity wooden grandstands and judges' towers are slowly collapsing in on themselves yet they still retain a tangible air of Alpine grandeur.

The origins of the district tournament, Torneo dei Sestieri, lie in Cortina's centuries-old tradition of country festivals. After the annexation of Cortina to the Kingdom of Italy in 1918, the Sestieri had lost much of their administrative value and so in an effort to reclaim each unique identity and to preserve the rich folkloric heritage, in February 1936 a cross-country skiing race was organised. Ending with a parade of Arcadian floats, over time this winter competition was integrated with summer activities including a summer 'palio' running race, tennis tournaments and from 1971, a summer football tournament that has survived to become one of the oldest of its kind in Italy. Shaped by a fierce competitiveness, each event raises often substantial funds which are then ploughed back into sports training programmes for the children of Alverà, Azon, Cadin, Chiave, Cortina and Zuel.

As the youngsters leave the pitch after the final of the junior tournament, the floodlights flicker into action and high above, the Trampolino Olimpico begins its slow disappearance into the inky night. Zuel and Alverà have reached the men's final this year and both are represented by a good and noisy support among the crowd of around 600. I am invited to share a long wooden bench table with a family from Alverà who after 30 minutes have opened a fourth bottle of red. Knödel dumplings are passed around as kids challenge one another to see how far up the ski slope they can go under the thin yellow glow of the lights. All around the atmosphere crackles with conviviality. Zuel win the trophy 2-0 but by the time the game ends, most are too merry to notice. The players change then join friends and family around the banks, the party destined to go on for some while yet.

Estadio Santiago Bernabéu

MADRID // SPAIN // REAL MADRID

It is said that no amount of money can buy you style. In the case of Real Madrid this may well be true as the Bernabéu's shiny new 'second skin' has left it looking like an enormous stainless steel air fryer. Class, however, is permanent and thankfully inside, the Bernabéu still has it in spades. As such an integral part of the national fabric, Real needed this gear shift more than ever. Although we are used to seeing them break records on the pitch and the bank off it, even for them the €1.8bn spent on renovating their tired old stadium was an eye-watering sum. But by stretching the bounds of innovation and sticking with their address on the prestigious Paseo de la Castellana, the club finally have a stadium befitting of their enormous global appeal. Tourists and part-time vloggers may have been overheard bemoaning the narrowness of the new seating rows or the queues for the toilets but for those most affected, the Madridistas who turn up week in week out, the all-new Bernabéu has been greeted with almost undivided positivity.

Long before FIFA's darlings were awarded the title of 'Best Club of the 20th Century', before Raúl, Camacho, Gento and Di Stéfano, it was on a roped-off field in Moncloa that a fledgling club named (Sociedad) Sky Football began. Founded in 1897 by Cambridge and Oxford graduates, a conflict of interests in 1900 led to members splitting from Sky to form a new club, Nueva Sociedad de Football. A year later, this team would be renamed Madrid Football Club and when King Alfonso XIII granted them the royal title in 1920, Real Madrid. The original Sky club continued under the name of the New Foot-Ball Club until being dissolved in 1903 although they did compete in the 1902 Copa de la Coronación, a tournament that proved such a success that a year later the Copa del Rey was created and inaugurated. All matches in the one-off Copa de la Coronación were played at the old Hipódromo de Madrid which stood until 1933 on La Castellana, just a block south of where the Bernabéu would be built in 1947.

Real would go on to play at two grounds in the city centre, firstly Campo de la Estrada close to the Prado and then on a pitch between the present-day Goya metro station and the Palacio Deportes. But it was in October 1912 that the club played Sporting de Irún in their opening match at Campo de O'Donnell, the first ground with any real substance. Further along the very same boulevard, another small ground with the same name would be opened a year later by a team calling itself Atlético Madrid. From a stretch of road less than 200m, one of European football's greatest rivalries began. Although Atlético's O'Donnell was the larger of the two and had the privilege of hosting Madrid's very first international in 1921, Real's O'Donnell was chosen for four Copa del Rey finals. With a wooden grandstand for 200, famously ventilated toilets and a perimeter fence erected by none other than a young Santiago Bernabéu and his brother Marcelo, Real left Calles O'Donnell in 1923. And as if mirroring each other's every move, so did Atlético. Both headed north, Atlético to Estadio Metropolitano next to the university and Real to Ciudad Lineal where they would build their fabulously homey Estadio Chamartín.

Opened for a match against Newcastle United on 17 May 1924, Chamartín's capacity would grow from 15,000 to 22,500 by the end. Architect José María Castell designed a 4,000-seater grandstand for the ground which, with its pointed central gable, reflected the work of Archibald Leitch at many British stadiums of the time. But for Santiago Bernabéu, who had risen from fence erector and speedy inside-forward to secretary and club president by 1944, it still wasn't big enough. Bernabéu signed off the purchase of five hectares of land wedged between Estadio Chamartín and Paseo de la Castellana and in October 1944, he broke ground himself on the site. At a cost of 38 million pesetas, early signs of Real's big spending were there even then. But for their money, architects Luis Alemany Soler and Manuel Munoz Monasterio had given Real a very special stadium. With a capacity of 80,000, Bernabéu would have been thrilled as finally Real's domination of the European game could begin. It was elegant too: three wraparound uncovered double-decker stands, a low terrace where the old ground had stood and behind this, a fine neoclassical tower similar to the one still standing at La Coruña's Estadio de Riazor. Renamed Estadio Santiago Bernabéu on 4

January 1955, the stadium has changed beyond recognition in the intervening seven decades but as is the Real Madrid way, always with a finger on the pulse.

With Barcelona's Camp Nou undergoing its own complete overhaul at the time of writing and therefore omitted, the Bernabéu's new capacity of 85,000 makes it the largest stadium in this list. Regardless of the colossal wealth (and debt) synonymous with the club, it has evolved to become the most recognisable stadium in world football. In football parlance the word iconic has become a cliche but for this one we must make allowances. Anfield may be deemed iconic by virtue of its Kop, the San Siro through its appearance or Stade Vélodrome because of the fan noise. But the Bernabéu has achieved such status simply through the talent that has walked out on to the pitch since the very first game against Belenenses on 14 December 1947. It is testament to Real's stubborn refusal to not be knocked off their perch. At any cost.

Why then has this stadium ranked just 56? Put bluntly, the Bernabéu can be a let-down. Every year, tens of thousands from across the world go into the stadium filled with the same expectation that they are about to be part of a world-beating atmosphere, one befitting of the team and ground. It inevitably ends in disappointment. Spanish football supporters are among the most knowledgeable and passionate in all of Europe but unlike the Italians for example, theirs is a more composed, family-orientated support that reflects the characteristics of the people as a whole. Much of the noise will come from the Grada de Animación's 2,000 fans who, since president Florentino Pérez banned the old far-right Ultras Sur group in 2013, now have to follow a strict set of rules imposed by the club. But even Madrid's 'White Wall' falls a long way short of Dortmund's 'Yellow Wall' and with other sections of the stadium watching with restraint, it can sometimes feel a little chilly. If it's the stars you want, however, the Bernabéu is football's Hollywood. Love it or loathe it, that cannot be argued.

Stadion FK Viktoria Žižkov

PRAGUE // CZECH REPUBLIC // FK VIKTORIA ŽIŽKOV

055 // Stadion FK Viktoria Žižkov

PRAGUE // CZECH REPUBLIC // FK VIKTORIA ŽIŽKOV

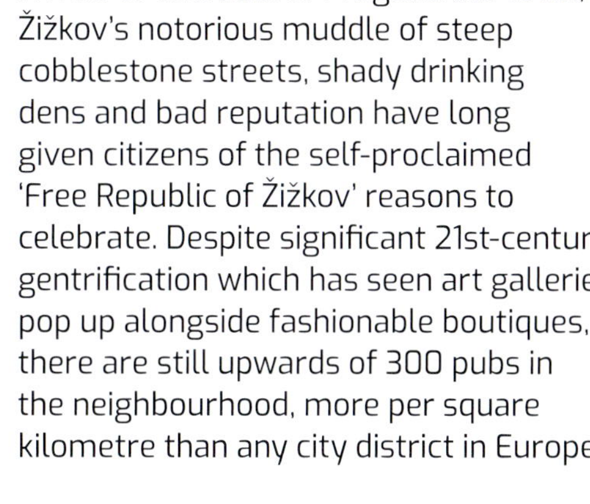

A mile or two east of Prague's old town, Žižkov's notorious muddle of steep cobblestone streets, shady drinking dens and bad reputation have long given citizens of the self-proclaimed 'Free Republic of Žižkov' reasons to celebrate. Despite significant 21st-century gentrification which has seen art galleries pop up alongside fashionable boutiques, there are still upwards of 300 pubs in the neighbourhood, more per square kilometre than any city district in Europe.

For football-loving Žižkovians waking with sore heads on a Sunday morning, the cure is always found at the bottom of hill at Stadion Viktoria where matches in the Czech National League kick off at 10.30am. Although crowds rarely peak above 1,500, they make enough noise for 5,000, singing away hangovers and drinking themselves towards a new one. Prague is crammed with a myriad of football grounds, many with far larger capacities than Stadion Viktoria's 5,600. Indeed, up on Petřín Hill sits Great Strahov, the largest of them all with a capacity of 250,000 which now operates as Sparta Prague's training centre. None however, quite match the homeliness of Viktoria.

Keeping up with the changing environment, Stadion Viktoria is also moving with the times. In the years between my first visit in 2016 and second in 2023, the main stadium access roads from Na Seifertova have been reconfigured and three new entrance points created. Gone is the eastern end's unsightly scaffold stand beneath which smoke from grilling *klobasas* would rise and sting the eyes of those sitting above, and in its place, new refreshment units have been constructed. The shabby uncovered seating that ran from the western end along three-quarters of the southern side has been torn up and the once-perilous terracing has been stabilised. Most impressive of all is the new two-storey, bright crimson press centre with facilities for TV crews, separate treatment rooms for athletes and spectators and members' bar. With the name of the adjacent tram stop now changed from Husinecká to Viktoria Žižkov and

an enormous club crest on the press centre facade welcoming fans approaching through Náměstí Radost park, Viktoria Žižkov have given themselves a refreshing new identity in the neighbourhood. From being entirely obscured from view, everyone now knows who plays here.

Much of Prague's industrial past can be traced to Žižkov. Stadion Viktoria itself stands on land that was once Plynárna Žižkov, the 'light and heat factory' which gas powered many of the city's eastern districts. The plant closed in 1926 and after the gasometer and seven of the eight brick chimneys were demolished seven years later, the land was left to nature. Next door a munitions factory had also shut its doors and the site became a playground for local children who would often be heard beckoning friends to 'come play in the gas house!' Littered with abandoned tanks and projectiles, parents of the Žižkov young must have been spare with worry. In 2019 modifications to Stadion Viktoria saw Plynárna Žižkov's last surviving wall on Krásova street pulled down, leaving a lone chimney on Jeseniova as the final tangible reminder of its past.

After the second world war the site was cleared by the Prague 3 Municipality. A new grass field with spectator terracing along the southern side was opened and in 1965 offered to Viktoria. By this point the club were languishing in the regional leagues but desperate to reclaim their reputation as one of Czech football's most-feared clubs, the facility represented a golden ticket back to the top. They left behind their Na Třebešíně home in Strašnice (now Velodrom Třebešín) and in 1968 erected the 2,000-seat grandstand we see today. Yet it would take two decades and the exodus of Slovak clubs after the Velvet Divorce before Viktoria returned to the First League in 1993. For most it was seen as a welcome and more than a little romantic return for one of Czechoslovakia's true pioneers of the game, a club that until 1948 were the country's third-most successful. Viktoria had won seven Czechoslovak Cups before the outbreak of the second world war and in 1928, playing at their original Nad Ohradou ground (near the Ohrada tram stop), a single First League title where they finished two points above Slavia and four ahead of Sparta. The idea of Viktoria repeating this in 1993 would have been preposterous but remarkably, they twice came third and even held Chelsea to a draw in the UEFA Cup with a team inspired by a 22-year-old Karel Poborský.

It has now been over a decade since top-flight football was last played at Stadion Viktoria. But somehow that doesn't seem to matter quite as much as it used to. Ultras Žižkoland and the club's fanbase grow year on year while Viktoria have established themselves as a firm favourite among the district's student population. Winning matches remains the fans' priority but nowadays there is now a greater emphasis on simply having fun. Always with a few drinks, of course.

Much of Prague's industrial past can be traced to Žižkov. Stadion Viktoria itself stands on land that was once Plynárna Žižkov, the 'light and heat factory' which gas-powered many of the city's eastern districts.

Gemeentelijk Parkstadion

BOOM // BELGIUM // RUPEL BOOM

Boom's history as the heart of Belgium's brick-making industry is such that by 1900 the town was churning out over one billion bricks annually. Seventy years on from the closure of the pits and kilns, its history can still be felt everywhere.

Numerous drying tunnels criss-cross beneath Boom's modern streets and railway lines while on the banks of the Rupel river, Blauwe Pan Alley's enormous sheds, ring kilns and banded chimneys still dominate the landscape. Meanwhile, east of the town centre an old clay pit called De Schorre has been repurposed as the venue of Tomorrowland, one of Europe's leading electronic dance music festivals. Unsurprisingly the football team are known as *De Steenbakkers* (the Brickmakers), a club that once had Boom's most famous son, Romelu Lukaku, on their books as a five-year-old. The town's history therefore should make up for any disappointment felt upon learning that Boom translates as nothing more than 'tree'.

Gemeentelijk Parkstadion is one of few surviving Belgian stadiums set within the boundaries of a public park. Moreover, it is a place that manages to effortlessly distil all the good stuff from Belgian football past into a single intoxicating brew: abundant terracing, the pitch-level clubhouse view, a masterful grandstand and of course bounteous quirks at every turn. Within Belgium's dwindling pool of classic football grounds there are many older and more famous than Boom's, Antwerp's heavily modernised Bosuilstadion and Berchem's sadly butchered Ludo Coeckstadion 15km and 13km up the road respectively, for example. But anchored between Belgian football's unprosperous postwar years and thrilling resurrection of the national team, it is Parkstadion's changelessness that sets it apart.

Unsurprising for a small commuter town of under 20,000, the locations of Rupel Boom's former homes are separated within an area of less than a square mile. As Turnkring Boom from 1907 and Boom FC from 1913, the

054

club had played on the site of the old De Klamp clay pit on Molenstraat. With few financial resources available at the time, Richard Lamot (future club chairman and then owner of Boom and Mechelen's Lamot breweries) paid for the enclosure of the ground, enabling the club to begin collecting entrance fees from their growing fanbase. But as the 1930s rolled in and with a first promotion to the Belgian First Division on the horizon, Boom found themselves in desperate need of a ground more suitable for hosting contemporaries Anderlecht, Beerschot and Royal Antwerp. Shortly before 1938's promotion and the addition of the royal epithet to their name, they packed up and headed across De Klamp to Velodroomstraat.

While the French have the Tour de France and the Italians the Giro d'Italia, it is a widely held view that Flanders is the beating heart of the sport. Boom's velodrome was one of hundreds of provincial cycling arenas in Belgium that had been built in the early 20th century. There exists a single photograph of an expectant Velodroomstraat crowd, thousands gathered for a Royal Boom match beneath the canopy of the grandstand and on flanking terraces. When the site was sold in 1967 and Boom moved in with neighbours Rupel at Gemeentepark, a thoroughly basic enclosure in comparison, it must have come as a blow to all *Steenbakkers* fans regardless of the club's plight in the lower divisions. Nowadays the site is covered by a Colruyt supermarket while just beyond, De Klamp remains an open space earmarked for development.

Back then all that existed at Gemeentepark was a few rudimentary steps of terracing on the park side and next to the changing rooms opposite on Acacialaan. Rupel had played here since 1941 but with little success in the amateur leagues. However, with the park under the auspices of the municipality by 1970 and with a new board of directors dreaming big, Boom's Parkstadion quickly began to take shape. First came the grandstand, its steep design likely influenced by the stands at nearby Lier's Vanderpoortenstadion but with a whole new level of bathmophobia thrown in for

While the French have the Tour de France and the Italians the Giro d'Italia, it is a widely held view that Flanders is the beating heart of the sport. Boom's velodrome was one of hundreds of provincial cycling arenas in Belgium that had been built in the early 20th century.

those with a fear of slopes. With a 43-degree angle, more than a few will have had to use both feet and hands to pull themselves up to its uppermost rows. From its 1,800 seats, however, the reward is an unmatchable view of the action and verdant oasis of Gemeentepark beyond. Similarly elevated terracing was then constructed behind the northern end, symmetrically curved around each corner, while the park side was given a roof to keep those of a more boisterous nature happy. And on a bitterly cold, foggy December evening in 1972 the floodlights were first switched on for a match against Hungarians Ferencváros.

Boom last played in the Belgian top flight in 1992/93. Serious financial problems and a slide into liquidation quickly followed before Royal Boom and Rupel merged, albeit without the former's prized matricule number 58 which was subsequently erased. The new Rupel Boom club refer to their home as a 'cosy' one and you'd be hard pushed to find a single member of their 800-strong fanbase who doesn't agree. It may not suit those seeking the boom of the smoke bomb but in its delightful tree-fringed setting, this municipal park is the finest of its kind.

Wellesley Recreation Ground

GREAT YARMOUTH // ENGLAND // GREAT YARMOUTH TOWN

With one foot in the heyday of saucy postcards and penny arcades and the other in the very real present-day battle against deprivation, Great Yarmouth is typical of the 21st-century Great British seaside town. In 2023, over a third of its population were living in areas that were among the 20 per cent most deprived in the country. It is the kind of place you might just spot a tattered Union Jack in the window of a boarded-up guesthouse while a few yards on, a listed art nouveau theatre or a 17th-century merchant's house. For a town built on wealth and trade, Yarmouth's modern plight can be both jarring and saddening. Just north of the Hippodrome, hidden from the seafront by a collection of grand gabled hotels, we find another of the town's overabundance of listed buildings. The Wellesley Recreation Ground's remarkable 1892 grandstand is recorded by Historic England, the governmental body responsible for the protection of the country's historic buildings, as 'possibly the earliest football grandstand surviving in England'. If ever it was possible to prove, it would therefore make it the oldest in the world.

Back in the early 1880s, the town's embryonic football scene was taking place on the North and South Denes, rough beachside land at either end of the town walls. Matches on the South Denes were played behind a backdrop of thousands of wooden barrels stacked perilously high. At a time when Yarmouth was establishing itself as a major holiday destination, the humble herring was also bringing renewed prosperity. With the fish-salting industry in full swing on the town's open spaces, the port of Yarmouth had been revived as one of the most important in the country. But the town still needed a real sports facility, something grand to reflect its great affluence, and so on 21 September 1885, the town council's Lands Committee came together and proposed to build on an undeveloped site next to a now long gone railway loop, likely used for transportation of the herring barrels. Two estimates to level the three-hectare site were presented and surprisingly, the committee chose the cheaper of road scrapings and market sweepings rather than good soil.

By 1887, a cinder cycling track had been laid out and the site fenced off with oak palings. A cast-iron gate was ordered which still stands today in the south-west corner on Wellesley Street. Officially opened by the town's mayor on 6 August 1888, a bank holiday, a temporary grandstand able to hold 600 was erected on the east side. Such was the success of the day, an estimated 3,000 turning up to watch running, cycling, tricycling and walking events – further sports were added to the roster in the following months including cricket and tennis. Yet it would take a further two years for football to make an appearance when on 11 April 1890, a match between Yarmouth (not Great Yarmouth Town who were founded in 1897) and a County Captain's Team took place.

Still the need for a proper grandstand persisted, however, and in September 1891, the Recreation Committee awarded the tender to local builder Mr A.E. Bond. Built for a sum of £1,015, when opened on 11 June 1892 for an athletics and cycling tournament watched by 4,200, the *Yarmouth Mercury* newspaper described the grandstand as 'perhaps the finest in East Anglia'. I wonder if Mr Bond ever had an inkling of just how celebrated his masterpiece would become? With the plots of land on Marine Parade behind the stand still vacant (the hotels would not be built until the early 1900s), the site would have afforded spectacular views out over the North Sea where a fleet of 65 fishing boats bobbed on its waters.

Great Yarmouth Town moved in for the 1901/02 season having played their first four years on the neighbouring New Recreation Ground (now the Beaconsfield Recreation Ground). With the Wellesley known as the Old Recreation Ground, to avoid confusion, in 1908 each acquired their current names. A low-slung wooden stand about a shallow terrace was erected on the Wellesley Road side and in time became known as the Chicken Run, and although track and field still held sway over the locals until the 1920s, the football club were beginning to attract their own, different type of supporter. Founder members of the regional Eastern Counties League in 1935, the Bloaters began a two-decade period straddling the Second World War in which they twice reached the second round of the FA Cup. Having played Wrexham at the Wellesley in front of 6,963, a year later on 21 November 1953 they beat Third Division Crystal Palace before a crowd of 8,944. Thousands dressed in long coats

and flat caps stood on makeshift terracing of stacked fruit boxes to watch. The events of that afternoon will likely never be repeated and will remain the club's finest hour.

As a young enthusiast of the game keen for experiences further afield, the Wellesley has been something of a go-to for me over the years. I have seen it in rain and shine, both dilapidated and sparkling and populated by 40 and 400. The current wave of supporters have brought with them a new impetus, an amber army with songs and a drum which have recently carried the Bloaters to a long-overdue promotion.

The grandstand too has had a lick of paint, the heritage green shade naturally, while funding of nearly £1m has been spent on a new adjacent training facility. On a late-summer afternoon, walking to a game along Marine Parade with a bag of chips might just be the most authentically English approach to a football ground while inside, the Victorian aesthetics are a portal into a lost world of elegance and derring-do. Other than perhaps Wimbledon, a handful of suburban bowling lawns or real tennis clubs, few other English sports venues deliver such refinement in the 21st century.

052

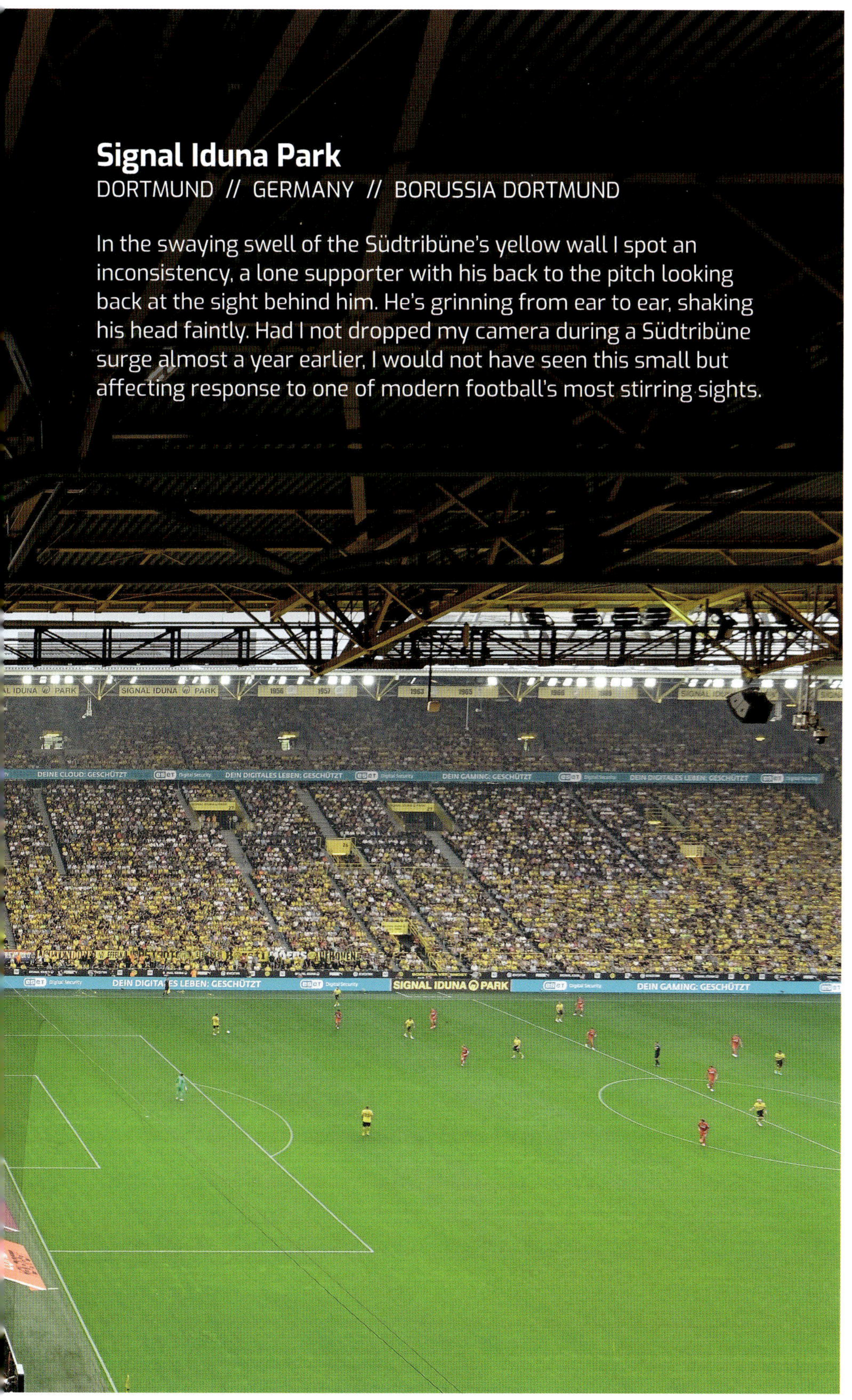

Signal Iduna Park

DORTMUND // GERMANY // BORUSSIA DORTMUND

In the swaying swell of the Südtribüne's yellow wall I spot an inconsistency, a lone supporter with his back to the pitch looking back at the sight behind him. He's grinning from ear to ear, shaking his head faintly. Had I not dropped my camera during a Südtribüne surge almost a year earlier, I would not have seen this small but affecting response to one of modern football's most stirring sights.

This time I am sitting in the more sedate south-eastern corner, roughly level with the halfway point of arguably Europe's most famous terrace. I use my new camera to zoom in but there is nothing to focus on, only an unbroken sea of yellow above which 24,454 floating heads bob in unison to the beat of the drums. To put this into perspective, that's a goal-end stand with a capacity larger than Union Berlin's entire Stadion An der Alten Försterei and twice the size of AFC Bournemouth's Dean Court. Hyperbole and 21st-century football are largely inseparable but if you're lucky enough to catch *Die Gelbe Wand* (the Yellow Wall) at its very best, all superlatives can justifiably be piled on.

The fluctuation of corporate naming rights on stadiums can leave fans at a loss to know exactly what to call them. Supporters of clubs whose homes are less modern and were once known by their original name will aim to keep tradition alive by bypassing altogether any new sponsorship-led rebranding. For Borussia Dortmund, however, whose partnership with insurance brand Signal Iduna began in 1974 and will continue at least until 2031, their stadium's more authentic name, Westfalenstadion, is one gradually being lost, only kept alive in its metro stop, Westfalenpark. Dwarfed in the shadow of the Osttribüne next door, the club's original home, Stadion Rote Erde ('Red Earth'), has no such fussy moniker. It serves as a yardstick to gauge just how far Borussia have come since becoming the first German club to win a European club competition in 1966. Moreover, paired against its successor it offers a fascinating snapshot of the progress German stadiums have made as a whole. After a 376-day period of renovation between March 2022 and April 2023, Stadion Rote Erde has recently been brought back up to scratch. With a capacity now trimmed by two-thirds to 9,999, it is still seen as consecrated ground for legions of Borussia fans who continue to fill its 1925 terraces for under-23 matches.

In the early 1970s Borussia Dortmund were still two decades away from becoming the club we now recognise as one of Europe's elite. Kings of the domestic game were then Borussia Mönchengladbach, Schalke 04 and Bayern Munich, while Rot-Weiß Oberhausen and Kickers Offenbach were busy pulling up more trees than

Dortmund. In comparison with today, Bundesliga attendances were still low, but Borussia's 1971/72 average of just 18,118 at Rote Erde was middling at best. We can pinpoint the first wave of the club's transformation to three key events during this time: Cologne's withdrawal as a host city for the 1974 World Cup and subsequent reallocation of stadium funding to Dortmund, the soaring popularity in the game following West Germany's victory (without a single Borussia player in the squad) and Borussia Dortmund's return to the Bundesliga for the 1976/77 season.

It is interesting to note that had funds been more readily available, Signal Iduna Park would have been a 60,000-capacity oval-shaped arena with an athletics track. Instead a more English-styled stadium for 54,000 was constructed for half the price, a template which in future decades would be used to expand the stadium to its current capacity of 81,365. Opened on 2 April 1974 for the Ruhr derby against Schalke 04, six weeks later it hosted Zaire v Scotland, the first of its four World Cup matches as the only non-Bundesliga stadium used.

In terms of size, Signal Iduna Park finds itself sandwiched between Paris's Stade de France and Milan's San Siro. As Europe's fifth-largest football stadium, therefore, it may come as a surprise to some to see it ranked as low as 52 in this book. Many will claim with some justification that it is worthy of a top-five position for much the same reason as Newcastle United's St James' Park is. However, take the goosebump-inducing crowds out of the stadium for a moment and Signal Iduna Park reveals itself as an elephantine colossus, short on looks and behind the club's colour scheme, as grey as the Ruhr skies in wintertime. Architecturally, Dortmund's cathedral of the game is neither stylish nor inventive. It lacks both the head-turning appeal of the San Siro or the seductive elegance of the Bernabéu. Yet it is the one ground most fans would trade for their own. Why? Because of its simplicity. Four boxy but immensely proportioned stands packed steep and tight above the pitch, a representation of what to most fans all stadiums should look like.

After successive Bundesliga titles between 1994 and 1996, and 1997's Champions League victory, Borussia's popularity skyrocketed. From selling out just five matches during the 1992/93 season, every game was now a hot ticket which led to the club's decision in 1997 to expand Signal Iduna Park for a second time in three years. The Nordtribüne was enlarged considerably while opposite, the Südtribüne was remodelled as the largest free-standing grandstand of its kind in Europe. With that came the Yellow Wall and Signal Iduna Park's status in popular culture as one of European football's most atmospheric grounds. There can be no argument with this. On a good day very few European stadiums come close to achieving what Signal Iduna Park does on a visual level. In Germany the decibels at Kaiserslautern's Fritz-Walter-Stadion may sound a little louder but having a modern-day version of Celtic Park's Jungle or Anfield's Kop at our disposal is a very special thing indeed.

BVB
09
Familienblock
64-68
DORTMUND
GROßKREUTZ
19
AUBAMEYANG

051

Stadion im. Mieczysława Słabego

PRZEMYŚL // POLAND // KS CZUWAJ PRZEMYŚL

On an early morning bus from Kraków to Košice in late spring, I awoke to find we had stopped in Zakopane near the Polish-Slovak border. Once Poland's informal cultural capital and early 20th century getaway destination for the Nouveau Riche, this is where the lowlands of Lesser Poland climb to meet the Tatra mountains. Through the window, I squinted at a scene of green sunlit slopes, dotted with elegant wooden villas built in a style that two months earlier, I had become so familiar with. These were *Styl Zakopiański* houses, a style of architecture conceived by Stanisław Witkiewicz in the 1890s and embraced by Podhale's highland communities. Combining wooden frames made from halved logs with elements of Art Nouveau and traditional folk motifs, the main features include steep gables, radiant suns, intricate flower carvings and the six-petal rosette solar symbol. Yet the building I had enthusiastically photographed had not been awaiting its next party of skiers in the Tatra Mountains. Instead it occupied a space between a tatty residential street full of blockish 1970s apartments and the grey water of the San River. And it was 350km away near the Ukrainian border in the small city of Przemyśl.

Very few football grounds have a feature quite as extraordinary as Stadion im. Mieczysława Słabego. Even fewer have one with the age of Czuwaj's clubhouse, especially in Poland whose historic stadiums have all but been wiped from the map. It seems implausible that such a building should exist in Przemyśl, one which in architectural circles across the world is regarded among the most beautiful of its type. Przemyśl itself is far from an unattractive city, but loaded with baroque architecture it has more in common with its big brother Lviv over the border rather than anything remotely Carpathian. To establish how it ended up here, we need to travel back to Czuwaj Przemyśl's beginnings and the early days of the Polish scouting movement.

Poland wasn't even on a map when Baden Powell's idea of scouting first reached the youth of Przemyśl in 1909 having been under Russian, Prussian and Austrian occupation for over 100 years. With the Polish Republic reborn at the end of the First World War, all existing scout groups were amalgamated in 1918 to become the ZHP, the Polish Scouting Association which in time would grow to become one of the largest social and educational associations in Poland. Unlike the bivouac-building boy scouts of western Europe however, members of the ZHP were trained to fight in battle and were often drafted in to join forces with the military. Thousands of scouts fought in the Polish-Bolshevik War and the Silesian Uprisings.

It was one of its earliest sons, Mieczysław Słaby, who in 1918 founded Sports Club Czuwaj (meaning 'watch'), the city's second football club with the help of scouts from the city's junior high school. Across the city nine years earlier, the Polonia club had been born yet the pair wouldn't meet in competitive football until 1935. Czuwaj had almost exclusively spent their early years playing fellow scout troops including Jewish and Ukrainian teams before they joined the district league of the Lviv FA. Here the fierce rivalry took hold, one marked by a political hatred which still bubbles today. A fixture in 1938 was cancelled when Polonia activists pasted match posters across the city only in Polish which Czuwaj responded to by doing the same but in Ukrainian. It caused outrage, the Polish press branding Czuwaj a 'chauvinistic Russian club'.

During the club's first general meeting in 1922, it was agreed to professionalise official activities, and soon afterwards the need for a proper football stadium began to arise. Several scouts had attended an orienteering and cartography weekend in Podhale and had stayed in a Zakopane-style hostel. It was suggested that such a building should be built in Przemyśl; a large clubhouse to serve the growing number of sports on offer at the Czuwaj club while acting as a symbol of its scouting tradition. With engineer Gustaw Krupiński appointed as club president by 1931 and donations rolling in from Przemyśl's wealthy elite, including Mieczysław

Słaby who had gone on to become a major in the Polish army, carpenters and craftsmen were brought in from Zakopane to begin their designs. Their only instruction was 'to disregard the conventional'. And how they did. With the cornerstone laid on 28 June 1931, the stadium was officially opened in March 1932 with a capacity of 2,500. The complex included two tennis courts, a basketball court and a football pitch which was transformed during the winter months into an ice rink, much to the delight of Przemyśl's young. Images of the new clubhouse from the time illustrate just how imposing it was, its timber as black as the Tatras in twilight, its gable end sunbursts resplendent and its hexagonal glass observation tower giving it a palatial touch.

For Czuwaj the golden years continued, the club adding handball, motorsports, boxing and ice hockey to their roster as their members swelled to over 2,000. But by the end of the Second World War, the stadium had been bombed, shot at and flooded by the San River; it lay in ruins, neglected for 15 years as the club's members dwindled and its athletes allied with other associations in the city. The footballers stayed loyal, however, and against all odds Czuwaj reached Liga II, the third tier of Polish football, in 1950. By now under the ownership of the Ministry of Railways, the stadium was tidied up with a new pitch laid and reopened on 16 August 1959 for the Przemyśl derby. Despite drifting back into district football through the 1960s and 70s, they made a surprise return to Liga II in 1997. Shorn of any support from the ministries, however, the club having been jettisoned and promptly forgotten in similar fashion to Lech Poznań and Polonia Warszawa, it was left to Czuwaj supporters to prepare the stadium in readiness. Within weeks, six rows of low, shallow terracing had been added in a horseshoe

With the cornerstone laid on 28 June 1931, the stadium was officially opened in March 1932 with a capacity of 2,500. The complex included two tennis courts, a basketball court and a football pitch which was transformed during the winter months into an ice rink, much to the delight of Przemyśl's young.

shape around the oval which in the early 2010s were garnished with the red and yellow seating we see today. That season saw 6,000 turn up for the visit of champions-elect GKS Bełchatów, a game which in the collective consciousness of the Czuwaj supporter is the very peak of the club's achievements,

In 2023, Czuwaj are back in the Podkarpackie district league again playing their final game of the campaign; they haven't been beaten all season. A crowd of 500 turn up of which around half light flares and chant through the entire match. It is a very different club than the one 100 years ago, the only surviving connection to its scouting origins being the clubhouse whose impact on the landscape has undoubtedly been weakened by the buildings which have grown up around it on 22 Stycznia Street. It looks indestructible yet faded and shabby. Inside, rooms are stuffed with ancient sporting detritus, the central hall, which once saw players gather post-match to play billiards by candlelight in the days before electricity, littered with empty energy drink bottles and a thick film of dust. For the time being however, any conservation will likely have to wait. Mounting debts in recent years have threatened the very existence of the club who play on with their heads barely above water. For the sake of such a unique sporting venue, we must hope that the people of Przemyśl's widely held affection for its centrepiece will one day materialise into giving it the maintenance it so clearly needs.

050

Campo Municipal das Velas

VELAS // PORTUGAL // GD VELENSE

Visiting the Azores out of season was among the great highlights of my European tour. While a six-hour layover in Terceira exposed the archipelago's self-proclaimed party island to be operating in a strange limbo between the tourists and winter closures, São Jorge uncloaked itself as a peaceful subtropical backwater in virtual hibernation.

Here the stillness was punctuated only by the occasional puttering pick-up, the air heavy with the scent of woodland bonfires. In the western parish of Velas I found just a single cafe open during my two-day stay serving burger and fries for €3, a single illuminated building in an otherwise shut-up town. No buses were running between the towns and villages on São Jorge's populated southern edge, communities built under steep volcanic slopes on flat cape-like *fajã*, debris fields formed by lava flows or landslides. So other than a taxi to nearby Urzelina to watch FC Urzelinense (one of just four clubs on the island), I spent my time trekking up the volcanic cliffs of Morro das Velas and Morro de Lemos where, steeling myself, I would occasionally peer down upon the spectacular Campo Municipal das Velas, a stadium built in perhaps the most audacious location in Europe.

Football took its time in reaching São Jorge. Of the nine islands in an archipelago roughly 1,000 miles off the coast of Portugal, São Jorge's original club, Marítimo Velense, were not founded until 1964. Fifty-five years earlier, Fayal Sport Club were established on neighbouring Faial as the Azores' first club, handing that island the fuel for fiery debates over which island is the true pioneer of Azorean football. In fact, aside from remote Corvo with no competitive football and tiny Flores whose Boavista club began in 1966, São Jorge was the last island to join the party. Azorean football is competitive and club rivalries fierce. Teams play in individual island championships with the winners going on to contest for the title of overall Azorean champion in what is the fifth tier of Portuguese football. From here, it becomes a straightforward pyramid system, a once unthinkable pathway for Azores clubs to compete in national competitions on the mainland. Six 21st-century appearances in Portugal's Primeira Liga has not only established the Santa Clara club from São Miguel island as the most successful, it has ushered in a newfound belief which has spread throughout the archipelago. Through forays into UEFA club competitions, Santa Clara have single-handedly put these nine tiny specks firmly on the footballing map. In turn, clubs have begun to raise playing standards, create more professionalised infrastructures and tidy up decrepit, weather-beaten stadiums.

Grupo Desportivo Velense came into existence two years after Marítimo Velense, both clubs using the rudimentary Campo Vila das Velas in the town centre which would eventually make way for a new secondary school in the 1980s. The project for the new stadium began in the summer of 1978 and while flat land is always at a premium on São Jorge the municipality identified a clifftop plane at the Miradouro Entre Morros, a deep bay and headland where ancient volcanic formation had given rise to the two towering Morros hills either side. Civically the location made perfect sense; Velas was beginning to expand in a north-westerly direction and the new swimming pool, running track and football stadium would serve the needs of younger families moving into the new apartment complexes. The execution of the build would be painless too, the surface almost ready-prepared for development through a century of cultivation by hand. Only mild levels of anxiety were reported during the construction of the access lane as diggers performed three-point turns in the narrow space between the stadium's grandstand and a perilous 100-foot drop into the blue.

By the spring of 1980 Campo Municipal das Velas was ready for its inauguration, a celebration involving a philharmonic group-led procession from the town centre followed by a quadrangular football tournament. It would take the appearance on the pitch of Eusébio in the 1990s to surpass the opening-day crowd, a municipality-led drive to promote local football mobilising the entire island and attracting visitors from across the central Azores. Over the years the stadium has kept up with the demands of increased participation, especially among the young. In 1997 the first artificial pitch was laid followed by a complete remodelling in 2000. That summer, the two seating areas either side of the changing rooms and press gallery were given roofs, finally putting an end to pesky sea haar and all buildings including the bar in the north-east corner were painted in the white, red and blue of the Velas coat of arms. Meanwhile, the municipality designated the entire rim of the headland a tourist spot and set about beautifying the area around the stadium with gardens, nature walkways and a viewing platform.

Less urgent than the previous day's fare at Urzelinense who had battled hard against an excellent side from Graciosa island in the league above, Velas take on Calheta from the centre of São Jorge. A crowd of 300 gather to watch, most sat on grass banking close enough to the bar and out of the direct glare of the sun. I join them but after a particularly tedious first half, I find my myself in something of a reverie, gazing up at the Kelly-green pastures rolling down to the sheer edge of the cliff tops. Just below and soaring up behind the grandstand, there is a single red-brown volcanic stack. And then turquoise water all the way to Pico. Such is the beauty of this place, I come round to find two players have been sent off and Velas have scored two goals.

049

Naturarena Hohe Warte

VIENNA // AUSTRIA // FIRST VIENNA

Entirely befitting for a club founded by gardeners from the nearby Rothschild estate, First Vienna's green suburban oasis has now kept the city council busy for over a century. Advances in garden machinery may have rendered the mower on a rope trick obsolete but just keeping Hohe Warte's enormous grass embankment trim remains a demanding task.

Of all European football's larger grounds, only Charlton Athletic have had a similar topography to work with, theirs an old chalk pit and First Vienna's a result of clay extraction used for tile manufacturing. Whereas The Valley's steep banking was developed over time into steep concrete terracing with the titanic East Stand its crowning glory, Hohe Warte has altered little since 85,000 once congregated on its slopes. With only the grandstand replaced in 1974, it now embraces its newfound conservational status as the Naturarena. Moreover, with Austria's very first football club still performing adeptly in the country's second tier, Hohe Warte is now the perfect pick-me-up for any fans tiring of the effort and money needed for the modern game.

West of the Danube, Vienna's northernmost district of Döbling is where the city gives way to the countryside. Most supporters will arrive at Heiligenstadt U-bahn station where after passing through an arch beneath Karl-Marx-Hof, one of the world's longest single residential buildings at 1,100m, it is a steep climb up to Hohe Warte. It is a route that millions have taken since 19 June 1921 when the stadium was opened for a championship game against Vienna's pre-eminent Jewish club, SK Hakoah. A year earlier First Vienna had turned to Eduard Schönecker, a 35-year-old architect responsible for Rapid Vienna's Stadion Pfarrweise in 1912. Adding to the pertinence of the appointment, Schönecker as a player had represented both Rapid and the Austrian national

Nowadays matches are watched by crowds of around 1,800, many with an 'against modern football' outlook. Although most stick to the grandstand, a few will take pints up on to the hillside and lean against a battered crush barrier.

team while in track and field he competed at the 1908 London Olympic Games. Although only 12,000 witnessed the first match, Hohe Warte had an estimated capacity of 50,000, making it likely the largest stadium in continental Europe at the time. More lopsided than even Dukla Prague's Stadion Juliska, the original grandstand on the eastern aspect was a low-slung wooden affair opposite which numerous rows of terrace steps had been cut into the fearsome hillside. These still exist, overgrown and out of sync, another special reminder of Hohe Warte's place as the cradle of Austrian football.

On 23 April 1922 Austria played the first of 35 internationals at the new Hohe Warte, the country's first permanent home having spent two decades flitting between Cricketer Platz (next to where the Praterstadion would be built), WAC Platz (still the oldest stadium in Austria) and Simmeringer Had (Austria's largest stadium until Hohe Warte was built). A crowd of 70,000 saw the match against Germany, surpassed almost exactly one year later when an estimated 85,000 gathered beneath leaden skies for the visit of Italy. The wet weather that day, combined with the heavy footfall, resulted in sections of the embankment subsiding, a situation that was avoided thereafter by curbing each step with concrete supports. Meanwhile, First were busy winning Austrian Cups, a first league title in 1931 and the Mitropa Cup, a central European predecessor to UEFA competitions.

Coinciding with the emergence of Austria's Wunderteam, Vienna's Praterstadion (now the Ernst-Happel-Stadion) was constructed on the banks of the Danube in the more central district of Leopoldstadt. Austria's farewell match at Hohe Warte is still spoken of in hushed reverence today, an 8-2 victory over arch-enemies Hungary in front of 60,000. First Vienna played on in the Third Reich-enforced Gauliga and won the Tschammerpokal (the predecessor of the German Cup) in 1943 but after four further Austrian titles in the 1940s and 50s, the glory years came to an end. At the end of the 1991/92 season First Vienna were relegated from the Austrian Bundesliga; they have yet to return.

Nowadays matches are watched by crowds of around 1,800, many with an 'against modern football' outlook. Although most stick to the grandstand, a few will take pints up on to the hillside and lean against a battered crush barrier. The views from up here across the ever-changing Viennese skyline is sensational but it pays to sidestep your way down, especially when wet. From the grandstand the scale of the hillside can truly be appreciated. Just beyond are the Central Institute for Meteorology's radar tower and the gardens of Döbling's elegant residences. Hohe Warte has a quiet, stately ambience. And as such a key component in the story of Austrian football it receives all the necessary care and attention it deserves. Although it could never again receive a five-figure crowd, in its changelessness you can picture what a match in 1931 would have looked like here. It might just be the finest 1920s stadium still in use.

gemeinsam besser leben
UNIQA
REISSWOLF
JÜRGEN SCHMIDT
DVB
PLANTER'S

Grigoris Lambrakis Stadium

ATHENS // GREECE // ATHENS KALLITHEA

From the barrios of Malaga to the banlieues of Marseille, European city neighbourhoods teem with football clubs. Their role of representing the neighbourhood's few square miles of territory is an important one and has led to the cultivation of fierce and often historic rivalries. Many are older than the senior clubs of the city and can trace their roots to long-forgotten local industries, ties to the church or athletics clubs. Some represent the diaspora of ethnic minorities across the continent; others were founded in tribute to a larger club for whom players were supporters.

The individuality and identity of the neighbourhood and its club is often mirrored in the football ground. Where once they would have taken up a couple of blocks on city plans, the skyward creep of urbanisation sees many now dwarfed by commercial buildings or apartment blocks as seen at Red Star in Paris and CE Europa in Barcelona. As much part of the social fabric as the church or the restaurant, they act as sanctuary for inhabitants, ingrained in people's lives and routines. Once a fortnight they become the beating heart of the community, a place where dignitaries chatter with labourers in bars beneath grandstands. Corridors are collaged with photographic memories of former players and local folk who played a small part in the club's story. Kids will graffiti their allegiances on to any spare inch of space on surrounding walls while Ultras debut well-rehearsed flag and flare routines.

In Athens, more than 20 such neighbourhood clubs continue to thrive. An excellent example is Panionios from the district of Nea Smyrna. Founded by refugees from the former Greek city of Smyrna, now İzmir in Turkey, they are Greece's oldest football club with over 130 years of history behind them. Despite a troubled recent history, their support base remains strong and matches here can be as visually visceral as those at Panathinaikos.

Two miles south-west of Kallimarmaro, the Panathenaic grandfather of all stadiums, lies one of the most densely populated city neighbourhoods in the world, Kallithea. Here, obscured behind a tumble of sloping, fetid streets and lofty apartment complexes, hides the Grigoris Lambrakis Municipal Stadium, or as the locals fondly refer to it, El Paso. There is nothing immediately to explain away the reference to the Texan border city or indeed the plentiful daubing of 'Desperadoes' on the perimeter walls. It's all fairly conventional, ordinary. Only once the climb up one of two exterior stairwells is made, themselves having the appearance of scaffold movie-filming towers, does El Paso's exoticism become apparent. Like the half-built set of a spaghetti western, a toytown Rio Grande, limestone cliffs roll around half the pitch. Bizarre off-centre seating blocks are built into the rock while apartments teeter on the edge above. It can be simultaneously sunbaked and windswept too and often cast in shadow from the loom of the buildings all around. The nickname Kallithea's supporters christened it with at once seems faultless.

Europa

In the mid-1960s, Greece's love-in with the Western movies of the day coincided with the building of Kallithea Stadium.

In the mid-1960s, Greece's love-in with the Western movies of the day coincided with the building of Kallithea Stadium. When Sergio Leone's *For a Few Dollars More* was released in 1965 under the name *Duel in El Paso* for Greek audiences, it signalled a high point in the genre. Within a few short months it had smashed box-office records across the country and the fervour for all things Western was carried by supporters to the new Kallithea Stadium. To this day, Kallithea run on to the pitch to the dustbowl strains of Ennio Morricone's score.

With promotion to the top division in 2002, Kallithea set about modernising El Paso, firstly reroofing the large south stand and making the stadium all-seater. New lights were then added and work began on a 2,500-capacity open stand which would follow the curvature of the cliff face behind the eastern goal. At a cost of €1.4m, this stand would prove technically challenging as constructing it flush against the cliff face required strengthening of the rock surface. However, before supporters had an opportunity to make themselves comfortable in their new environs, Kallithea found themselves relegated back to the second division. With a seating capacity of 6,300, ideal for visits from the likes of Panathinaikos and Olympiakos, the Desperadoes had shot themselves in the foot. From here the club would free-fall to the fourth division and by 2020 attendances had dwindled to below 1,000. Such overreaching has led to the abandonment of the curious curved stand which accumulates debris jettisoned from Milonos Street above. The seating, which once picked out the name Kallithea in inverse, has all but gone, torn up by vandals or repurposed in the main stand. The entrance gates are padlocked shut, rusted and topped with coils of barbed wire, a tumbleweed bounces around behind.

Despite such a costly blunder, the Grigoris Lambrakis Stadium is still a handsome if tatty ground and as the club emerges into a new dawn, it needs to be. In September 2022, the club undertook a programme of rebranding which briefly propelled the Desperadoes into a world of fashion and culture. Under the new ownership of US hedge-fund manager Andrew Barroway, the club's name was changed to Athens Kallithea in an attempt to popularise the club across the city and beyond. The crest, colours and kit were given a working over by German design studio Bureau Borsche who had executed Inter Milan's rebranding a year earlier. Such was the success, the Milanese sports lifestyle magazine *Rivista Undici* called it 'the most beautiful restyling of the year' whereas London-based *Versus* claimed it was 'one of the cleanest rebrands ever'.

All this appears to have driven a wedge in between the club and fans. On an overcast Monday afternoon in early December, Kallithea are playing a Super League 2 game against AEK reserves. Barely 500 are inside the stadium for the game although I am told there would have been twice as many before the club's 15 minutes of fame. The other half are up on Milonos Street, watching through railings, steadfastly boycotting the club due to the change of name. Where Kallithea go from here remains to be seen and who the real desperadoes are is debatable.

Stadion Plovdiv

PLOVDIV // BULGARIA // SPARTAK PLOVDIV

Our third visit to Bulgaria brings us to its second city, one with a strong claim to being the oldest continually inhabited city in Europe. Immediately more laid-back than Sofia, Plovdiv is imbued with a mood locals call *aylyak*, a virtually untranslatable word which loosely describes a feeling of being supremely relaxed or of being receptive to the pleasures of existence. Plovdivians are kings of kicking back. On a warm Sunday afternoon, people amble languidly along the city's side streets.

Others sip Turkish coffee endlessly outside attractive cafes or gather in the shade of Park Tsar Simeon's linden trees for a game of chess. A few hours later and I am one of 92 spectators inside a stadium more shadowy and forbidding than any other in this book, one with a greater capacity than Napoli's Stadio Diego Maradona or Newcastle's St James' Park. Barely three kilometres from the charm of the old town, Plovdiv's 'Big House' with a capacity of 55,000 remains the largest football ground in Bulgaria and its greatest shame; tenebrous ruin-porn for the ages where snap-happy urbexers come to gawp.

There are three other large-scale stadiums in Plovdiv which, in recent years especially, have inadvertently played a significant role in sounding its death knell. Botev's Stadion Hristo Botev was initially earmarked for an overhaul in 2012 while the first designs for the rebuilding of Stadion Lokomotiv emerged as far back as 2010. However, Plovdiv's big two would have to wait. Years of reconstruction setbacks fused with typical *aylyak* and in Botev's case, president Tsvetan Vasilev's indictment for embezzlement in what Reuters described as 'one of the Balkans' biggest post-communist fraud investigations', meant that by 2023 both were only just getting comfortable in their new homes. Indeed, without 2020's timely central government funding for Plovdiv's sporting infrastructure, it is likely both projects would still be stuck in a state of suspension. And then there is Plovdiv's crowning glory, the very antithesis of Stadion Plovdiv. Part-hidden beneath upmarket boutiques and restaurants in the heart of the city centre, the ancient Stadium of Philipopolis is never far from top spot in lists of tourist must-sees. All solid marble seating and granite ashlars, it is one of the best examples of a Roman Empire stadium in Europe and as such, relies on the continued funding from the municipality for its conservation.

Two sparkling new 21st-century stadiums and a first-century touristic delight have ultimately done for poor old Stadion Plovdiv. Once championed as the future national stadium of Bulgaria, it now finds itself scrubbed entirely from governmental plans for future redevelopment. Out of sight and out of mind with next to no chance of being granted any form of safety certificate for large-scale events, guano gathers in its darker recesses and nature creeps unfettered through its cracks. On its upper floor, in unfinished blockwork shells, bags of cement lay abandoned three decades on from the last and final attempt to finish the job. The entire stadium has become a Shangri-la for local graffiti artists, its doors open at all times as a single weary guard dog, tied behind a steel gate, offers little in the way of a deterrent. And yet, as we will see in Chiatura further on, through the deterioration and half-finished upgrades, there is no doubt that this is still a spectacular stadium. There are immense sweeps of curved terracing, handsome tiled walkways, lattice-work gates and four floodlight towers as behemothic and recognisable as any that have stood guard over Europe's great football stadiums.

Imported from Poland in the summer of 1991, the 70m steel pylons, each with unique elongated hexagonal mounts, should have represented both the rebirth and finally the completion of Stadion Plovdiv. At the time, work was in full swing to complete the stadium's second tier, uniting Sector B with the rest of 1962's top level. An electronic scoreboard was installed and a roof added above the main stand, its wavy design typical of the early 1990s, a Balkan interpretation of Watford's Graham Taylor Stand perhaps. Things were looking good, a national stadium in Plovdiv within touching distance. But when the money ran out shortly before completion, so did the will.

Stadion Plovdiv has limped on with little love ever since. A single Metallica concert in June 1999 was the only event to draw anything remotely like the crowds which once saw Botev and Lokomotiv play Barcelona, Juventus, Bayern Munich and Lazio here. Over the years, all Plovdiv's senior football clubs have had a go at making it home. Botev, Lokomotiv and Spartak played here from its opening in 1954 until 1961, 1967 and 1983 respectively and for three years at the end of the 1960s, Maritsa Plovdiv. Yet aside from Lokomotiv's record-breaking B Group attendance of 40,000 here against Beroe Stara Zagora in 1983, it is the lesser-known Spartak Plovdiv who played perhaps the stadium's defining football match. In 1963 Spartak held Eusébio and his Benfica to a draw in the Inter-Cities Fairs Cup, reportedly in front of a capacity crowd. Somewhat fittingly therefore, it is Spartak who plough on indefinitely at Stadion Plovdiv until the rebuilding of their own Stadion Todor Diev, affectionately known as Plovdiv's Loftus Road after the team's blue and white hoops, is complete. When it is, Spartak will likely be the last football team to play football here, leaving Stadion Plovdiv to join the likes of Brno's Stadion Za Lužánkami in perfect abandonment; enormous, stylish postwar stadiums that simply proved too costly to maintain but too much of a headache to bulldoze.

046

Parken

COPENHAGEN // DENMARK // FC COPENHAGEN

As we approach the second quarter of the 21st century, ask any young football supporter what they most want from their stadium and even before a successful football team, most will say high-speed wifi. We are now at the stage where the gauge of a good new stadium hinges on its technological capabilities and comfort as much as its architectural merit. Technology now powers everything from ticketing and retail through to giant screens, advanced audio systems and pitchside advertising.

Many have already implemented biometric entry, checkoutless retail and mobile ordering and very soon stadiums will be equipped with crowd management platforms delivering real-time information on crowd density, traffic and movement patterns. Football is now operating in a world unthinkable when our previous entry, poor old Plovdiv Stadion, was jilted in the 1990s.

The delivery of free high-speed wifi to all spectators in 2014 was just another in a long line of home comforts brought to Parken, Denmark's national stadium and the home of FC Copenhagen. Perhaps the most extravagant can be found up on the eighth floor where a three Michelin-starred restaurant serves a meat-free menu and was in 2023 voted as the best in the world. Although not directly linked to any football activities, some may view such concessions to modernity as just another nail in the game's coffin. Yet Parken is the leading example of how to keep the fire burning in an arena equipped with all the gear. Its ability to straddle both the new world and the impassioned one of old is its greatest success.

Danish football fans are often portrayed as a hedonistic bunch, impassioned and fun but always on the right side of what's acceptable and what's not. It was in Denmark in the 1980s that the roligan movement emerged on the terraces to oppose the hooliganism so rife elsewhere; easy-going and respectful, but with unwaveringly rabid support for their teams. Nowadays we have become accustomed to witnessing spine-tingling renditions of 'Der er et yndigt land' belted out by a sea of red at summer tournaments. The all-round trust Copehagen's authorities have in their supporters has made it easy to give them what they want, in Parken's case plenty of space to bounce and if they choose, celebrate a goal with the now familiar mass beer-throwing. Such displays may be frowned upon elsewhere but here they are seen as symbolic of the conviviality in the stands. Indeed, after FC Copenhagen's fans roared their team to the last 16 of the Champions League in 2023, the city gave supporters 30,000 free beers as a thank you.

Parken stands on the site of the old Idrætsparken national stadium. When the original ground opened for a Copenhagen XI v Sheffield Wednesday game on 25 May 1911, a wonderful grandstand designed like a Palladian villa with 325 seats for officials and journalists was situated on the halfway line. With no facilities for athletics, a separate enclosure was then opened in 1912 on the northern side with a running track and Denmark's first reinforced concrete building, the stunning Idrætshuset. No visit to the modern Parken would be complete without a peek at its little brother. The atmospheric Østerbro Stadion is home to nine-time Danish champions B.93 (Boldklubben 1893) and for games in the Fenix Trophy (see chapter 27) Boldklubben Skjold, one of the country's largest football clubs in terms of membership. Opposite the Idrætshuset, the grandstand opened in 1958 is usually opened to the public before Denmark internationals to give fans a place to warm up with a few drinks and perhaps lose themselves in a little of its history.

When the original ground opened for a Copenhagen XI v Sheffield Wednesday game on 25 May 1911, a wonderful grandstand designed like a Palladian villa with 325 seats for officials and journalists was situated on the halfway line.

When Idrætsparken was expanded and rebuilt between 1990 and 1992, only the main stand was preserved. The layout was turned 90 degrees and for 640m Danish kroner (€86m in today's money), three towering, visually separate English-style stands were constructed. In time the corners were built up with and given over to commercial use. Between 2007 and 2009 the original main stand was demolished and in its place was a new two-tier edifice styled similar to those on the west and south to pull together the whole appearance. Only the North Stand with its multiple stacked glass-fronted boxes has seating spread over just a single tier. With 38,065 bright crimson seats, there can be no doubt that this is Denmark's manor but for FC Copenhagen's matches attended by an average of 28,154 in 2023/24, the abundance of white and blue can be a little jarring.

With contemporary Copenhagen having embraced the Danish modern style, Parken's exterior was kept light and uniform so as to harmonise with Edvard Glæsel's vast Fælledparken, the parkland which wraps around the stadium's north and west sides. Even Parken's main access road, Øster Allé, is uniformly lined with trees, further enhancing the sensation of having stepped out of the city into an idyllic hinterland despite being just five minutes from the Little Mermaid. I remember my first visit in 2015 for a Denmark match, the Øster Allé thronged with fans sporting Viking hats and standing around trolleys loaded with cases of beer which had been wheeled in from all over. The atmosphere crackled with positivity as a group of octogenarian ladies sipped from cans and shared songs with fans half their age. This is Parken, a place where regardless of nationality, if you've got the stamina for it you can jump wildly in the South Stand, arms wrapped around the shoulders of supporters next to you. If not, perhaps just kick back and order a stadion platte on the mobile app, enjoying the luxury provided elsewhere.

Glebe Park

BRECHIN // SCOTLAND
BRECHIN CITY

While Brechin City's 2022 relegation from the Scottish Football League may have fleetingly thrilled the mileage-worriers, it was met almost unanimously with a resigned sadness by those with an abiding love for the Scottish game. A pillar of tradition in a country slowly being overtaken by the modern game, for almost a century the club had blazed a trail for Scotland's smaller, outlying communities.

Surrounded by Brechin Park and its ornate cast-iron bandstand, the town's cemetery and a whisky distillery, Glebe Park has been home to the club since 1919.

In losing Brechin to the non-league game, the Scottish league also said goodbye to one of its most beloved grounds. Glebe Park is a place where rather than the terrace garb of the cities, you'll find gilets on the shoulders of young Angus cattle farmers. Club officials dress as they have done for a century, immaculately in blazer and tie meeting and greeting over drams of whisky. Threadbare hand-knitted scarves, wooden rattles and a fiercely loyal mindset are all brought to games as Brechin begin a new dawn and shoot for Scottish footballing history. Most believed they would immediately become the first club to beat the pyramid system and regain entry to the league. That they've now missed out as champions of the Highland League only to lose in the play-offs and by a goal difference of just four in successive seasons has been a double hammer blow for all concerned.

Brechin is a beguiling place. With barely ten shops, a smattering of pubs and no mainline railway station, it is to all intents and purposes a village-sized outpost. A city only in the traditional sense by virtue of its small cathedral, its handsome purple-grey sandstone streets are as sleepy as the surrounding farmsteads. Before the game, I spend an hour walking around. Two primary school-aged girls are out on an Easter egg hunt and pass me regularly as they excitedly tick off their finds displayed in shop windows. It is otherwise empty, the scene faintly reminiscent of those filmed in Kirkcudbright for the 1973 film *The Wicker Man*. In stark contrast, my last visit here was in 2012 when over 3,000 Rangers supporters wearing expressions of bewilderment flooded the streets and bars, Brechin representing not just their opening fixture, but their strange new reality after the club's demotion to the Third Division.

Surrounded by Brechin Park and its ornate cast-iron bandstand, the town's cemetery and a whisky distillery, Glebe Park has been home to the club since 1919. Until then Brechin City had used Nursery Park in the lower town, the former home of Brechin Harp and still used as a football ground by the town's junior club Brechin Victoria. For the first-time visitor, Glebe Park is likely to appear both extraordinary and puzzling, one half firmly in the realms of professional football and the other a delightful anachronism. Its fabulously

unorthodox look has largely been informed by the peculiarity in the divisional sizes of the Scottish league's top four tiers. Twelve Premiership teams and ten in each of the three divisions below means that part-time clubs on a promotional bounce from the bottom division can be mixing it in the Championship with a giant relegated from the top division within a few short years. Brechin themselves, averaging attendances of just 400 the season before, found themselves in the second tier in 2017/18 coming up against the likes of Dundee United, fresh from the Premiership with an average crowd of almost 8,000. Add to that the seasonal possibility of a home draw in the two cup competitions against one of the Old Firm, and stadiums need to be prepared for both eventualities which is why from Stranraer to Brechin, an ancient covered terrace or tiny grandstand, perfect for a crowd of three or four hundred, is often dwarfed by a modern all-seater stand.

Passing through turnstiles thought to have been sourced from Manchester City's Hyde Road stadium upon their departure to Maine Road in 1923 (it is rumoured another set found their way to Raith Rovers), the vast beige-gold frontage of the David H. Will Stand sets everything up for a modern football experience. Constructed in the early 1990s and architecturally influenced by the stands at St Johnstone's McDiarmid Park, which was opened in 1989, the David H. Will Stand is Glebe Park's only real concession to modernity. Built behind the north goal and able to seat 1,228, it was named not in vanity but in recognition of the former Brechin City chairman, president of the Scottish Football Association and latterly vice-president of FIFA. Will had overseen the development of Glebe Park throughout the 1970s including the installation of the club's curiously squat floodlights in the mid-70s. Opposite, the Cemetery End covered terrace was erected in 1960, its low, cranked roof propped by 13 steel supports abutting the final resting place of several Polish soldiers.

It is tempting to cast Glebe Park's famous beech hedge as its absolute highlight. Indeed, between May and October, its verdant splendour completes the ground perfectly. Its existence has not been without complication, however, and in 2009 Brechin entered a tug-of-war with the SFA over the width of their pitch. Falling two metres short of UEFA requirements and constrained by the hedge on the ground's north-eastern aspect, the club were faced with the very real prospect of having to dig it up, move floodlights and terracing and to top it off, pay a hefty fine. Ultimately common sense prevailed and after minor alterations, the fine was suspended. There was a time the hedge enclosed Glebe Park in its entirety and as recently as the 1970s, it ran the length of the pitch. Halfway along, where the hedge abruptly gives way to a breeze block wall (built after a section of hedge died off through waterlogging) there is a small and inconspicuous door. Here, young ball retrieval operatives would perch themselves on a ladder behind the hedge, watching the game but always ready to rush wayward balls back through the door.

We finish with my own favourite piece of Glebe Park, its central grandstand. Constructed between 1980 and 1981 and opened for a friendly with Alex Ferguson's Aberdeen, it replaced a dark wooden grandstand of a similar shape which was believed to have come from the Angus agricultural show. Although relatively small, its boxy loftiness and elegant glass screen-ends, backdropped by the spire of the former West and St. Columba's parish church, set it apart as one of the most beautiful 20th-century grandstands in Scotland. Although the team's current predicament has seen a growth in numbers attending matches and new, more local friendships forged, we must hope that Glebe Park is reinstated as a league ground sooner rather than later. For without it, the Scottish Football League is a poorer place.

Football stadiums next to bodies of water are not uncommon; after all coastal land is usually good, flat land upon which to play the game. Fourteen miles south of Brechin, Arbroath's Gayfield Park sits just a few yards from the gunmetal waters of the North Sea and is oft-lauded as Europe's closest stadium to the sea. But elsewhere, just down the road from the Galician fishing villa of Muxía, the local club's Arliña beach ground is similarly buffeted by brutal sea squalls in a location that would require a tape measure to determine a winner between the two. In another fishing village 3,000km away, Kassiopi's Dimotiko Gipedo stadium in Corfu rests atop a promontory, surrounded by the turquoise Mediterranean on three of its sides and sharing topographical similarities with Sportplatz's 'Treasure Island' in Greiz, Germany.

044

Stadio Comunale G. Sinigaglia

COMO // ITALY // COMO 1907

044 // Stadio Comunale G. Sinigaglia

COMO // ITALY // COMO 1907

You would assume that other than the proximity to the water's edge of the town's two main stadiums, any similarities between Arbroath and Como would end there. However, for a while during the last century both were places of fresh fish lunches by the marina and Italian ice cream on the beach. Holidaymakers would speak of Arbroath as though it were itself on Lake Como and of it being the most sun-blessed town in Scotland. Nowadays it is a faded veneer that cloaks both, Como's of old money gentility that lures over a million tourists each year and Arbroath's of lost industry and lost hope. In Como, heavy blooms of bougainvillea tug on the render of its palatial villas while in Arbroath, buddleia bursts through the blackened brickwork of obsolete industrial buildings. Although any demand for twinning remains unlikely, both have football teams backed by small but intensely passionate fan bases that in recent years, have carried their clubs to the cusp of promotion to their respective top divisions.

In December 1926, six months after 'Greater Gayfield' was repositioned and reopened, construction of Como's new stadium began. Quick to recognise the power of sport in achieving political ambitions, Mussolini's fascist regime had embraced sport in all its forms. New stadiums were going up all over Italy's provinces during the 1920s and 30s, lasting monuments to the country's industrial might and its sporting superiority which culminated in back-to-back World Cups in 1934 and 1938. The building of a new stadium on Lake Como had come at Mussolini's behest, 50km from where 19 years later he would be captured and executed by local partisans. Entrusted with the stadium's design was Milanese architect Giovanni Greppi. Greppi's early work had largely involved small-scale residential buildings in Milan although his stock would rise considerably throughout the 1930s when commissioned with a series of important war memorials including Italy's largest First World War military ossuary on the summit of Monte Grappa in the Venetian Prealps.

Given a square of uncultivated land called 'Garibaldi' to work with by Mayor Baragiola, Greppi chose subtlety over substance. Recognising the existing harmony between the adjacent public gardens and the lake in an area still free from buildings at that time, his design incorporated low, modest tribunes and two decorative entrances with columns inspired by ancient Rome. Opened on 30 July 1927 at the height of city-wide celebrations dedicated to Como native Alessandro Volta (inventor of the electric battery, who had died 100 years earlier), the inaugural football matches took place in September. Present during the triangular tournament involving Como, Genoa and Internazionale (for whom future World Cup winner Giuseppe Meazza made his debut) was Antonietta Porta Sinigaglia, godmother of the event and mother of rowing champion Giuseppe in whose honour the new stadium was named.

Stadio G. Sinigaglia would go on to become a stadium synonymous with some of sport's greatest postwar names. Eddy Merckx, Felice Gimondi and Tom Simpson all won the Giro di Lombardia on the Sinigaglia track while in 1952, Faustino Coppi won a stage of the Giro d'Italia here. That year Coppi would cement his reputation as the finest Italian cyclist of the day, winning both the Giro d'Italia and the Tour de France. Como's football team has played 13 seasons in Serie A at Sinigaglia, never finishing above sixth. On 15 May 1988 Arrigo Sacchi's Milan arrived needing a point to clinch their 11th *scudetto* and first under the presidentship of Silvio Berlusconi. With a team including Paolo Maldini, Franco Baresi, Ruud Gullit and Marco van Basten, Como held the *Rossoneri* to a 1-1 draw. Images captured that day show Milan's unbridled joy upon hearing the final whistle, a backdrop of a thousand flags and distant dreamy hills dotted with elegant villas. They remain some of the most recognisable and romantic in Serie A history.

Walking to the match along the water's edge, down Viale Puecher passing Giuseppe Terragni's 1931 hydroplane hangar and Como Yacht Club, English accents mingle with Italian. Dennis Wise, Thierry Henry and Cesc Fàbregas have all taken roles at the club in recent seasons, the knock-on effect of which is a growing English fanbase.

We can be thankful that little has altered at Sinigaglia over the years. The architect of all things aquatic, Gianni Mantero followed up his 1931 masterwork, the fabulous reinforced concrete three-tier diving tower for the Canottieri Lario rowing club behind the stadium, by accepting a commission to design a swimming pool and gymnasium beneath the grandstand. Mantero also designed a cantilever roof for Sinigaglia's grandstand which during its complete renovation between 1990 and 1991 was finally constructed in accordance with his original drawings. Where once stood the beloved 'Curva Azzurra' at the western end, its temporary-now-permanent 2002 scaffold pipe replacement is finally beginning to find some love among the diehards for whom it has become 'Curva Como'.

Walking to the match along the water's edge, down Viale Puecher passing Giuseppe Terragni's 1931 hydroplane hangar and Como Yacht Club, English accents mingle with Italian. Dennis Wise, Thierry Henry and Cesc Fàbregas have all taken roles at the club in recent seasons, the knock-on effect of which is a growing English fanbase. Many gather on the steps beneath the Monumento ai Caduti war memorial, another of Terragni's many works dotted along the shoreline, basking in the sun and awaiting kick-off. Less than 5,000 will come but of those that do, you'd be hard pushed to find anyone not of the opinion that Sinigaglia is the most perfectly situated football stadium in Europe.

1907

Sportpark Goed Genoeg

AMSTERDAM // THE NETHERLANDS // AMSTERDAMSCHE FOOTBALL CLUB

From Ajax and Achilles to Xerxes and Heracles, the Dutch have a rich panoply of mythologically named football clubs. While the English were busy suffixing clubs with Rovers and Rangers, the Netherlands adopted football as something of an elitist pastime in much the same way they had cricket a few decades earlier. Rather than the working man's game it would become, it attracted the intellectually minded who in seeking avenues to popularise their clubs, borrowed liberally from Greek and Roman classical literature.

Beneath the skin-deep grandiosity, however, the Dutch have always been a modest bunch, prone to self-deprecation and mordant wit. When Amsterdam's oldest amateur club left their first home between the ponds of the Vondelpark in 1906 and kicked off alongside a tumbledown farm on the Watergraafsmeer polder, they took inspiration from its self-effacing name, one which they have held on to dearly ever since across a variety of settings: Good Enough. Some 120 years later, Amsterdamsche Football Club find themselves residing at a small but perfectly formed new stadium among the most expensive real estate in the entire country. Yet despite the high-profile, high-value surroundings, Sportpark Goed Genoeg firmly reflects the amateur spirit of the club carrying with it the same unpretentious motto of old; if it's good enough for you, it's good enough for me. Amsterdam's second club may be less well-known than Rotterdam's or Eindhoven's but their all-inclusive philosophy has seen them grow to become the largest in the city with a staggering 158 teams in operation for the 2023/24 season. Many wait in the wings for membership which unless more pitches are created, the club simply cannot offer.

It is tempting to consider how big a name in European football AFC could have become had they followed their peers through the unstoppable 1950s movement towards professionalism. In the years immediately after the First World War, AFC were regularly beating Ajax and Feyenoord in front of crowds of 20,000. Yet on the eve of the first professional league, created from a merger of the KNVB and the unofficial breakaway NBVB competition on 25 November 1954, AFC's members pulled rank to maintain their amateur status. It is likely that professionalism simply came a little too late for AFC who at the time were enduring a success-starved three decades at their Zuidelijke Wandelweg stadium in Amsterdam-Zuid, a mile east of their current home. Membership was never a problem, 727

043 // Sportpark Goed Genoeg

AMSTERDAM // THE NETHERLANDS // AMSTERDAMSCHE FOOTBALL CLUB

in 1945, but the early success had dwindled as talented players swerved AFC for more progressive clubs. At Zuidelijke Wandelweg the crowds remained healthy, regularly topping 1,000 which created the need for a pitch-length grandstand that was constructed in the late 1950s and stood alongside an elegant two-storey clubhouse. It would only serve for a few years as in 1962 a narrow tract of land with development potential was made available to the club on De Boelelaan in Zuidas. Shortly after, they upped sticks and began building their new Goed Genoeg.

An image of Goed Genoeg from 1975 perfectly illustrates the startling rapidity with which Zuidas and Amsterdam-Zuid as a whole has developed. A faintly pastoral scene, uncultivated land bisected by a mud-brown dyke has given way to a 100m-high building named Valley. All mirrored glass and boxy

It is rare to find a new stadium meeting in perfect alignment with its surroundings. AFC's new home in the heart of Amsterdam's Financial Mile is a fabulous success.

protuberances, Valley is a 'symphony of life' according to its architect where people live, work, shop and barbecue on their sky patios. Looking north, the only giveaway that this is the same place is the then-stubby Telecomtoren, a tower which has since grown an additional 50m in height. And in the centre, Goed Genoeg's single football pitch, fenced, rudimentary and without furniture, as unassuming as the original version would have been.

By 2007 AFC had created a new show pitch in a move which would be repeated in 2019 when in keeping with the ever-changing Zuidas skyline, the current Goed Genoeg began to take shape. To make room for 1,350 new homes the entire site was shifted 100m north. Here, everything was constructed from scratch leaving no trace of the original ground, the site of which is now under the Ravel residential development. Three new pitches were added at the Beethovenstraat end, the most westerly of which would soon be dwarfed by the arrival of Valley in the autumn of 2022. Forty-two trees were felled to make way, replacements for which were planted along the north and south perimeter of the park and on the sloping banks of the river into which many footballs continue to meet their fate. The arrangement of the four outside pitches, all of which seem to be in constant use, occupy a north to south aspect while the new stadium sits in an east-westerly position accessed via a new road off Vivaldistraat.

It is rare to find a new stadium meeting in perfect alignment with its surroundings. AFC's new home in the heart of Amsterdam's Financial Mile is a fabulous success, not least because of its aesthetic appeal; the grid-like rigidity of the layout allows the abstract forms of the Valley to really dance, the low, green oasis of pitches giving some much needed breathing space among the sky soaring angles. AFC have worked hard with city planners to achieve something great without losing their identity, from the sustainable design of the clubhouse to the overall functionality of the park. Specially commissioned benches in the club's red and black colours are dotted around, and a large Omega timepiece affixed to a floodlight pylon is perhaps a tongue-in-cheek nod to Wall Street. Here among the professionals, these amateurs have a home fit for purpose for the next 100 years.

Satellite imagery of La Rioja, Spain's smallest region, renders its northernmost half as a tortilla-coloured land, bleached by sun and portioned up into an incongruous patchwork of narrow oblongs. These are the famous grapevines of Rioja Alta, gnarled and endless as they stretch off towards the Sistema Ibérico mountains. Down on the ground the road from Logroño to Nájera winds through a landscape of rocky outcrops crowned with timeworn pueblos, each with one or more opulent bodegas where wine tasting and accommodation is available for those that can afford it.

Estadio La Salera

NÁJERA // SPAIN // NAXARA CD

042

In Nájera itself, a sleepy town of 8,000 and former capital of the Kingdom of Navarra, face-in-the hole effigies of saints stand in the shadow of the monastery of Santa María la Real offering photo opportunities for pilgrims on the French Way, the most travelled path on the Camino de Santiago. Most on the path will be unaware that the unmarked track they will soon pass leads to a woodland glade where in 1966, the people of Nájera crafted out of the red earth one of Europe's wackiest football stadiums.

Completely at odds with the heat and dust of the region, Estadio La Salera is a cool Sylvanian wonderland. Wild bears are often spotted padding across the pitch while the club groundsman's annual battle is with the deep settling of woodland pollen on the playing surface during early springtime. It has an almost Scandinavian feel; it's early February and we are 666m up in the slopes of Monte Calavera, the air chilly beneath the forest's dark canopy and sharp with the scent of conifers and leaf mould. Today, under porridgy skies, Naxara will look to strengthen their grip on the Rioja group of Spain's fifth tier with a derby against Anguiano. Space in the 1,000-capacity stadium is always at a premium so supporters will need to get creative with their vantage points. Luckily the video platform game assortment of ramps, tiers and pathways, some more precarious than others, offers plenty of solutions for those with a certain nimbleness.

Back in 2010 with Naxara set to become champions of their group in the fourth tier, a group of ticketless young fans rekindled the lost childhood pastime of den-building. Down through the forest they came with armfuls of wooden planks and plywood, a few chairs and multiple crates of beer to claim their own vantage point, high above the western goal where the tree line ends on the edge of a 20ft drop. Although La Salera has a very fine grandstand for 350 people in the south-eastern corner, it is this rudimentary arrangement, cobbled together on top of the steep red cliff, which gained media attention. Images of the Ultras celebrating the title from their lair with smoke bombs and flags, raining down streamers on to spectators and the pitch below, have served to give the club a unique identity in Spanish football, a fixed idea that Naxara do things their own way. Yet not everyone is happy with the situation.

Thirty minutes before kick-off a set of headlights appears deep in the forest's gloom followed by three or four motorbikes. These supporters have bypassed La Salera's entrance to take up their position in the lair. Paying supporters in the stand point and jeer and I am told that while it is simply not possible to stop fans coming through the *puertas al monte*, the gates of the mountain, they can try and change the consciousness of young supporters. At the very least, the club encourages walking. Over the years the club has been threatened with possible sanctions regarding the safety of the stadium and surroundings, not least the very real risk of fire from the pyrotechnics.

Naxara's regular success and ambition on the field together with ever more stringent health and safety regulations from the Spanish FA dictates that La Salera will eventually be remodelled. Working in conjunction with the stadium's owner, the town council, there have been tentative discussions to lay a new pitch on Monte Calavera. It will see better access and a perimeter fence around an artificial pitch fully screening out the forest's lower slopes. While such progress is inevitable, we can only hope that Naxara continue to do things in their own inimitable style. In Rioja, only here will you experience the hoary Navarrese hard rock band Barricada roaring from the PA, ham and wine raffle tickets being plucked from an old wooden clock and supporters whose allegiance lies solely with their local club and not those in the realms of the professional game.

Grýluvöllur

HVERAGERÐI // ICELAND // HAMAR HVERAGERÐI

Just beneath the surface of Grýluvöllur's immaculate pitch, boiling underground rivers run hot enough to cook an egg. Fumarole vents near the touchline and in neighbouring backyards belch plumes of sulphuric steam into the ether, larger and angrier up on the slopes of the Grændalur volcano. The landscape here is so viscerally raw that until the mid-20th century, people avoided the little village of Hveragerði out of genuine fear. Add to the mix ancient tales of folkloric dread and regular earthquakes, and the name Hveragerði (which translates as 'hot spring garden') had been a byword for danger.

Endogenous factors began to change this in the early 1950s as people started to harness the immense energy of the Earth, using the rivers to cook food, heat greenhouses warm enough to grow bananas and wash football kits. Then came the artists, musicians and poets from Reykjavík, all inspired by a landscape that would alter dramatically from one minute to the next before their very eyes. In the 21st century, Hveragerði is a must-see tick for thousands of tourists travelling Iceland's Golden Circle route. Through it all, since 1956 in fact, the people of Hveragerði had played football at a pair of remarkable fields among one of the most alien landscapes in Europe.

Grýluvöllur takes its name from the Grýla geyser which now lies dormant just 70m from the pitch. 'Völlur' means field and prefixes the majority of Icelandic football grounds. Until the late 1990s Grýla would often shoot boiling jets of water up to 12m high during a match, bringing new meaning to the phrase 'the ground erupts'. It could also be triggered by pouring soap into it. If that sounds like fun, the alternative meaning of the word is altogether darker suggesting an intangible feeling that something terrible is going to happen. If you were an Icelandic child, however, it gets worse for your dreams will almost certainly have been haunted by Grýla. Capturing badly behaved children in a sack, legend tells us she cooked them in her cauldron and ate them for supper. I am relieved when 15 minutes into Hamar's fourth division match, an inebriated young man wearing nothing but a luminous green leotard suddenly appears on the pitch. Evading a couple of challenges from an official wielding a corner flag, he runs the length of the pitch before disappearing over a hill and into his mate's car. The small crowd of 200 are floored with laughter. In the distance, golfers lazily play out their nine holes on the Gufudalsvöllur course. The sun beats down, the bar does a brisk trade and the local football team score eight. There is little to fear here.

041

Crushed lava was collected in great quantities from nearby Þurá farm and used as a base for the pitch with a network of drainage pipes filtering water out. That summer, teenagers working summer jobs for the municipality helped level the site and lay the town's first grass football pitch.

Under the banner UFHÖ, sport in Hveragerði was ever present from 1935 until 1989 with football joining the existing divisions of swimming, handball and badminton in 1956. Eight years later, UFHÖ participated for the first time in the Icelandic Football Championship where on a gravel pitch in the town they would yoyo between the fourth and fifth tiers but never higher. That pitch, although now built over, would keep the football team in business up until the 1990s when during early spring Grýluvöllur's grass would often not be ready. In the spring of 1987 construction of the Grýluvöllur football ground began. Crushed lava was collected in great quantities from nearby Þurá farm and used as a base for the pitch with a network of drainage pipes filtering water out. That summer, teenagers working summer jobs for the municipality helped level the site and lay the town's first grass football pitch. Shortly after, the wooden clubhouse was built and final trimmings added around the pitch.

To finance the work, UFHÖ had introduced a club lottery scratchcard which had become popular in Iceland during the late 1980s. Initially a success, spiralling production costs and decreasing sales left UFHÖ penniless by 1989. Despite having built a fabulous new football facility, the envy of much larger settlements, they filed for bankruptcy shortly after and in doing so joined a small band of Icelandic sports clubs to be wound up. It had all begun so well. On 3 July 1988, daily newspaper *DV* ran with the headline 'Grýla gaus 9 sinnum!' following Grýluvöllur's inaugural match the previous day. Translated as 'Grýla erupted 9 times!' in reference to how many goals UFHÖ scored against their visitors Léttir from Reykjavík, the report continued, 'Hveragerði are on a fast cruise. They walked over Léttir on their splendid new grass field next to geyser Grýla.'

Named after a small, steaming hillside in Hveragerði, Hamar came into existence in 1992 and began using Grýluvöllur for competitive football a year later. They would go on to become a mainstay in the lower reaches of the Icelandic league system, playing in the third tier between 2008 until 2014 before dropping into the fourth and fifth tiers. Perennial underdogs, on 19 June 2008, Hamar beat neighbours Selfoss to reach the last 16 of the national cup in front of a Grýluvöllur crowd estimated at 1,000. Selfoss fielded three players who would a few years later be playing for the great Icelandic team of the mid-2010s including Jón Daði Böðvarsson who continues his career in England with Bolton Wanderers. In a land of such enormous emptiness, the Icelandic football family is unsurprisingly a small one. Seeking the recipe for the successes of the national team and those of its club sides in European competition continues to leave many more knowledgeable than myself scratching their heads. However, we can be certain that it begins on fields such as Grýluvöllur where maybe, just maybe, there is something in the water.

Stade Maurice Beraud

MONTARGIS // FRANCE // USM MONTARGIS

Those visiting Montargis having bought into its self-styled claim to being the Venice of Gâtinais may find themselves a little underwhelmed. Certainly there are bridges and a lot of water; Gâtinais is a historic province of France between the Seine and the Loire rivers. But La Serenissima it is not. For the thousands of provincial backwaters in France, finding an exclusive angle to lure tourists can be a tricky business. In recent years the Montargis tourist board has fixed its attention on the town's Chinese heritage. Here in the early 20th century Li Shizeng founded the Work-Study Movement, which focused on bringing young Chinese radicals to France to learn French culture and western science. Thousands came to Montargis, including future leaders of the Chinese Communist Party who would adopt many of the movement's key principles.

Stepping out of the train station, I pass through Place Deng Xiaoping before reaching a bridge where a group of young Chinese students are huddled in the rain, busily taking selfies in front of a bronze statue of the revolutionary. Soon after, they will make their way to the Museum of French-Chinese Friendship. In the tourist office there is no reference to the town's football stadium while in the library, the assistant is at pains to find anything significant for me to read. Yet when I post an image of Stade Maurice Beraud online a few days later, the reactions are those of unbridled joy. One person was so enamoured by the ornamental grandstand he had quickly begun researching his own route from the UK. Whether or not Montargis has missed a trick in omitting Stade Beraud from its tourist maps is both debatable and perhaps unimportant. It is, after all, 'only' a football ground and home to a club largely forgotten – if indeed they were ever really known at all. In all likelihood, it will see out its days as a fanciful folly for curious connoisseurs, serving the same club it has since 1925.

USM Montargis' success amounts to three short seasons in the French third tier and a last-64 cup tie away at Marseille in 1956. Rarely playing in front of crowds above 100, the club are indicative of French football's lack of appeal as a spectator sport below the professional game. Montargis is, after all, a reasonably sized town of 14,000 people with no professional club within 70km. Just how it came to have a stadium quite like Stade Beraud remains a little hazy, as architect Louis Philippon's many commissions in Montargis bear no similarities to his 1925 stadium. For example, the town hall opened the same year and widely considered his masterpiece is a work of neoclassicism, full of colourful art nouveau interior design. Given land just beyond the tree line of the national forest, it is likely Philippon sought inspiration from the neo-Basque architectural style popular at the time in the forested areas of south-west France. Stade Beraud's only sporting comparable is Stade Rémy Goalard, a rugby stadium in Soustons, near Biarritz, although that wasn't constructed until 1938.

Although much of the grandstand's ornamentation is purely for show, the whole structure serves as a focal point in a woodland theatre. Entering beneath an arched gate

alongside one of two surviving gatehouses, there is a sense of having wandered into the stately grounds of a French chateau: trees pruned, grass trimmed and everything swept clean in readiness for an evening of bourgeois entertainment. Although the pair of gazebo kiosks at either end of the grandstand are pure decorative folly, they serve to visually connect the forest to the arena. Beneath the western tower is a small raised floor accessed by a steep flight of wooden steps, a spot once designated for reporters but in lieu of the club's plight in the modern era rarely used nowadays. Considering the age of the timber used for the grandstand, everything is in remarkably good condition, the pay-off for a century of professional repairs and careful repaints, always in the same canary yellow with navy blue trim.

Any illusion that the stand is a complete work in wood, however, is shattered below where the brick and render block it sits atop houses the clubhouse, changing rooms and toilet facilities. A single shelf sparse with trophies occupies one wall. Floors are polished, spaces kept tidy and in the absence of the usual football detritus clogging up corridors, the impression is one of everything being kept uncomplicated for the purpose of protecting the building itself. Pitchside are two sunken concrete dugouts of the kind rarely seen anymore, the surface itself prepared to an exemplary standard. Out of time and out of place, Stade Maurice Beraud is a little-known piece of 1920s French chic.

039

Hillsborough

SHEFFIELD // ENGLAND // SHEFFIELD WEDNESDAY

With each passing season, what we refer to as the 'classic' English football ground moves ominously closer to extinction. Stadiums that once served as templates for much of Europe and helped define the original character of the game have, in the upper echelons of the game at least, dwindled down to fewer than 40. But while names such as Highbury, Roker Park or the Baseball Ground will usually be met with a wistfulness in those above 40, we can rest assured that in 70 years' time today's future classics will all be greeted with similar levels of reverence.

Future generations may learn of Goodison Park or Kenilworth Road from a grandfather but having no experiences of such places; for them it will be Tottenham Hotspur Stadium, Brentford Community Stadium and Everton's stunning new dockside stadium that spark similarly strong emotions. The highs and lows of their clubs will infuse them with their own special character and from the footfall of millions, they too will take on a more mature appearance and eventually become outdated. Football's thirst for progress cannot be stopped and money, technology and fashion will continue to dictate the appearance of its homes just as it always has done.

History hides within Hillsborough's every nook and cranny. It is a chimera, a disparate assortment of bits and pieces that cobbled together serve as a reminder of the extreme highs and the appalling lows of England's 20th-century game.

Scunthorpe United's arrival at Glanford Park in 1988 marked a sea change in the construction of football grounds. With 1990's Taylor Report following the Hillsborough disaster recommending all major stadiums convert to all-seater models, it firmed up the idea that the 'complete stadium' was the way forward: off-the-shelf models which would become the accepted way to build a stadium regardless of size, style or substance. Until then, grounds had largely been developed in a piecemeal fashion, individual components added, demolished or updated when and as necessary depending on finances. This gave us the 'hodgepodge' factor, clashing styles built decades apart which in

stark contrast to the perfect symmetry of today all seems fairly quaint when looking back. But it is the loss of this vital aspect of the 'classic' ground that is perhaps felt more keenly than any other. Hillsborough, for example, offers the opportunity to sit in a stand constructed in the year of Emily Davison's suffragette protest at Epsom Racecourse. Or you could choose the North Stand, opened 70 days after work began on the Berlin Wall. Meanwhile, in the Spion Kop, still one of the largest single-tier stands in Britain, you'll be sat beneath a roof that went up the same year as the Chernobyl disaster.

When Sheffield Wednesday moved from Olive Grove to Owlerton in 1899 it was considered a huge risk. Three miles north of the city centre, thinly populated and with few public transport links, the more attractive option had appeared to be a site in Carbrook. A year earlier a poll among club members was taken and Carbrook had won easily with 4,767 votes to Owlerton's 4,115. But with the Sheffield city mayor promising to push through an Owlerton branch of the city's tram system if Wednesday headed north, the club ignored the result. The land was purchased from famous Sheffield silversmith James Dixon for £4,783, a sum that was met by director and future chairman of the FA Charles Clegg taking out a £3,000 mortgage. Close to the old Wadsley Bridge (now High Bridge), it largely consisted of dandelion-filled meadowlands on the banks of the River Don. When Hillsborough was opened on 2 September 1899 for a match against Chesterfield, there was no bridge over the river for spectators accessing the Leppings Lane turnstile. For some time afterwards, fans would use the stepping stones in the river to cross, some even swimming across especially if dared to do so. Those 'leaping' stones became the lepping stones from which the street and stand (now the West Stand) took its name. It is of course where, 90 years later, the worst disaster in British sporting history occurred.

Wednesday had moved their 2,000-capacity grandstand from Olive Grove to Owlerton brick by brick where between 1899 and 1903 it was reconstructed on the ground's southern aspect. By 1912 the club's rapidly expanding fanbase had led to record profits being turned over. It was decided that Hillsborough should be given a brand new stand which reflected Wednesday's ambitions and with that, architect Archibald Leitch was brought in to oversee its design. If this was a book solely about the British football ground, Leitch by now would have had countless mentions as the man most responsible for their appearance. By the late 1920s 16 of the 22 clubs in England's First Division had hired Leitch's company at one time or another. His South Stand for Hillsborough remains the oldest and most impressive on the site. So good was it when it opened that up in Edinburgh, Hearts demanded a replica of their own for Tynecastle. Improvements including 1965's conversion to an all-seater in readiness for the 1966 World Cup and an upper tier added for the European Championship of 1996 have served it well. While pesky roof supports obstruct spectator views at either end of the ground to this day, the single-span, 500-tonne girder added during the construction of 1995's new tier allows for uninterrupted views. Up on the roof, the ornate ironwork finial may be a replica of Leitch's original but the copper football held within is very much original. When it was discovered to have been inscribed with the wrong date of the club's formation, it was corrected from 1866 to 1867 during the 1947/48 season.

History hides within Hillsborough's every nook and cranny. It is a chimera, a disparate assortment of bits and pieces that cobbled together serve as a reminder of the extreme highs and the appalling lows of England's 20th-century game. Tony Christie's Ozzie Owl nightclub behind the South Stand may be long since closed but among all that red brick, so characteristic of the north's industrial past, there is enough here to keep the football romantics happy for years. With Wednesday a shadow of the team they once were at the time of writing, Hillsborough may just stick around for a good while yet.

Titanbet
Sign up at titanbet.co.uk/swfc
Titanbet
Bet in-play now
Titanbet
Sheffield Wednesday - Hillsborough

038

Lahden Stadion

LAHTI // FINLAND // FC LAHTI

Football's coexistence with winter sports is unusual but not unheard of. High in the Taebaek Mountains in South Korea, Gangwon FC have in recent years played at the Alpensia Ski Jumping Stadium where the outrun doubles as the club's pitch. Meanwhile, after the snowmelt in Austria's Tyrolean Alps, the pitches beneath Seefeld Sports Arena's jumps are regularly used by the likes of Manchester City, Galatasaray and RB Leipzig for summer training matches.

We have already looked at Cortina d'Ampezzo's remarkable repurposing of its Trampolino Olimpico's outrun, while in 1961 a 45m-high jump was erected on the pitch at London's Wembley Stadium, complete with 50 tonnes of crushed ice. That event was merely a fundraiser for British skiing but in the surprisingly industrial Finnish city of Lahti, a more senior example of such compatibility can still be found. Lahden Stadion may be adorned with ski-themed sculptures (one even created by Moomins author Tove Jansson's father Viktor) but in the summer months it becomes home to a club who have been absent from Finland's Premier League for just one season since 1999.

Close to the town of Hanko on Finland's southern coast to Joensuu near the border with Karelia, the Salpausselkä ridge system crosses the country for almost 500km. Formed by retreating glaciers during the last ice age, many natural depressions were left from the melting of colossal blocks of frozen ice. In 1922 one such geological pocket, known as Mäkimonttu, was selected as the site for what would become one of Scandinavia's most beloved winter sports stadiums. Although primitive upon completion with a single jumping hill, a slalom track and solitary maintenance building, the horseshoe-shaped arrangement of the stands allowed spectators to surround both the start and finish areas. With the jumping hills reaching a height of 224m above sea level and creating a spectacular natural amphitheatre, the Salpausselkä Sports Park quickly became Finland's premier winter sports venue. Home since 1923 of the annual Lahti Ski Games, it would go on to host numerous world skiing championships.

Back in the midst of time there was a football team immortalised in Subbuteo colours (ref. 243) and as the original club of Finland's most famous footballing son, Jari Litmanen. Although the name is preserved in a reformed club, the original Lahden Reipas were three times champions of Finland in the 1960s. Founded in 1891 in the town of Viipuri, the Reipas name was carried to Lahti by evacuees during the First World War where they moved into the city's Kisapuisto Stadion after it was built for the 1952 Olympic Games football tournament. With Reipas mainstays in European competition throughout the 1970s and city rivals Kuusysi about to embark upon a run of five Finnish championships from the narrow confines of Kisapuisto, the Lahti municipality and Ministry of Education initiated a project for a new stadium next door to Salpausselkä. Operating as a versatile summer sports stadium, it would also cater for the increased popularity in winter cross-country and biathlon events where spectators could witness thrilling race finishes.

To make way, the 90m jump was repositioned further west while the oldest remaining building on the site, the 1923 Finnish log sauna, was moved east. Work began in 1977 on land just a few metres east of Mäkimonttu's outrun but significantly higher. Designed by architects Esko Koivisto, Pekka Salminen and Juhani Siivola, the 5,000-seat grandstand was built over two levels with a cantilever roof supported by concrete panel columns. The top tier contains a single corridor from which 15 elegant glass-fronted skyboxes are accessed. With a curved bank of terracing for 7,000 standing spectators wrapped around the eastern end, a further 2,000 seating places were created on the southern side. By carving rows into the wooded slope and installing delightfully rustic log benches (now fitted with blue plastic seats), it offsets the fierce modernism of the grandstand perfectly. Opened for the 1978 edition of the Nordic World Ski Championships, football took up residency in 1981 and although Reipas and Kuusysi would continue league games at Kisapuisto, Liverpool, Paris Saint-Germain and Steaua Bucharest would all visit Kuusysi at Lahden Stadion in European competitions. When Reipas and Kuusysi met in 1988, 13,533 watched – not a huge attendance by other countries' standards perhaps but in a land where skiing is king, it represented an enormous one.

Work began in 1977 on land just a few metres east of Mäkimonttu's outrun but significantly higher. Designed by architects Esko Koivisto, Pekka Salminen and Juhani Siivola, the 5,000-seat grandstand was built over two levels with a cantilever roof supported by concrete panel columns.

I visit in 2023 for a league match between FC Lahti and FC Honka, of Espoo. The name FC Lahti is the result of the 1996 merger of Reipas and Kuusysi and although the success of yesteryear has so far eluded them crowds remain healthy. Beyond the giant scoreboard, Salpausselkä now has a full deck of jumps and despite the summer haze being thick enough to cut with a knife, it looks a picture. Down on the outrun at the foot of the 90m jump, a swimming pool swells with summer bathers. On woodland paths people are visiting the protected trenches and potholes left behind from the Finnish Civil War while others amble along the trail of sculptures dedicated to Finland's skiing legends. There is nothing else quite like it, a scarcely believable backdrop to the football taking place. However, with Kisapuisto earmarked for a brand new stadium that would see the club return to their spiritual home, it may be that like so many great football oddities its days are numbered. Another case then of get there and get there quick if you want to experience football in this most unlikely of settings.

Lahti
PARTURI
SHALA
&
SAQI
02:56
LEIKKAUS 20-22 €, VAPAUDENKATU 10
PLANMILL
Halton
NYT

Melach Road

KEMATEN IN TIROL // AUSTRIA // SV KEMATEN

When in 2022 SV Kematen chairman Arno Bucher officially renamed Kematen in Tirol's football field 'Melach Road', it represented the latest in a series of Anglicisations which began at West Ham United. There, at a 2016 memorabilia auction of fixtures and fittings from the soon to be demolished Boleyn Ground, Bucher ended up with a pair of claret roll-through turnstiles which a few months later would be installed at the new entrance gate of Sportplatz Kematen. Around this time, the team began to run on to the pitch to crackly audio of an English crowd singing 'Come on You Blues'. This ditty would later find its way on to items of merchandise in the new club shop and be belted out with occasional variation by Kematen's small but tight band of supporters.

Football fans across the continent have long since borrowed cultish elements of the game. Tifos have been unveiled in Aberdeen and Poznań danced in Venice. There are Kops in Guingamp and Belfast, the Viking Clap in Lens, pyrotechnic displays in Tórshavn. And of course there is nothing unusual nowadays hearing songs from around the world being adapted into chants by fans, whether it's the *Azzurri's* 'Campioni del Mondo' to the tune of 'Seven Nation Army' or 'Polska, Bialoczerwoni' underpinned by the Village People's 'Go West'. But at Melach Road, in particular when celebrity neighbours Wacker Innsbruck roll into town and lift the crowd into four figures, all this adopted Englishness serves to create a jarring sensory overload. A hullabaloo in one of the most tranquil locations imaginable. It is as unlikely as it is charming.

Melach Road was opened in 1968, a purpose-built replacement for SV Kematen's original ground in the south of the village known locally as simply 'Lager' or 'Camp' where they had played since their formation in 1947.

Although the mountains around Kematen are fairly tame in comparison to those further west where the football grounds of Lermoos and Ehrwald hide beneath the alpine primordial landscape of the Zugspitze, the close proximity of Martinswand (Martin's Wall) gives Melach Road a very unique appearance. Rising vertically 594m behind the north goal, its impressive scale renders Kematen and neighbouring Zirl into little more than model villages held within its daunting embrace. In reality, the foot of Martinswand is separated from Kematen by the River Inn scuppering any chance of the ultimate game of Wall Ball, yet its overhanging ledges give it an imperious presence and Melach Road a feeling of tight confinement. It is probably a good idea to not look up if troubled by pangs of acrophobia. Such anxieties beset a youthful Emperor Maximilian on the face of Martinswand in 1484. Hunting chamois and ibexes he became trapped on the rock face for three days and three nights, frozen with fear, too afraid to move forward or back. The drama was all played out before an amused general public watching from the ground below, quite possibly from the spot where Kematen now play an altogether more agreeable sport.

Melach Road was opened in 1968, a purpose-built replacement for SV Kematen's original ground in the south of the village known locally as simply 'Lager' or 'Camp' where they had played since their formation in 1947. Photographs from the inaugural match show a 50m-long uncovered grandstand with bench seating carved into the natural banking on the western side. From Voralberg to Burgenland similar uncovered seating solutions are still typical at Austrian amateur grounds where football is only played during the warmer months and adjoining hillsides provide natural rake. Informing the current oval shape of Melach Road was a sand running track which was eventually removed and grassed over in 2015. In 1980, in a move which foreshadowed Bucher's later reclamation of sporting artefacts, the club purchased the 'Austria House' from the 1978 World Ski Championships in Garmisch-Partenkirchen. A traditional alpine lodge, it was disassembled, transported and rebuilt behind the southern goal at Melach Road to serve as the club's canteen. Although modernised in 2015, its cosy interior retains its traditional charm, woody fragrances mingling with the sour tang of Austrian beer.

Under Bucher's guidance, the 21st century has seen Melach Road transformed into a modern and stylish football ground. The tactful knitting together of concrete, steel and glass unites it with the rockbound vista. Rebuilt in 2000, the grandstand was given a polished concrete cantilever roof and 272 royal blue plastic bucket seats. From here, sweeping around the south-western corner towards the entrance is a continuous balcony area, paved with grey flagstones and fronted by a curving glass and steel barrier. Built on top of new changing rooms it is from this elevated position that the majority of supporters gather to watch the game in the archetypal manner of the Austrian football fan, a beer never far from hand. Upon my arrival, my question 'Do you know Arno Bucher?' is met with 'Everybody knows Arno!' When those beers are raised to greet the team, I suspect that the fans in their COYB! scarves are also raising a glass to the chairman who has made this football ground what it is, the envy of so many in Tirol.

Johan Cruijff ArenA

AMSTERDAM // THE NETHERLANDS // AJAX

Despite the seasonal slew of sparkling new stadiums, the Johan Cruijff ArenA's status as a groundbreaker in the field appears to be holding firm. Almost 30 years have passed since it first wowed onlookers from across the globe and although it has long since fallen into the category marked vintage, its aesthetic impact still delivers hard. Indeed, Amsterdam's arena hasn't been allowed to rest on its laurels. Significant improvements throughout the years have been undertaken, most recently 2020's completion of exterior renovations which have further enhanced its likeness to a gigantic armoured beetle.

Any Ajax fans previously tiring of its presence will surely be delighted by the Government of Amsterdam's continued investment in their home. It may still have a few detractors among those Sons of the Gods who still pine for an atmosphere comparable with Ajax's rough old De Meer Stadion but by and large, it is as good a modern football stadium as there is.

De Meer had been the club's ground from 1934 until the arrival of the Amsterdam Arena in 1996. The home of Rinus Michels' Total Football, it was a surprisingly modest venue for one associated with the grace of Cruyff and with a capacity of just 27,000, always much too small for the waves Ajax were busy making in the European game. Five kilometres north of the arena, the site is now covered by residential apartment blocks. But for any students of the game, it is well worth a visit as De Meer's legacy is kept alive in not only the placement of old stand signs and a series of wooden bridges honouring the names of Ajax greats, but by a show-stopping mural of Cruyff on the corner of Wembleylaan and Anfieldroad. Just a few streets from where he grew up at Akkerstraat 32 in neighbouring Betondorp, it is a powerful reminder that this was once the Flying Dutchman's bailiwick.

After attempts to bring the 1992 Olympic Games to Amsterdam were thwarted by the Barcelona bid, plans to replace the city's 1920 Olympisch Stadion (where Ajax had been playing European and evening matches) were shelved. The proposed location had been a site in the Biljmermeer which at the time was an overcrowded urban hell of dilapidated tenements, drug addiction and streets piled high with rubbish. Back in 1966, Biljmer had been envisioned as a modern new 'radiant city', one which would solve Amsterdam's great housing shortage after the Second World War. But by the end of the decade, the Dutch middle classes for whom the blocks had been developed had begun seeking less uniform family homes, ones with gardens and clean air, and were moving out

AMSTERDAMSCHE FOOTBALL CLUB AJAX SINDS 18 MAART
AJAX
VS
-LUDOGORETS
31 AUG. 2023

of Amsterdam altogether. With many of the high-rise apartments standing empty and the mass influx of underprivileged and unemployed Surinamese immigrants moving in, by the 1980s Biljmer had the distinct profile of a poor black neighbourhood. It was even declared nationally as the first and only Dutch ghetto in the Netherlands.

Nowadays those high-rise apartments that were once used as video backdrops for aspiring rappers have been razed or converted to larger family homes. Biljmer has a new profile, one of creative promise and great vibrancy. It has become something of a hipster neighbourhood. Everywhere residents are sporting replica Ajax shirts, testament to the club's huge multicultural appeal, while just to the west, the Amsterdam Arena rises from the flat land, its colossal impact on the landscape similar to Milan's San Siro. The original designs for the Olympic Stadium had in 1990 been reworked following the creation in 1987 of the Stichting Amsterdam Sportstad (Amsterdam Sports City Foundation) and with Ajax by this stage desperate for a new home having just landed the UEFA Cup, the new stadium was finally given the green light. With the deep foundations' first pile placed on 26 November 1993, the construction took three years and cost €140m but when it was officially opened by Queen Beatrix on 14 August 1996, Amsterdammers saw for the first time just what the money had been spent on.

Architect Rob Schuurman's modified design for Grabowsky & Poort had done away with the running track, lost seating sections in favour of bringing stands closer to the pitch and above it all, gone with an idea that would change the face of large-scale European football stadium design forever. Although a prototype for the retractable roof had been unveiled at Pittsburgh's Civic Arena as far back as 1961 and a first fully retractable version opened at Toronto's Rogers Centre in 1988, Amsterdam Arena was the first to be constructed on European soil. It wasn't without teething problems, however, and for a long time Ajax fans remained unenthusiastic. Endless blank concrete walls bearing little reference to their club, hideous patterns picked out in the seating blocks and a pitch cast in permanent shadow from the roof requiring it to be ripped up and replaced up to four times a year were among Amsterdam Arena's biggest failings early on. Yet it didn't stop Ajax with a team including Patrick Kluivert, Frank Rijkaard, Edgar Davids and Clarence Seedorf from winning the following year's UEFA Champions League and through the team's on-field successes and rectification of the stadium's problems, fans gradually began to fall in love with their new home.

Still warming up in the traditional manner of drinks in the city's Rembrandt Square before taking the metro south, Ajax fans are nowadays greeted by all new widened concourses outside the arena and a series of enormous portraits of Johan Cruyff, after whom the stadium was renamed for the 2018/19 season. The dizzying new facades now appear like the world's largest Snakes and Ladders board, transparent tubular escalators vying for room with horizontal walkways, A-frame structural supports and vertical ornamental columns. There is now car parking space for up to 12,000 vehicles and the surrounding area has taken on the look of a futuristic mini-city with hotels, restaurants and shopping options continuing to spring up. By standing by their convictions and ironing out the multifarious issues, the Government of Amsterdam has overseen the transmogrification of the Johan Cruijff ArenA and moreover, the Biljmer neighbourhood. In keeping with the city's great tradition of modern architecture and forward-thinking, it is now a thrilling place to enjoy the modern, out-of-town matchday experience.

Kaffeetälchen

TIEFENORT // GERMANY // KALI WERRA TIEFENORT

Kali Werra Tiefenort welcomed in 2024 with a big public announcement. The capacity of their historic woodland home would be increased from 8,000 to 8,006 following archivist Heiko Adler's discovery of two old GDR-era benches in neighbouring undergrowth. Supporters were urged to purchase season tickets without haste, adding that the new seats would be snapped up quickly.

It is often best to make light of a situation when the chips are down. For Kali Werra, a club languishing in the murky basement of German football, watched by barely 100 in a stadium they once regularly attracted 8,000 supporters to, their predicament has become the source of good humour. And it needs to be. Aside from the current football team, Adler and the small band of club volunteers have roles which require enormous dedication and time in maintaining a veritable goldmine of German football history. As with the self-assembled archeology team that in 2015 descended on the site of Bradford's old Park Avenue stadium, their enjoyment is in unearthing and preserving traces of a lost footballing world. For Adler especially, a former Kali Werra player in the GDR second division, it is particularly poignant. Between them they continue to conserve Kaffeetälchen to such a high standard that it has become something approaching an unofficial museum of East German football.

Before we unpick the story of one of Germany's most romantic stadiums, we must address the name Kaffeetälchen, a word that sounds as curious in the German tongue as it will in any language. Twenty-four hours after my visit to Tiefenort I was watching Lokomotive Leipzig, another great old GDR club, with the club's press officer. I mentioned I had been to Kaffeetälchen, a remark which left him rolling the word around his tongue. Although the name Kali Werra Tiefenort had drawn a nostalgic smile, to him I had made a faux pas, apparently throwing two unrelated German words together. The story goes that in the forest gorge high

035

BSG
Aktivist

above Tiefenort, long before the miners' football field was opened on 11 September 1926, there stood a small wooden cafe popular with weekend excursionists. Approaching the forest, the scent of roasting coffee beans would drift enticingly through the trees leading to it becoming known locally as the coffee valley: Kaffeetälchen. Until recently, the story was something of a myth, one which had begun taking on a life of its own as it was swapped between football nostalgists the length and breadth of Germany. But in 2022 Kali Werra's very own time team finally discovered evidence of the cafe and that it also sold a delicious cake, presenting the information in an exhibition entitled '100 Years of Football in Tiefenort'.

In Thuringia, Tiefenort and its 4,000 inhabitants occupy a position virtually in the bullseye of Germany. Its football club's postwar history is inexorably entwined with the Kaiseroda potassium mines, a place that took on a darker context in April 1945 when the US Army discovered 30 miles of underground art galleries and sacks of gold stolen by the Nazis. At the founding of the German Democratic Republic in 1949, all civic football clubs were forced to dissolve as the new command economy decreed that sporting organisations affiliate themselves with local industries. Tiefenort's players were offered employment at the mining company who in turn began funding the expansion and maintenance of Kaffeetälchen. In recognition of the partnership and to widen their appeal, the club became BSG 'Aktivist' Kali Werra Tiefenort in 1963, 'Aktivist' being just one of many new Soviet-sounding prefixes added to sporting clubs to demonstrate East Germany's industrial clout.

Kali and Werra were adopted to reflect the name of the mine and the nearby river while 'Aktivist' refers to mining. In Chemie Leipzig, Motor Altenburg, Turbine Potsdam and Dynamo Dresden the industries with which those clubs were affiliated live on, namely the chemical, automobile and electricity industries and the interior ministry or Stasi. Any new band having a tilt at the Krautrock genre but stuck on a name could do a lot worse than delve into the wonderful world of East German football club names. Among those long forgotten we find gems such as Kernkraftwerk Greifswald, Funkwerk Kölleda, Robotron Sömmerda and Zuckerfabrik Goldbeck.

In 1964, Kaffeetälchen was given its first grass pitch, replacing the sand surface which had served them since 1926. In time it would become known as the 'Holy Turf', one the finest pitches in East Germany upon which Kali Werra's golden years were played in the GDR second division. With four successive top-six finishes between 1959 and 1963, fans from across the region began travelling to watch the team, cramming Kaffeetälchen's steep curved terraces to capacity. The 14 rows of terracing, constructed with upright concrete slabs and gravel, have such a sharp rake that to imagine them full is to picture a wall of bodies standing upon each other's shoulders. When Germany's reunification arrived in 1990, East German clubs immediately lost the support of the industries. In Kali Werra's case, the Ernst Thälmann potash company was swiftly liquidated, leaving players without jobs and financial and maintenance agreements severed. Many of the old GDR stadiums, especially those further down the leagues, have either fallen into disrepair or been demolished entirely. Those that remain are unanimously treasured by stadium aficionados, especially those which retain original fixtures and fittings. Although Kaffeetälchen lost its announcement tower in the 1990s, there are few better preserved football stadiums from the old GDR. Right down to the pitch gate with its hammer and pick symbols, everything is as it was. Better still, on matchdays in the forest you can now get the best Thüringer Bratwurst to go with your coffee.

St James' Park

NEWCASTLE-UPON-TYNE // ENGLAND // NEWCASTLE UNITED

Sitting high and mighty (but never pretty) above the city, St James' Park has evolved in almost a century and a half from a rough patch of grazing land to one of England's most celebrated and historic football stadiums. To illustrate the endurance of the site which would become the home of Newcastle United in 1892, just three decades before a ball was kicked on Town Moor the sport of the day was in full swing. On a spot known as the 'Gallows Hole', yards from where the infamous Gallowgate End banking would be developed, public executions were taking place for crimes as piddly as forging a bank note and stealing a horse. Heaven knows what the punishment would have been for Lee Bowyer and Kieran Dyer's same-side scrapping a century and a half later. Thankfully, what the *Newcastle Guardian* described as a 'Saturnalia of blood' had been taken inside prison walls by 1863 and in 1919, the city's relationship with capital punishment ended.

Exactly 100 years after the Magpies tied the knot with their new home, I moved to Newcastle as a student. Although at the time I was unaware that my third year digs on Hartford Street was situated just yards from the site of Heaton Junction, the club's home until 1892, I vividly recall how between 1992 and 1996 St James' Park shot up above the city. My first experience was one of being lashed by freezing horizontal rain on an uncovered Gallowgate terrace, the team playing out a dismal First Division draw with Derby County in front of 20,000 cheerless fans. But by 1996, St James' Park was welcoming Zinedine Zidane, Brian Laudrup and 20,000 overseas fans to Euro 96 and its Eurofest Village.

Barely a month after the game with Derby, Sir John Hall had arrived announcing his masterplan to create a multi-sport institution along similar lines to Barcelona. After so many years in the doldrums, supporters naturally scoffed. But having installed Kevin Keegan in the managerial hot-seat, Newcastle quickly went from the brink of relegation to the Third Division to being nailed-on Premier League winners in 1996 only to famously fall at the final hurdle. Corresponding with every sparkling new signing or momentous victory, a new piece of the St James' Park jigsaw seemed to be fitted into place. In the spring of 1995, I watched the final of a county cup tournament from a seat in the half-built second tier of the Leazes End. Surrounded by a gigantic steel framework, the old ground was being transformed before the public's very eyes.

While it has long been accepted that the 1892 amalgamation of the city's East End and West End clubs marks the moment Newcastle United came into existence, an intriguing new theory has in recent years emerged to challenge this. It is now believed that no merger took place; rather, Newcastle East End simply renamed themselves United. As East End had begun life in 1881 as a club named Stanley, if correct this would age Newcastle United by an additional 11 years. Furthermore, instead of the widely held view that East End's aforementioned Heaton Junction was the club's first home, three additional sites used by the fledgling club have

034

now been identified in Byker, Heaton's southern neighbour on the north bank of the River Tyne.

Stanley had been established on the long since vanished Stanley Street from which they took their name. Kicking off on a piece of open land close to where St Peter's Social Club now stands, Stanley soon regrouped as East End and began their creep northwards, moving into a new ground behind St Michael's Vicarage inside what is now the famous Byker Wall Estate. After a stint next to the railway sidings on Dalton Street, they eventually ended up at Heaton Junction, a tidy football ground with a large wooden pavilion and one of the sport's first press boxes. Here, just off Chillingham Road on Hartford Street, East End would regularly attract crowds upwards of 5,000 for derbies with Sunderland and West End.

Back in the city centre on Town Moor, an area of common land larger than Manhattan's Central Park, Newcastle West End had in 1886 taken over the 14-year lease of the pitch from a club named Newcastle Rangers. By 1889, West End had laid down wooden boards for spectators to keep their feet dry and, on the Leazes Terrace side, they erected their own press box. Nearby St James' Street and St James' Terrace were at the time two of the most exclusive addresses in the city, populated by wine dealers, drapers and several gentlemen of the city. When West End were wound up in 1892 and Newcastle United moved in, St James' Park became the preferred name. One year later United joined the Football League and set about fixing the ground's many problems, not least the slope which was reduced by about four feet from north to south. Terracing was then cut

into the banking at the Leazes Park End and Leazes Terrace side and the ground was enclosed by enormous fences of corrugated iron, giving St James' Park the impression of a hippodrome according to sportswriters of the day, Gibson and Pickford.

Across the world people marvel at the Geordies' unwavering passion for football. Even during the club's formative years it was bubbling, testing the capacity of St James' Park time and time again. From 28,000 in 1901, by 1906 the ground had been expanded to 60,000 with a fine new stand on the western side built for £11,000 and increased banking all around. The Leazes End was given a roof in 1930, the same year a record 68,386 turned up on 3 September to see Magpies legend Hughie Gallacher's return with his new Chelsea side. But until the 1990s, the stadium achieved only modest expansion as over the decades, lack of finance and poor team performances saw multiple plans shelved.

Nowadays St James' Park has an all-seated capacity of 52,350. If you ever hear a radio commentator mention that they are 'up in the gods', you know they are reporting live from Newcastle. From up in the Leazes fourth tier and from its big brother the Milburn Stand, the views over Newcastle and its Quayside bridges are sensational. By virtue of the Gallowgate and East stands' comparatively regular scale, it is even possible to spot the Byker Wall three miles away and the place it all began. Tyneside's 'San Siro' still has a little way to go if it is going to reach the giddy heights of 70,000 but with the new Saudi-led backing, anything seems possible. The sky is no longer the limit, it would seem.

033

Cnoc Na Mònadh

ERISKAY // SCOTLAND // ERISKAY

Eriskay Football Club are one of the smallest teams in our 100. Their pitch, known for decades as the 'Hill of the Moor' in dwindling Gaelic tongue, is the smallest to the point that anywhere else it would be deemed unsuitable for football. The landmass upon which they play, an island barely 4km in length and the width of the Champs-Élysées, is the smallest. And it will come as no surprise that Eriskay's population of 143 is one of the smallest to support a football club in Europe. On maps, it appears as the tiny stop beneath the Uists exclamation mark. This is a land in miniature, accentuated by enormous Hebridean skies and the endless iridescent turquoise sea beyond the pale shell sands of its beaches.

From the causeway, Eriskay's single road bumps through a thin cluster of houses, past the pub and football field then on through a treeless landscape dominated by the greys and greens of its rock slopes before dead-ending in the middle of the island, just beyond its last house. The journey takes about five minutes. It's a rugged place, its appearance reflecting its endurance against the hardships wrought by nature and history. Over the past 150 years, the abandonment of many of the 36 main islands which make up Scotland's Outer Hebrides archipelago has been stark. From Taransay to Scarp in the north to Mingulay and Berneray in the south, they serve as reminders of just how difficult eking out a life in such extreme remoteness was. On the once thriving Mingulay for example, 30 families in a population similar to Eriskay's, had survived on crofting and fishing until 1912 when the island was abandoned. A recently discovered school log paints a sobering picture of the hardships detailing children being unable to attend class due to the teacher running out of coal for the fire. The next delivery would take anything up to four weeks by boat.

Games would signal the end of the week and were always played on a Sunday afternoon after Mass, a time to unwind and cast aside the worries of the working week.

For those islands whose population clung on during the Highland Clearances and exoduses, they find themselves reaping the rewards on offer in the 21st century. Arts and crafts enclaves have sprung up, distillery tours on even the driest of the Presbyterian islands in the north are a touristic rite. Climbers, ramblers and twitchers from all walks of life visit. For Eriskay, the opening of Eriskay Causeway in 2001 was the final link in the Uist chains spinal route and has made travel for the more adventurous relatively straightforward. Travel websites wax lyrical over Eriskay's untamed beauty, tourists come for the indigenous ponies and land of 'Whisky Galore!'. And in recent years, a new kind of tourist has been spotted on the island. When in 2015 the FIFA World Football Museum selected the Cnoc Na Mònadh pitch for its 'Planet Football' showcase, the club began a courtship with celebrity which shows no sign of abating despite the fundamental struggles of pulling together 11 players for Uist and Barra League games.

In recognising Eriskay's pitch as one of the eight most remarkable places in the world to play football, FIFA kick-started a love-in with the club which has seen devotees of the game descend upon the island. Award-winning Scottish actor Martin Compston rocked up at Cnoc Na Mònadh and was soon after spotted wearing Eriskay's Celtic hoops in Las Vegas. A chartered flight of German football bucket-listers made the trip while many other media channels have trilled over its authenticity. Most leave with the impression that Eriskay and its imperfect pitch is the perfect antidote to the gloss of the professional game, redolent of a more innocent era. Most will connect memories of awful childhood pitches to Eriskay's wobbly lines, distinctly hilly south-western corner where the corner flag is as high as the crossbar and the occasional stray sheep making a beeline for the centre circle during a match. And most will have stopped for a pint in the island's only pub, Am Politician, close to where the first seeds were sown with early evening kick-abouts through the 1940s and 50s on a patch of land now covered by the community hall and village shop.

Islanders' roles within such small communities are often doubled, tripled even and on Eriskay we find Stephen Campbell, club captain and part-owner of Am Politician. Stephen's wife Julia recalls days before the Causeway was built when her father's boat was used to bring rowdy away supporters over from South Uist and before that, her grandfather's boat. Most football supporters at the beginning of a season will earmark that away-day fixture which represents a good day out and for the supporters of teams on South Uist and Barra, Eriskay was just that. Games would signal the end of the week and were always played on a Sunday afternoon after Mass, a time to unwind and cast aside the worries of the working week. With little else on offer on the island, it was not unusual for Eriskay's people to gather in their entirety. Pre-match at Am Politician, inter-island acquaintances would be renewed, gossip shared and copious amounts of beer drunk, not least by the players. And then the throng would wander down the hill to Cnoc Na Mònadh for the match where Eriskay's fans would stand on the huge embedded rocks at the sea end and travelling supporters opposite on the grass banking. Those rocks have thinned out over the years, a result of 1993's blasting to enlarge the pitch, but not nearly as much as the crowds.

In a way, the busyness of 21st-century work lives and routines on the islands have become the hardships of today. People's lives are too occupied to give up a day just for a football match. It's a story repeated across Europe where clubs with a century and more of history fall by the wayside weekly, often from much larger communities than Eriskay. Since the Uist and Barra League united the islands by welcoming in teams from North Uist, the guarantee of a traditional Sunday afternoon football match has all but gone. It has been replaced by a fixture list of games spread across the week to take into account the extra travel. The collective commitment to keep the game alive by the people of Eriskay and indeed their brothers in similarly remote places is immeasurable. Some have even suggested a miracle. But if those ingrained hardships of yesteryear have taught the people of Eriskay one thing, it is to survive.

Estadi Nacional

ANDORRA LA VELLA // ANDORRA

From the turquoise seas of tiny Eriskay we arrive in the tiny landlocked mountain principality of Andorra. Only the hardest of hearts would not agree that *Els Tricolors* are due a little luck. Since a 6-1 international debut defeat to Estonia in 1996, Andorra have gone on to win just 13 matches in 210 attempts. In FIFA's world rankings, at the time of writing they are positioned 153, sandwiched between Yemen and the Dominican Republic. While not quite the levels of awfulness fans of San Marino have to put up with, Andorra's plight does not sit well with their supporters. Over in Serravalle, that great minnow cliche 'we're just happy to be playing at this level' may appease some after the latest avalanche of goals but in Andorra la Vella, it simply doesn't wash. Fuelled by a desire for success and an inherent competitiveness, hardly surprising with big brothers France and Spain breathing down their neck, Andorrans have become embarrassed by how their football is perceived across the continent.

In recent years, however, there has been a glimmer of hope, one not centred on the national team but rather the upturn in fortunes of FC Andorra. Although traditionally the principality's biggest and most successful team, in December 2018 the footballing world raised a collective eyebrow when Barcelona defender Gerard Piqué bought the club. Financially fast-tracked into the third tier of Spanish football at the expense of the beleaguered Reus Deportiu, by 2022/23 they had reached the giddy heights of the Segunda División. There, for two seasons until relegation in June 2024, FC Andorra found themselves watched by crowds often larger than those present for national team matches. Moreover, games against such heavyweights as Espanyol and Real Valladolid appeared on televisions in bars from Las Palmas to Lugo as Andorra la Vella's fun-sized Estadi Nacional became a familiar sight. Despite doing it all without a single native Andorran in the squad, a modicum of pride had been restored.

Before the Estadi Nacional was opened in 2014, every international match on home soil had been played a few hundred yards west at Andorra la Vella's Estadi Comunal. Primarily an athletics venue restricted by its tight confines, plans for a proper national football stadium had been in place since the turn of the millennium. But only in 2011 would funds be secured, largely because of a €2m grant from UEFA HatTrick, a programme that redistributes two-thirds of the revenue from the European Championship to help fund football development projects. Next, the government opened a competition for all Andorran architects to design the new stadium, won by Julià Call Reig and supported by two Barcelona-based firms. Work began in May 2013 on a site that since 1971 had been the Camp d'Esports del M.I. Consell General, a small football and rugby ground squeezed between the banks of the Valira River and the studios of RTVA, Andorra's radio and television network.

At 1,023m above sea level, Europe's highest national football stadium was inaugurated for the Euro 2016 qualifier with Wales on 9 September 2014. Andorran team sports were finally united in a single, central hub as the stadium was integrated with the adjacent Poliesportiu d'Andorra, a 5,000-capacity indoor arena opened in 1991 for basketball, handball, futsal and hockey. It is the hall's pitched roof peeking out from behind the flat-roofed grandstand, a modern twist on the traditional football gable, that gives the western side of the ground its character.

Partly to ensure the stadium does not look too empty when only a couple of thousand turn up and partly to allow the magnificent 'twisting' floodlights to dance against the mountainous backdrop, the overall concept was for everything to be kept low and unobtrusive.

And it works sublimely. The three individual stands (the fourth side is tightly hemmed in by apartment buildings) are connected together by rectangular corner blocks. Access to the southern end is via a new footbridge over the Valira River while on Baixada del Moli on the northern aspect, a convex concrete facade represents the stadium's main entrance. There may only be seating for 3,306 but the Estadi Nacional is a lesson in how to give small things a big personality.

Elsewhere across the microstate, it may come as a surprise to learn that there are a healthy number of other well-furnished football grounds. Many are used by the 12 clubs competing in the principality's own Primera and Segona Divisió and most have grandstands resplendent in the blue, yellow and red tricolour. Those not carved directly from the side of a Pyrenean mountain will at the very least have a spectacular view of one. The maverick FC Andorra, founded as the first Andorran club in 1942 and soon competing over the border by virtue of their affiliation to the Catalan Football Federation, traditionally played at the now-demolished Camp d'Esports de les Valls. From there they moved to Camp d'Esports d'Aixovall in 1983, a much-loved ground in the southern parish of Sant Julià de Lòria which too has now sadly been lost to development.

031

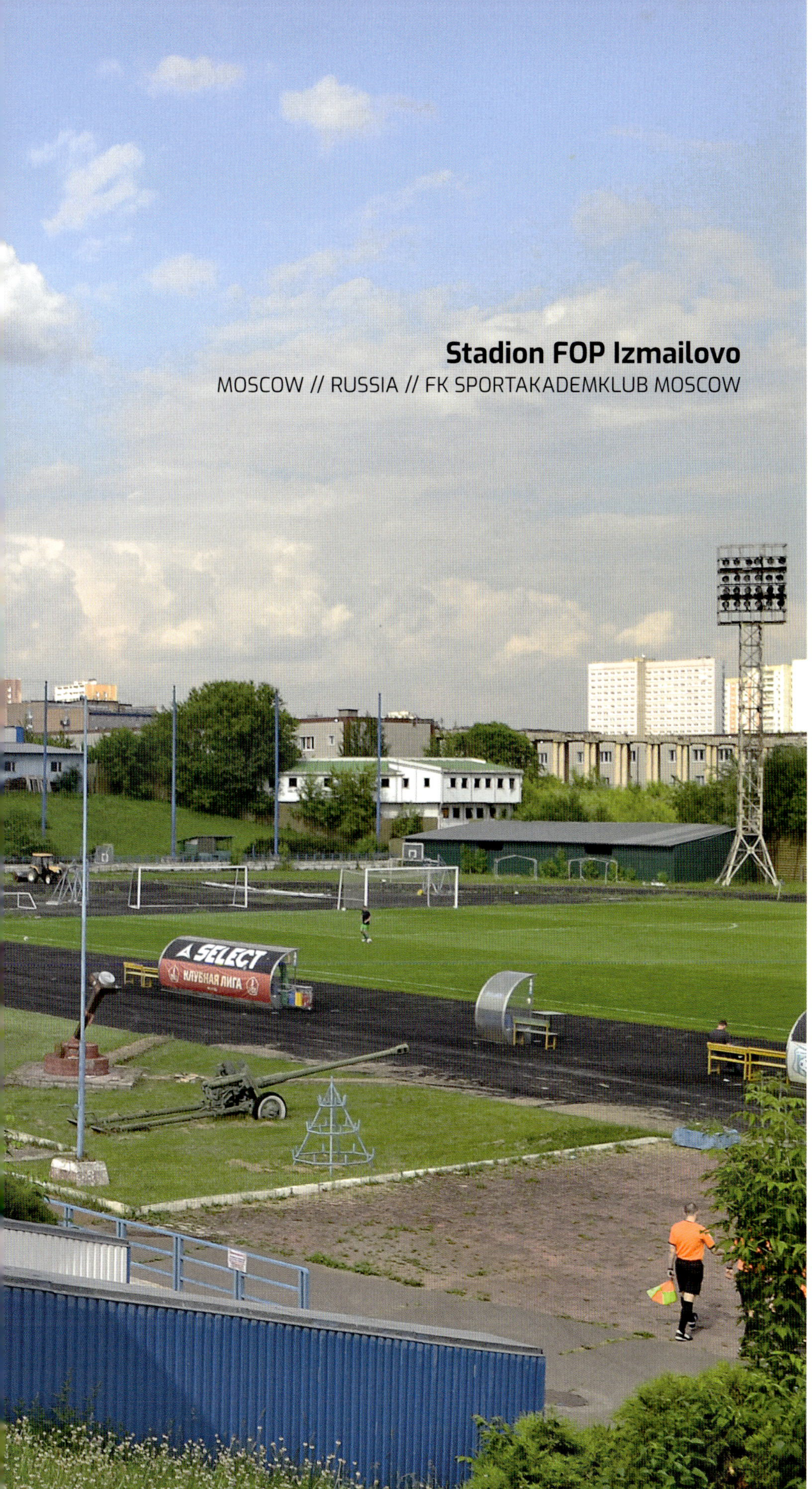

Stadion FOP Izmailovo

MOSCOW // RUSSIA // FK SPORTAKADEMKLUB MOSCOW

Some football grounds in Europe have become snug with some truly bizarre paraphernalia. Until recently, in the Belgian town of Maldegem a corner-taker could rest up against a rust-streaked train carriage before his kick. This carriage carried the provenance of having been seized by Hitler following the annexation of Lithuania before going on to serve Queen Elizabeth II on state visits to Germany.

All around FC Sobemai's pitch stood hulking rolling stock, engines and carriages poxed with oxidation and unidentifiable lumps of railwayana. For 40 years they quietly decayed awaiting the development of a theme park which never materialised. Again in Belgium, the SIDMAR Post 4 stadium of amateur side St. Kruis-Winkel sat in the middle of a rusting steelworks plant the size of a small city, dwarfed by overhead pipework and ringed by belching ground-level steam vents. Beyond, distant slag heaps in a dystopian landscape straight from the mind of David Lynch. There were concrete cows grazing in a corner of MK Dons' old hockey stadium, enormous Cold War radomes alongside Bad Aibling's Sportpark Mietraching in Bavaria, an upside down house next to Tartu JK's Holm Jalgpallipark in Estonia.

Yet nothing quite compares to FOP Izmailovo, Moscow's forgotten stadium where the players of fourth-tier Sportakademklub turn out among the grim junk of Stalinist warfare. Here, an L-29 Delfin fighter jet stands primed for take-off directly over the away team's bench. BMP-1 tanks guard the car park, and heavy artillery surrounds the pitch, guns pointing skywards. Beneath the pitch it gets even stranger as legend has it a top secret metro station exists, one with a line straight to the Kremlin 15km away. The supporting evidence for this comes directly from Stalin's bunker next door, built to house the Soviet high command during the Second World War and now a museum complex. Here, the guided tours unsurprisingly neither confirm nor deny the existence of 'Metro-2' under the stadium, speculation over

Original designs for the stadium drawn up in the 1930s envisage a 129,000-seater bowl reminiscent of Berlin's Olympic Stadium. By 1935 however, the USSR had already declared sport a propaganda battle while the magazine *Soviet Architecture* loudly stated that any showcase arena should honour the idea of the New Soviet Man.

which exploded upon the release of Vladimir Gonik's 1992 novel Preispodniaia and continues to rage on. It all serves to add a further layer of intrigue to a football stadium which already begs so many questions.

We are only a few streets from Cherkizovsky's infamous meat market and a stone's throw from Lokomotive's RZD Stadium. If history had followed a different path, FOP Izmailovo would likely have been Russia's pre-eminent sporting arena. Original designs for the stadium drawn up in the 1930s envisage a 129,000-seater bowl reminiscent of Berlin's Olympic Stadium. By 1935, however, the USSR had already declared sport a propaganda battle while the magazine *Soviet Architecture* loudly stated that any showcase arena should honour the idea of the New Soviet Man. Yet the impact of the 1936 Berlin Olympics across the continent underlined the idea's importance to the politburo and although the USSR snubbed the 'bourgeois' Olympic movement, it was clear that Moscow urgently needed a suitable home for its Spartakiad festival of sporting endeavour.

Construction of the stadium began the same year, a grass field laid out and a curved stand with 10,000 seats built on its western side. Eventually, three tiers would have been erected around the field with the lowest holding 36,800, the middle 22,000 and the upper tier a staggering 70,200 people. Progress on the stadium was halted with the advent of war and although briefly reignited afterwards, it was soon quietly shelved. Two events in the early 1950s finally sounded FOP Izmailovo's death knell. In 1952, Soviet athletes made their mark on the world stage, bringing home 22 gold medals from the Helsinki Summer Olympics. Such enormous success again highlighted the glaring need for a showcase stadium of their own. At this point, FOP Izmailovo may have still stood a chance but upon Stalin's death a few months later, his successor Khrushchev denounced his plentiful crimes and in doing so severed any link to the half-built stadium so intrinsically connected to the man. Instead, a more central location on a bend in the Moskva was chosen for Moscow's grand arena. Construction of the Central Lenin Stadium began in 1956 and it would go on to host the Olympic Games of 1980, the Champions League Final in 2008 and the 2018 World Cup Final. Under the name Luzhniki Stadium, it has become one of the most recognisable in world sport.

Meanwhile in Moscow's north-eastern corner, the projected Stalin Stadium slowly falls apart, a monument visited by few and loved by fewer. In the late 1980s it was turned into a local athletics facility and was briefly earmarked as a site for a world-class athletics arena. Other ventures have come and gone too, one faded panel recalling the short-lived Prince Kornienko orchestra, a military band that were based here from 1998 to 2002. Ultimately, it remains something of an encumbrance to the city, a white elephant if you like. Football continues in the Russian fourth division with Sportakademklub, a club formed as recently as 1992 and who played professionally in the Russian second tier in the early 2000s. Nowadays, crowds of barely 100 take up position in the 13,000-capacity grandstand. Surrounded by the heavy artillery and the clanking of nearby car workshops, matchdays here give new meaning to the word eerie. Its future is uncertain. For over a decade the area was on the radar of developers following the closure of the nearby Cherizovsky market but Russia's war in Ukraine has seen it fall even further from the minds of Moscovites. FOP Izmailovo remains an idea that never came to fruition, a half-built Stalinist dream that over the years has perhaps become Europe's strangest football ground of all.

Stade Louis II

MONACO // AS MONACO

Friday, 25 January 1985 marked a seminal moment in football stadium design. On a warm Monaco afternoon, Prince Rainier III inaugurated Henry Pottier's new Stade Louis II and in doing so sent architects and urban planners alike into a spin lasting for much of the next 40 years. Despite the following day's teething problems, the scoreboard erroneously announcing the score as 30-0 when AS Monaco scored their third goal against Lens, here was a stadium plucked straight from a future hitherto unknown.

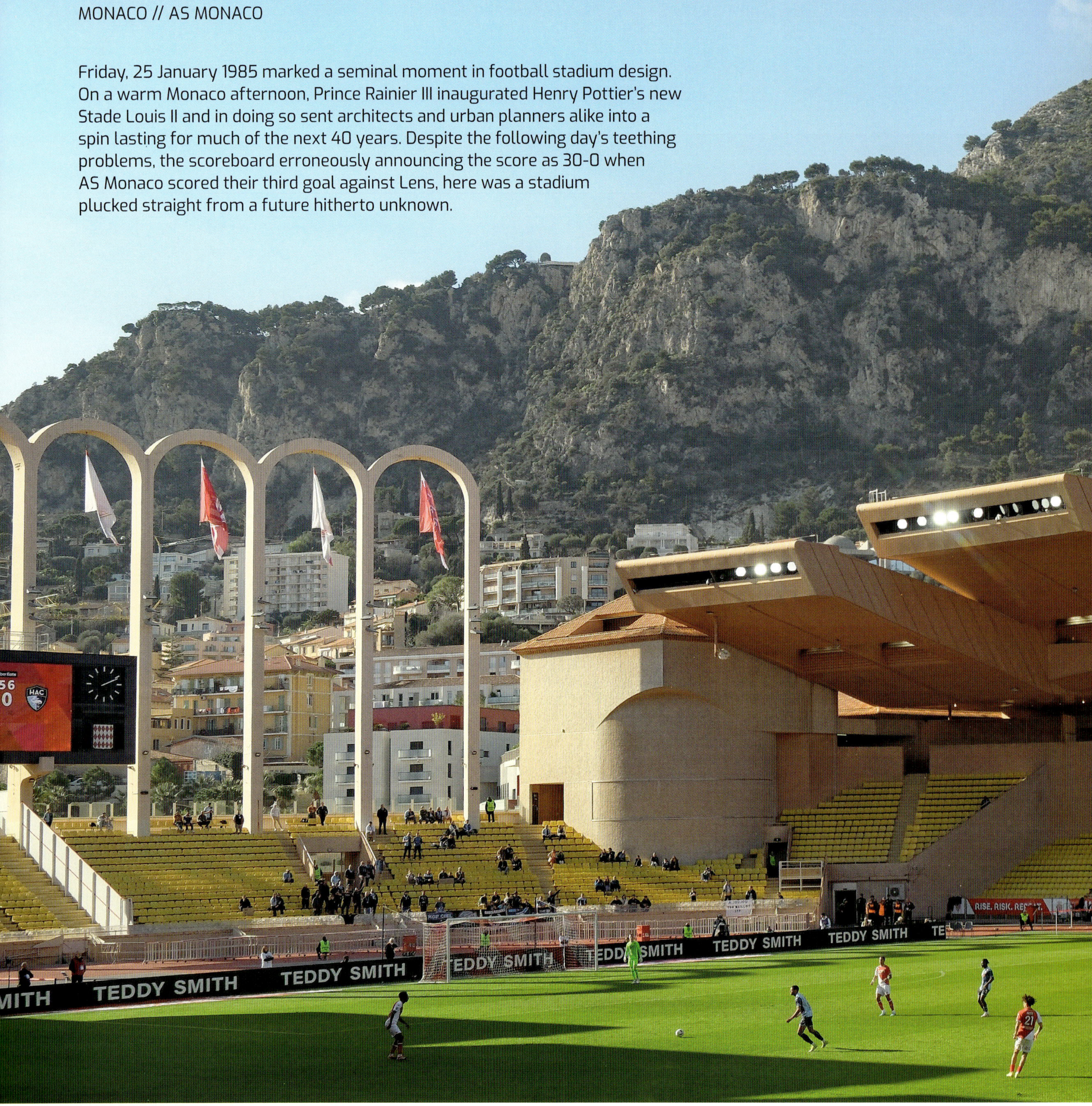

Many have since tried to emulate its jewellery box compartments with varying degrees of success but as yet, few have come close. Much like its team, it remains a fabulous anomaly on the map of European football. Of course, not everyone has at their disposal the colossal wealth of the Monégasque, less still 100 years of experience of engineering things into the tiniest of spaces. But as urban space in cities across Europe becomes ever more prized, Stade Louis II's revolutionary design is perhaps more relevant than ever.

Most with a passing interest in football grounds will be aware that hidden beneath Stade Louis II's rooftop stadium is a car park. Built over four storeys from the basement to the third floor, it occupies around one half of the space within and until additional storage spaces were added in the 2000s, it had the capacity for 1,800 vehicles. In the second half, however, there is an Olympic-sized swimming complex with seating for 500, several gymnasiums, a sports hall with 4,560 seats (home to Monaco's Roca basketball team), shops, a university, restaurants and vast corridors of office space, all compartments interiorised without infringing upon one another's activities. This allows the stadium's facilities to operate individually at any given time; for example a swimming gala could be taking place while AS Monaco kick off on the fourth floor and it is this total functionality which is the real triumph of Pottier's masterpiece.

Approaching on foot from Monte Carlo via an assortment of street elevators, it is not immediately obvious which of the tightly clustered high-rises is the actual stadium. Unaffected by the usual street grime and graffiti daubed across most French stadiums, its faceless facade is as modest as any other block in the Fontvieille neighbourhood. This blending is another of Pottier's key design components which extends right to the very top of the stadium. Peering down over Monaco from Le Centre Botanique or higher still from the Tête de Chien alp, Stade Louis II's traditional Provençal roof tiles integrate it seamlessly with its surroundings. No fussy floodlight columns here, the lights are instead tucked away in individual stepped roof fascias designed to pay homage to the front end of Prince Rainier's beloved Ferrari V8. Back down in Fontvieille, the stadium only really begins to reveal its palatial qualities as the elevators, housed within eight enormous cylindrical supports sunk deep into the sea bed, alight on the top floor. Every bit the penthouse suite, the football and athletics stadium is laid out as a lavish array of red and yellow seating blocks and subtle arches beneath a peach-gold roof. The south-western end is uncovered to allow for views of a more rugged nature through the now iconic nine white arches. It's hard not to look for flaws, age distress or ill-maintenance yet other than a few worn stairwell floors, Stade Louis II is still the immaculate 1980s icon it set out to be.

Monaco's original Stade Louis II was an altogether more humble affair. Its location one block from the present stadium, tightly squeezed between a railway line and the harbour's slipway, left little room to increase the capacity from 13,000 at a time when AS Monaco crowds were peaking. Opened on 23 April 1939, much to the relief of AS Monaco who had spent their formative years without a home before abandoning amateur status in 1933, its position abutting the Rock of Monaco gave Louis II a perfect view of the action from his palace above. After significant bomb damage during the Second World War, it was renovated to include a single-tier grandstand but little else before making way for its replacement after 45 years of service. During the 1960s, Prince Rainier's desire to enlarge the territory of the principality had seen the creation of a new ward. Designed by Gianfranco Gilardini, Fontvieille was built across 22 hectares of land reclaimed from the sea between 1965 and 1971. By 1979, the 'Builder Prince' had just over a hectare left to play with when he handed the chief architect of Paris's Front de Seine development, Henry Pottier, the task of creating not just a stadium for the new neighbourhood, but a world of sport to dazzle the entire principality.

Work began in 1981 with the aforementioned cylindrical towers creating the foundations for the entire stadium. Within the next 12 months, 9,000 tonnes of steel would be used for the structural work plus a further 2,000 tonnes of framework in an area covering just 145,000 square metres. With that in mind, it is not surprising to learn that the building is designed to withstand an earthquake of 8.3 on the Richter scale. By 1985, 2,100 individual doors had been fitted and a team of full-time staff employed as the final cost came in at just under 600m francs, an astronomical sum in 1985 as it would be in today's money. Prince Rainier treated himself to a luxury viewing box and why not? He did foot the bill after all. Forty years on, the question for any visitor is still, 'Was it worth it?' In terms of the football stadium with its capacity of just 16,360, only half of which is taken up by supporters for average Ligue 1 matches, many still argue that Stade Louis II is simply an opulent show of Monaco's wealth and that hosting UEFA Super Cups and Diamond League athletics meets does not justify the extravagance. But for the 2,000 schoolchildren and 3,000 members of the general public who use the facilities each week, it achieves exactly what Rainier wished for. Perhaps with a little too much class for some.

Marriott

029

Stadioni Temur Maghradze

CHIATURA // GEORGIA // FC MAGAROELI CHIATURA

If ever a football stadium was symbolic of its environment's economic decline, the Stadioni Temur Maghradze in Chiatura is it. Once the source of up to 50 per cent of the world's manganese, Chiatura's golden age ended together with the collapse of the Soviet Union. Left behind was a population barely one third of its mid-20th-century high and a post-apocalyptic landscape of blackened concrete and rusted cable cars swinging high above the town.

The abandonment and dereliction festered throughout the 1990s and on into the 21st century. The infamous rope roads built to transport passengers and ore are neglected yet still operating between the steep valleys. Visitors interested in a more ghoulish kind of tourism found their way to this ex-Soviet outpost. A film about Chiatura, City of the Sun, was made exploring themes of the human spirit enduring in the deserted town.

In the town's tiny library I am told that the people of Chiatura are simply 'sad'. Hopelessness, unemployment, extreme poverty and a large number of orphaned children persists while in the show cities of Tbilisi and Batumi, Georgia window-dresses itself in its bid to join the EU. And yet on a warm autumn morning there are signs that Chiatura is emerging into a new dawn. Many of the 'metal coffins' have been replaced by shiny new French-built cable cars and a slimmed-down network operated by a young team of employees. The grey monolithic apartment blocks standing sentry on the cliff tops have been earmarked for a makeover involving local artists and mural designs while the International Adventure Tourism Festival recently made its debut in Chiatura.

Back in the library there is no archival material about the town's football stadium. No photos, no press cuttings, no mention. In fact, of the six older ladies who have gathered to see what the fuss is all about, only one knows of its existence and even then she tells us it may be 'gone' with a hand gesture across the throat. Perhaps Magaroeli, the town's football team which translates as 'miner', brings back too many painful memories in its association with the town's industrial past.

Walking alongside the old railroad tracks to the ground, the first sign that the Stadioni Temur Maghradze does still exist is a single, rusted and bulbless floodlight poking out above the trees canopy. These lights once illuminated matches in the Soviet second league when in the late 1960s and 70s, Magaroeli represented the Georgian state in games against teams from as far afield as Belarus, Latvia and Turkmenistan. Teams with similar resources from neighbouring mining towns such as Tkibuli also made it into the upper echelons of the Soviet league. With the mines profitable and employing virtually the entire male population of the town, these would have been heady days for football supporters in Chiatura.

Opened in 1964, the Stadioni Temur Maghradze was built with funds supplied by the Chiaturmanganese company and included an indoor public swimming pool adorned with mosaic artwork, a gymnasium and football pitch. Alongside the pitch, two full-length stands designed in a brutalist style with Italian flourishes were constructed from poured concrete. Four English-style corner floodlights were added along with a typically bombastic Soviet electronic

It's a dangerous place, so much so that the Georgian Football Federation warned the club in 2016 that their stadium was in a critical condition.

scoreboard on the facade of the gymnasium. When Magaroeli won the Georgian championship in 1975, it is estimated over 11,000 people attended a game against Salkhino Gegechkori from Martvili. At the time of the dissolution of the Soviet Union, Magaroeli had spent four seasons in the Soviet second tier and although their light would briefly shine once more at the top level of Georgian football in the mid-2000s, the club has since sunk to the fourth tier. What is truly remarkable is that to this day they continue to play their matches at the Temur Maghradze, remarkable because this stadium is certainly the most dilapidated football ground in use anywhere in European football.

Walking through the Italianate colonnade beneath the main stand with its beautiful arches and circular reliefs, you can hear the decay; a barely audible crumbling as concrete turns to dust and falls from steel framework. Paint flakes swirl in the breeze, falling and collecting with other debris on the ground. Up above on the terracing, gaping holes the size of small cars open up to pitch darkness below. It's a dangerous place, so much so that the Georgian Football Federation warned the club in 2016 that their stadium was in a critical condition. And yet still the football goes on, supporters gather in small numbers and group themselves in areas of the stands less perilous than others. Over on the opposite side,

the stand backs on to the Kvirila river and is in even worse condition. Home to several varieties of lichen and spongy moss which streak the concrete in shades of green, a whole section of the terracing has collapsed, giving way to the inner framework of the building and the ground below strewn with the carcasses of wild animals.

A friend commented when seeing a photograph of this stadium that it looked like a set of a horror film and in a way, they were right. It's a place where the ghosts of the Soviet Union, of Chiatura and its lost miners and wealth, still roam. But there is also a real beauty to be found here. A beauty in the abandoned, the derelict. Every year thousands visit ancient ruins across the world, those interested in more recent history take organised tours to Pripyat or Hashima Island. Online, social media groups dedicated to exploring abandoned places including sports venues, are bulging with urbexers. Macabre tourism perhaps, or maybe it's simply that such places are incredibly evocative. They conjure feelings of nostalgia in a world that is increasingly becoming shiny and sleek.

In stark contrast, three hours west of Chiatura on the Black Sea, old foes Dinamo Batumi are playing their football in a €25m illuminated spaceship surrounded by skyscrapers. Chiatura's old stadium will have to be bulldozed eventually and whether funds become available for a new stadium or even just an artificial pitch, remains to be seen. In the meantime, Chiatura and its football stadium, set down in a spectacular landscape of deep gorges, valleys and mountains, belongs firmly to the old world.

028

Stadion Poljud

SPLIT // CROATIA // HAJDUK SPLIT

Driving through the castle towns around Kastela Bay towards Split, Stadion Poljud flits in and out of view across five miles of Adriatic water. In the haze of the Dalmatian sunshine, it shimmers beneath the city's high-rises resembling its fictional 1977 twin, Spielberg's spaceship in the film *Close Encounters of the Third Kind*; all metallic space-age curves and translucent Lexan panelling developed, appropriately enough, by the American space programme.

From this perspective, Poljud's low, squat profile respects the natural landscape, acting as a focal point and creating connections between the city and its backdrop, the Marjan hill in the south and the Kozjak mountain range in the Dalmatian Hinterland beyond. For a football team named after 17th-century Balkan bandits Hajduk's home is aptly exuberant. Fearless in its design and dazzling in appearance. After almost 50 years Poljud remains one of the most beautiful large stadiums in Europe.

The fact that a country with a population of just four million is so well represented in this book is a testament to its cultural re-emergence since independence in 1991. Of the six former Yugoslav republics, Croatia and Slovenia remain the wealthiest and most developed. The importance of cultural preservation of the arts, including its buildings, is seen as key to maintaining Croatia's identity and huge tourism economy. In 1979 Split was added to UNESCO's World Heritage list and in 2015, Stadion Poljud

was given protected status by the Croatian Ministry of Culture. While other similarly architecturally important football stadiums across Europe have either been wiped from the map or live on under the threat of demolition or imminent rebuilding, Poljud's future appears secure. For a stadium which still perfectly suits the modern game this is reassuring for both stadium and architecture enthusiasts alike. The people of Split affectionately refer to it as *Poljudska ljepotica*, the Poljud Beauty, while for Hajduk supporters their relationship with their home is one of unswerving love. As the years go by, it is easy to forget that for those supporters, it was far from love at first sight.

When Hajduk arrived at Poljud in 1979 on the back of a decade of domestic glory, things didn't begin well. Often referred to as 'the Poljud Curse', the 1980s saw the trophies dry up with supporters blaming the running track as Dinamo Zagreb and the Belgrade clubs reasserted their dominance on the Yugoslavian game. Ironically all four clubs played at stadiums with athletics tracks. A similar scenario would play out 37 years later in England as West Ham United and their fans struggled to adapt to life at the Olympic Stadium in London. Hajduk would never win another Yugoslavian League title at Poljud although in Europe, they continued to romp through to the latter stages of competitions. A record crowd of 52,000 filled the stadium for a European Cup quarter-final against Kevin Keegan's Hamburg and two years later, the

capacity for the Eternal Derby against Dinamo Zagreb was increased to 62,000.

Stadion Poljud was built to host the 1979 Mediterranean Games with football taking up residence shortly after. Ideas of a new stadium had been floated as early as 1953 with Split's leading clubs, including youth teams, all playing out of Stadion Stari Plac, a ground wedged into a narrow plot near the historic old town with a limited capacity and rapidly deteriorating facilities. With the overuse of this ground reaching critical levels, the clubs came together to lobby the local government for new pitches and a municipal stadium. While no progress was made in the short term, a small stadium was opened for RNK Split in 1955 which alleviated some of the congestion and allowed Hajduk to continue their upward trajectory at Stari Plac. Stadion Stari Plac, often referred to as Plinada (the Gasworks), survives as the home of Split rugby club albeit in a much-altered guise – upon Hajduk's departure in 1979, most of the terracing was immediately demolished while the floodlights were rebuilt at RNK.

During the 1970s at Stari Plac, under the guidance of firstly Branko Zebec and then Tomislav Ivić, Hajduk's golden generation swept aside all comers. The Yugoslavian League was won four times and the domestic cup five while European battles against the likes of Leeds United, Saint-Étienne and Arsenal etched the name of Hajduk Split into European football's collective consciousness. As their fanbase grew along with their trophy haul, again the need for a larger home became all-consuming. When the 1979 Mediterranean Games were awarded to Split and its legacy stadium to Hajduk and the Yugoslavia national team, the future of football in Split looked rosy.

Beneath two colossal quarter-moon roofs, described by Poljud's architect Boris Magaš in 1977 as 'a transparent vault of lace', the bare concrete base of the stadium is a not-so-distant cousin of Sarajevo's Asim Ferhatović-Hase Olympic Stadium in its sunken bowl design. Once inside spectators are actually lower than street level, which explains the cacophonous acoustics when the Torcida are in full voice. Those roofs, spanning 206m by 47m and constructed from an intricate latticework of translucent panelling, allow light to flood into the arena, an often orange-hued luminescence as the sun sets across the bay. Suspended from the west roof are 19 cabins which include a central referee's station and suites used by TV reporters. These cabins are interconnected and accessed by a walkway which runs beneath the entire roof. Twelve bridges around the entire perimeter, 30 to 40 metres apart lead spectators up and into the stadium; a design similar to another great spaceship stadium, the Stadio San Nicola in Bari just across the Adriatic waters.

Up close, the overall effect is one of lightness with any clunky maintenance or utility buildings hidden away below ground level. The main approach road up to the stadium is wide, lined with flagpoles and resembling a runway which again calls to mind scenes from *Close Encounters of the Third Kind* rather than the open seashell Magaš's design is intended to mimic. Manicured rose gardens surround the circular perimeter pathway, everything maintained to a high standard. When Tito opened Poljud on the opening day of the Mediterranean Games, it is said that the feeling of pride in Split was palpable. To this day, that pride is still evident here and indeed all over Split and towns of southern Croatia where the 25 red and white checkers of Hajduk's logo are tidily painted on walls and buildings, carefully maintained and rarely defaced.

Once inside spectators are actually lower than street level, which explains the cacophonous acoustics when the Torcida are in full voice.

otac ulica, majka torcida

027

Arena Civica

MILAN // ITALY

Five kilometres east of Stadio San Siro and a block south of Chinatown, Parco Sempione has offered the Milanese respite from the nearby hurry-scurry for over a century. Like Parque del Retiro in Madrid or Hyde Park in London, on summer afternoons its lawns are awash with frisbee throwers and lazy sunbathers. Some will have visited the Palazzo dell'Arte on the park's southern fringe, others the medieval Castello Sforzesco at the eastern end.

Those entering the park's northern aspect from Viale Elvezia will have passed the collection of neoclassical towers concealed behind an unbroken elliptical brick wall. Every 20ft, a bolted door topped with wrought iron fanlight gives the impression of a Napoleonic-era military facility, the craftsmanship of the balustrades suggesting a building of great importance. Unless you're a member of the Atletica Riccardi club entering through a small entrance door for a morning run, its role in Milan's rich sporting history may not be immediately obvious.

Arena Civica is the oldest stadium in this book. In fact, with the exception of Spain's bullrings, it is almost certainly the oldest surviving stadium still in use in Europe. To put Arena Civica's longevity into context, when Internazionale moved in on a permanent basis in 1930, it had already stood for 123 years, 60 of which predated the dawn of football in England's public schools. Nostalgists like to gripe about the loss of historic grounds but in Milan, here is one opened by Napoleon Bonaparte himself. Moreover, it is one where long after Inter departed for the San Siro in 1947, football continues for those intrepid enough to seek it out.

There are those who will argue that Arena Civica's legacy as a football stadium is a tenuous one. After all, it was conceived as Milan's primary amphitheatre for the purpose of horseracing, bullfights and mock naval battles. But try telling that to a generation of Inter supporters or to Alcione, the third in Milan's trio of professional football clubs, who have recently fought tooth and nail for the right to bring Serie C football to the stadium. Then there is Brera, a club named in honour of

Civica's official title of Arena Gianni Brera who held their very own Fenix Trophy competition here in 2023. Targeting clubs from across the continent who use their non-professional status to build something beyond merely football, the hosting of the Fenix Trophy semi-finals at Civica and the final at San Siro was the very embodiment of Milan's sporting heritage. For the thousands who came from across Europe, it resonated with historic significance.

Built at a time when Napoleon had just declared Milan the capital of the Kingdom of Italy, Arena Civica had been designed by Luigi Canonica, an exponent of neoclassicism and designated architect for the ephemeral Repubblica Cisalpina. Opened on 18 August 1807, a depiction of the world's first female parachutist, Jeanne Geneviève Labrosse, dropping in 17 years later shows the arena packed. Many of Milan's high-ranking bourgeoisie gather outside, the stadium's upper concourse planted with trees to give the impression of complete enclosure. While many of the trees have died off and the top hats and walking dresses are no longer de rigueur, there is little to suggest the structure itself has altered at all. Such is its spiritual and architectural value to the city, its maintenance

Arena Civica is the oldest stadium in this book. In fact, with the exception of Spain's bullrings, it is almost certainly the oldest surviving stadium still in use in Europe.

remains a seven-days-a-week job just to keep it looking handsome.

Inside, 2020's re-topping of the running track in a vivid orange and green colour scheme offsets the building's stately palette and brings it kicking and screaming into the 21st century. It has likely not looked this fresh and colourful since the days of Internazionale's *Nerazzurri*. We are fortunate enough to live in an age where football grounds are finally becoming accepted as serious monuments of social and sporting history. Europe has lost so much since the rebuilding boom of the 1990s which allowed a sentimentality for what has gone to creep in and now thrive. We all care greatly about our own sporting arenas but there is always someone who cares that little more. To Brera and the council of Milan, the football world owes you for keeping this remarkable stadium both active for sports and spick and span.

026

Olympiastadion

BERLIN // GERMANY // HERTHA BERLIN

On 14 July 2024, Berlin's Olympiastadion hosted the final of Euro 2024 and its sixth match of the tournament. Across the preceding four weeks, no other stadiums involved had appeared quite as handsome on televisions around the world. Dortmund's 'Yellow Wall' had been painted red by the Turkish while just down the A1 autobahn, Georgia had turned Cologne's RheinEnergieStadion into an effervescent colosseum of unbridled joy. In Munich, *Die Mannschaft* scored five but failed to dampen the spirits of Scotland's Tartan Army, who further illuminated Bayern's red-lit Allianz Arena. Yet despite not being a pure football stadium, Berlin's Olympiastadion's cool-blue palette, seductive elliptical curvature and occasionally glimpsed neoclassical flourishes gave the tournament a welcome sense of grandeur among all the modernity and a visual reminder of Germany's brilliant sporting past.

A few months before the tournament I had visited for a match between Hertha and Schalke in the depths of the 2. Bundesliga, German football's second tier. Despite the flagging fortunes of both, nearly 70,000 came, further highlighting the stadium as a great source of 'topophilia', a strong sense of place for Berliners. Recent studies have addressed the 'stadium atmosphere' as a phenomenon that is waning in quality, largely due to the prohibitive nature of the modern game. Yet here between the 1936 Marathon Gate and the endless concourses built of Franconian limestone, the decibel meter registers higher than most. The Olympiastadion may be located almost 12km from Berlin's Fernsehturm TV tower, a 20-minute journey on the S-Bahn, but that doesn't stop fans wanting a taste of its infectious atmosphere from coming.

Just south of the stadium is Teufelsberg, a man-made hill in the Grunewald forest built from the millions of tonnes of rubble that was East Berlin at the end of the Second World War. If the Olympiastadion's origins and its connection to the Nazi regime are too much, the 'Devil's Hill' serves as a reminder of just how Hitler's reign of terror ended. Furthermore, buried 300ft beneath the summit lies Albert Speer's unfinished Nazi military technical college. In 1931 Berlin had been awarded the 1936 Summer Olympic Games. By 1933 plans were already at an advanced stage for Werner March's enlargement of his father Otto's Deutsches Stadion near the northern boundary of the Grunewald Forest. Opened on 8 June 1913 next to the Grunewald racecourse (also designed by Otto March and whose ticket booths survive on Jesse-Owens-Allee), the Deutsches Stadion had been built for the 1916 Summer Olympics which were subsequently cancelled following the outbreak of the First World War. But in October 1933, the newly-elected Hitler visited the site and recognising its potential as a rallying point for youth and sport, promptly declared that the new stadium 'must be erected by the Reich'. Werner March was kept on but under the direct command of Hitler's inexperienced but favoured architect Albert Speer, his original vision was either altered or quashed entirely, piece by piece.

Firstly, Hitler threw out March's plans to use modern, stylish concrete in favour of limestone blocks as natural stone was seen as symbolic of the National Socialist ideology. Next, the stadium's old axis was moved 150m east to form a single, long vista from the main approach road. Overlooking the young architect's drawings which placed a swimming pool at the stadium's western end, Hitler then introduced his latest grandiose scheme: a 131-hectare Reichssportfeld on the northern aspect including hockey, riding and swimming stadiums. In addition, an ancient Greece-themed open-air amphitheatre with seating for 20,000 would be constructed at the end of the Maifeld (May Field). On the stadium's eastern approach, a wide ceremonial piazza was laid leading spectators up to the two 50m-high gate towers

between which the five Olympic Rings were strung. Until 1947, a single straight line would have carried the eye from Olympischer Platz in the east, through the gates and across the stadium itself to the western end's twin clock towers which in turn, framed the Maifeld's 77m-high bell tower. As Simon Inglis wrote, 'This was totalitarian architecture on a grand scale.'

Nearly a century on, Olympiastadion's association with the Nazis has almost been erased by virtue of the great many achievements witnessed here. Although its history should never fully be forgotten, the stadium's true legacy began in 1936 when Jesse Owens famously ran Hitler's Aryan supremacy agenda into the ground. The Maifeld's huge 11-hectare lawn upon which Mussolini once addressed 900,000 Germans is nowadays the home of Berlin's cricket clubs and for one weekend each summer, the Maifeld Derby music festival. Meanwhile, the enormous bell which dropped when its original tower was blown up by British engineers in 1947 now stands as a memorial alongside the stadium, forever silenced on its plinth. Even a week before writing this, Pearl Jam played a sold-out show at Werner March's amphitheatre, frontman Eddie Vedder's liberal leanings another delicious irony which would surely have had the Führer blowing his top.

As for the football, when the spectacular new renovations were unveiled to the public on 1 August 2004 for a series of Hertha friendly matches, its popularity among fans soared. Having lowered the playing surface by 2.6m, the lower tier was then completely rebuilt with additional seating bringing the capacity up to 74,475. Above it all, the Olympiastadion finally got its roof, a light cantilevering steel horseshoe opening in harmony with the Marathon Gate. Next came the 2006 World Cup Final, Materazzi versus Zidane, then Madonna, Depeche Mode, Bruce Springsteen and the 2015 UEFA Champions League Final won by Lionel Messi's Barcelona. When Berliners debated the stadium's future in 1998, many were in favour of its complete demolition. Others suggested it be left to ruin like Rome's Colosseum. Thankfully common sense prevailed. The Olympiastadion's role in the 21st century as a place anyone and everyone can enjoy, a place where great memories are made, is testament to mankind's inherent goodness.

026 // Olympiastadion
BERLIN // GERMANY // HERTHA BERLIN

025

Yenişehir Stadyumu

GÜMÜŞHANE // TURKEY // GÜMÜŞHANESPOR

Football supporters are capable of enormous feats of ingenuity when faced with the prospect of missing out. From Ninian Park's dextrous floodlight-scalers in the 1960s to West Ham United fans perched precariously on rooftops above Upton Park in the 70s, where there is a will there is usually a way.

Banished from their Yenişehir stadium for three games in February 2017, more than 1,000 supporters of Gümüşhanespor took to the snow-dusted goat tracks high above to support their team against Hatayspor. Rolling barbecues up the paths and carrying enormous banners proclaiming 'Our Hearts are With You', they danced the halay in zig-zagging conga lines throughout the match to an accompaniment of traditional drums and pipes. That afternoon the

Canca valley echoed with chants of 'Everywhere for us is a stadium' and 'We will make you a champion in the mountains, the stands, everywhere'.

Although nothing could condone the fan clashes with visiting Ankaragücü a few weeks earlier, this impromptu transformation of the mountainsides into a natural arena left me hooked. A Turkish friend had sent me the footage of the afternoon, making sure to point out city mayor Ercan Çimen and governor Okay Memiş, both cheering in defiance of the punishment next to a giant screen broadcasting the game. Until seeing those images, the idea that a football ground on the ancient Silk Road from China to Turkey would be included in this book would have been hard to grasp. But in January 2023 I set out from Istanbul to Trabzon on the Black Sea. From there, a hair-raising journey by minibus took me up into the Zigana mountains and on to the city of Gümüşhane, 3,970ft above sea level. That final leg, driven by an unbelted teenager taking hairpin bends at 60mph, remains one I am desperate to forget.

Closely following the route on patchy wifi, I knew the stadium would be approaching as we rounded the final cliff-hugging bend on the approach into Gümüşhane's western end. In a split-second the scene abruptly altered. The sky darkened and the mountains closed in. There in

In a split-second the scene abruptly altered. The sky darkened and the mountains closed in. There in front was the Yenişehir Stadyumu, enveloped in absolute solitude by towering walls of red rock.

front was the Yenişehir Stadyumu, enveloped in absolute solitude by towering walls of red rock. For the purpose of finding a spot from which to take photographs, in the weeks leading up to the trip I had mentally collaged together an idea of how the scene would look. While I hadn't quite been sculpting mashed potato into the shape of a stadium, this was a Richard Dreyfuss peering over Devil's Tower moment: a first impression more impactful than I ever could have imagined. The bus dropped me off and disappeared into a tunnel through the mountain. Kick-off was still two hours away and Yenişehir Stadyumu stood empty; modern, colourful, toy-sized at the base of the barren peaks.

Until the late 1990s a succession of clubs that would lay the foundations for the current team (15 Şubat, Aydın Doğan and Gümüşhane Doğanspor) had played at the city's old Atatürk stadium in the Karşıka neighbourhood. With Doğanspor departing the city limits in 2004 for the municipality's brand new Yenişehir complex in Canca, the stadium took on the role of Gümüşhane's unofficial dumping ground. By the time the site on Fuadeyi Caddesi was cleared in 2015 to make way for a new youth centre, the old ground including its goalposts had been entirely buried under a vast mound of refuse. That this was allowed to happen is still the source of profound sadness among older supporters, those who witnessed Gümüşhane's finest footballing achievements from its single grandstand. Set within the city's public gardens, it was a handsome place with a bare-earth pitch and the ubiquitous bust of Atatürk atop a column at the entrance gate. The forced move three miles out of town remains another cause for anger among some.

Back in Canca and smoke is rising behind the grandstand. The köfte sellers have fired up their grills and bicycles are being parked up by those who have travelled out from town. With nothing else out here other than a hillside cemetery, people arrive early to renew acquaintances and drink coffee in the concourse next to a state-of-the-art new training field. I watch Gümüşhanespor take on Kahramanmaraşspor who have travelled 675 miles from close to the Syrian border for the game in Turkey's fourth tier. Under 800 watch, the majority congregated in the 2,800-seat grandstand. The surrounding mountains cast a swathe of deep shadow across the pitch, leaving those in the small stand opposite periodically blinded when the sun appears between the peaks. Some avoid paying altogether by finding a spot up on the goat paths or gather on rocks lower down. The noise of the crowd ricochets off the mountains, bringing the valley to life. A journey of 2,600 miles is a long way to travel for a game of football but without Gümüşhane's highland wonder, this book of greatest grounds would be incomplete.

024

Stade Vélodrome

MARSEILLE // FRANCE // OLYMPIQUE DE MARSEILLE

Marseille's real beauty lies in the integration of its multifarious ethnicities, a coming together in which everyone learns from each other to make the word 'foreigner' a foreign word. It may be the ultimate outsider city and you won't need to travel far before witnessing a street drug deal take place, but the notoriety that once clung to France's 'black sheep' like a bad stink is beginning to disperse. The simple act of just turning up at Stade Vélodrome before a game can often be more thrilling than an entire 90 minutes at other French stadiums.

On both of my post-2014 visits, fans in their thousands have converged hours before kick-off on Boulevard Michelet to set off flares and launch fireworks into the Marseille night sky. Many of these ferociously dedicated Ultras will have given up time during the week to work with foodbanks. By handing out fruit and cakes to those most in need, especially the city's homeless immigrants whose number soared during the Covid-19 pandemic, they represent a movement built on passion and pride for the city and, moreover, OM's beating heart.

Despite the decent geographical spread of stadiums used for the 1938 World Cup in France, only five remain in use for football. Stade Vélodrome, Parc des Princes, Le Havre's Stade Jules Deschaseaux, Reims' Stade Auguste-Delaune and Strasbourg's Stade de la Meinau all continue to host top-flight matches while Stade Yves-du-Manoir in Colombes featured in the 2024 Paris Summer Olympics as the Games' field hockey venue. Meanwhile, the football pitch at Antibes' historic Stade du Fort Carré has been abandoned in favour of the artificial surface adjacent to the site. Although Paris Saint-Germain may have something to say about it, it is Stade Vélodrome that has developed into the very best of the bunch. Its status across the continent verges on the iconic. From the arcing roll of the uncovered stands at the 1998 World Cup to the present appearance of a battle-clad armadillo with its rollercoaster roof finally in place, it has for three decades been a stadium which has captured imaginations.

It didn't begin this way, however. When Henri Ploquin's Stade Vélodrome was opened on 13 June 1937 for an OM match against Torino, many of the 35,000 in attendance left with the fervent belief that it could never replace the club's spiritual Stade de l'Huveaune. So invested were fans in their original home next to Huveaune beach that during the 1920s they had paid for the construction of the stands from their own pockets. Now they were giving up the ground where they had just won their first French title and being moved into one which, during its inauguration, appeared to place more emphasis on the cyclists who opened the show on the new track. It would in fact take decades for *Les Phocéens* to truly fall in love with the Vélodrome, decades spent standing in the rain on filthy, uncovered terraces while a difficult relationship with their municipal landlords only got worse. So bad was it that for a second division match against Forbach on 23 April 1965, only 434 spectators bothered showing up.

On the edge of the precipice and close to bankruptcy, in came Marcel Leclerc who in his first season as club president recruited eight new players and won promotion back to the top flight. The most astonishing thing about that season was because of the municipality's reluctance to lower rent on Stade Vélodrome, Leclerc had taken OM back to Stade de l'Huveaune, which had been fixed up with a new pitch and rebuilt walls. Although the promotion dictated a return to the Vélodrome for the 1966/67 season, in the eyes of OM fans the renaissance had begun. Further good news for supporters was to come in 1970 when the cinder running track was torn up and replaced with new seats and terracing to bring the capacity up to 55,000. Although the club made a brief return to Stade de l'Huveaune for the 1982/83 season while the stadium was renovated in preparation for the 1984 European Championship, the old pink cycling track finally made way in 1985. By this point the flamboyant tycoon Bernard Tapie had arrived and OM's golden period was within touching distance.

In the same way many grew to love the ugly/beautiful nature of Milan's San Siro, by the end

All four of the Vélodrome's stands are named in honour of runners but it was the entirely rebuilt, 19,000-seat Jean Bouin stand and restored upper tier of the Gustave Ganay stand which lifted the capacity from 60,000 to 67,000.

of the 1998 World Cup a whole new generation of supporters were beginning to give in to Stade Vélodrome's primitive charms. It had already melted a few hearts in the early 1990s when a Marseille side featuring Didier Deschamps, Alen Bokšić, Rudi Völler and Basile Boli had won the 1992/93 Champions League. But six appearances in 1998 including a semi-final between Ronaldo's Brazil and the Netherlands really cemented its legacy. When tournament football again came knocking for the 2016 European Championship, this time Marseille really went to town. Eric Cantona once said of his birth city, 'Marseille is a football city where L'OM is like a religion. It's a cosmopolitan, passionate city and the people live for football.' Finally they were about to get the stadium to validate this.

All four of the Vélodrome's stands are named in honour of runners but it was the entirely rebuilt, 19,000-seat Jean Bouin stand and restored upper tier of the Gustave Ganay stand which lifted the capacity from 60,000 to 67,000. The figures for the materials used are mind-boggling: 40,000 cubic metres of concrete, a 6,000-tonne roof support and 3,800 tonnes of steel. It was even estimated that Vélodrome's terraces measured a total of 13km. Eventually the roof-supporting pillars were removed to reveal the jaw-dropping translucent roof, constructed of fibreglass canvas and stretched over a metal framework to give it an undulating silhouette like that of an enormous seashell. No more would those pesky mistral winds sting the faces of supporters. The total cost of the renovations came to €267m but remarkably OM continued to bring in revenue by playing in the ever-changing building site for almost three years. Nearly a decade on and Stade Vélodrome looks more spectacular than ever.

023

Stadio Vittorio de Sica

POSITANO // ITALY // SAN VITO POSITANO

What do you do if your town is simply too steep to build a football stadium? In the case of Positano you go up, up and then up some more – 1,500 steps up in fact. For almost 40 years the construction of a football stadium in the town seemed about as likely as the Colosseum being rebuilt on the side of Gran Paradiso. As synonymous with Italy's coastline as Venice or San Remo, the Amalfi Coast's 'vertical city' ranks as one of the the steepest human settlements in Europe, a 20-25 degree gradient in parts as it climbs out of the Tyrrhenian Sea up to the Lattari Mountains. John Steinbeck wrote of Positano in 1953, 'It is a dream place that isn't quite real ... its houses climb a hill so steep it would be a cliff except that stairs are cut in it.'

One year after Steinbeck's visit, Positano's first football team were formed. Like their Italian brothers nationwide, the Amalfitanis' innate appetite for *calcio* meant such trivialities as having no flat land to lay a pitch were shrugged off. Named Associazione San Vito Positano after the patron saint of the town, Raffaele Telamo would go on to become parish priest of Positano but in 1954, young Telamo had just taken his vows and was *calcio* crazy. Alongside Cosimo Picci, then manager of a recreational club and later San Vito club president, the pair entered a team into the Campania regional divisions and so began San Vito's nomadic journey as Italian football's ultimate wanderers.

While Brigitte Bardot and Sophia Loren lived *la dolce vita* in Positano's boutiques and cafes, San Vito began climbing the divisions 30km away on a pitch next to Agerola town hall. From here they would eventually end up sharing Sorrento's Stadio Italia in 1970 via everywhere in between except their hometown. The sacrifices of all those involved should not be overlooked; a zigzagging journey along the hair-raising Strada State Amalfitana would often take upwards of an hour and a half for a home match in Vico Equense or Massa Lubrense. As such, talk of building a stadium in Positano never fully went away and as San Vito won promotion to the regional first category in the mid-1970s, two village locations were identified by Picci: firstly Laurito to the east and then Montepertuso, a hamlet directly above Positano.

Montepertuso was and still is a ramshackle place. Clinging both to the mountainside and its old time family traditions, it sits just 1,500 steps above its sophisticated neighbour but a world apart. It was chosen over Laurito not least to give the village an opportunity to develop alongside its big brother. Yet decades on, walking into the village on matchday is to witness a lone farmer plucking garlic bulbs from his plot and the parish priest and his flock lazily making their way to Santa Maria

Local engineer Giuseppe Cinque was brought in to oversee the complete remodelling of the stadium including the building of walls 18m high on the southern side and 12 on the northern.

Delle Grazie, whose bell on the hour pierces the magisterial silence. In 1986 the municipal administration tasked Positano architect Gennaro Passerotti with designing the stadium. It was to be an extravagant sports citadel which would include tennis and basketball courts, a place future Amalfitani champions would be made. Yet the scale of the project which included *tombamento di un alveo* (literally the burial of a riverbed) proved too costly. Instead, Montepertuso and San Vito ended up with just a flat piece of land above a buried river, the foundations for a changing room building and a mountain of local government bureaucracy to navigate before a ball could even be kicked.

Any chance of homologating the field depended entirely on the safety of the new facility and with the kitty empty and no benefactor forthcoming, the project was shelved. For another six years. It took the feel good factor cultivated during the successful hosting of the 1990 World Cup to kick-start projects up and down the country. Local government funding became available for semi-professional clubs and San Vito, by this point rebranded as Polisportiva San Vito Positano, re-entered into a new collaboration with the municipal administration. Work was completed and almost 20 years after finding their home, San Vito were coming home. On 13 March 1994 the official inauguration of the stadium saw San Vito beat Interminori in a fierce derby watched by over 1,000 spectators.

A few years later the sports field was christened Stadio Vittorio de Sica after the neorealist film director and actor, a familiar face in Positano during the mid-20th century. De Sica's films are widely regarded by critics as bona fide classics and for his name to be attached to what would soon become one of European football's greats seems fitting. It was upon San Vito's historic 2000 promotion to the Eccellenza, Italy's fifth level, that the need for spectator facilities were identified. Local engineer Giuseppe Cinque was brought in to oversee the complete remodelling of the stadium including the building of walls 18m high on the southern side and 12 on the northern. To complement the mountainside terraces all around, local stone was used and 22 arched reliefs in concrete render built into the southern wall mimicking ancient ones in villa walls opposite. Below these, two small terraces were added in the narrow space between pitch and wall. However, as with the pitch (which was replaced with an artificial surface a year after my visit) these are often cast into deep shadow during matches and as such spectators tend to gather in long rows atop the walls. Two small platforms behind the western goal ingeniously make use of the little space available to serve as three levels of car parking while opposite, the ground opens up to a vista of deep blue sea.

San Vito and the Positano municipality have played the long game but in return for their sacrifices now have a spectacular football stadium. Spectators can simultaneously stand at the foot of the gods, Monte Gambera and its huge gaping hole, while peering down into a Gladiatorial Rancor pit where they can bait the opposition until their heart's content. Good things come to those who wait. And wait they have.

022

Stadion Rajko Mitić

BELGRADE // SERBIA // FK CRVENA ZVEZDA

Few matches in European club football stir the imagination quite like Belgrade's 'Eternal Derby'. Over the years, I have been fortunate enough to be in that number at Glasgow's Old Firm derby, the Merseyside derby and the north London derby. In Italy, I have experienced the boiling rivalries of the Sicilia and Capitale derbies while at Galatasaray's infamous old Ali Sami Yen Stadium, I felt genuine fear during the continent-spanning derby with Fenerbahçe. I have been lifted off my feet, carried 20m back and forth in the surge in Athens after a Panathinaikos winner in the Derby of the Eternal Rivals and on the streets of San Sebastián, I have walked alongside a united front of 20,000 singing Real Sociedad and Athletic songs towards the Basque derby.

Obscure lower-level derbies in the Polish hinterlands can be both simultaneously wild and terrifyingly militaristic while Stockholm and Copenhagen's derby day pyrotechnics and colossal tifos are usually enough to bring out the goosebumps. However, the Belgrade derby remains European football's purest and most thrilling spectacle, largely because it is allowed to simmer and seethe unhindered as supporters of both Red Star and Partizan express their bottomless animosity towards one another in the most vitriolic manner.

The 21st century has seen a dissolution of the fierceness in many such games; legacies scarred by violence are beginning to heal through a combination of the sanitising effects of modern all-seater stadiums and rigorous security measures. Bucket listers, stag weekenders and groundhoppers with a few quid in their bank accounts can easily buy tickets for the sold-out games from online vendors or even tour operators, often at vastly inflated prices resulting in large pockets of neutrality among once staunchly partisan crowds. While you'd be hard pushed not to overhear an American, German or English accent on Belgrade derby day, ticket prices are astonishingly inexpensive and easy to come by despite the city being one of eastern Europe's more expensive capitals. The stadiums themselves, the fabulously creaking Partizana and Red Star's undulating hillside Marakana, both lend themselves completely to the scenes – grubby, graffiti-riddled and dripping with history, there's little issue with standing on seats and launching fireworks at either. Indeed, Red Star replace on average 300 seats after each derby, most ripped from the South Stand by Partizan fans.

Linked by Maglajska, a surprisingly leafy street lined with an architectural pick 'n' mix of some of Belgrade's most elegant residences, just 400 yards separate the two. To Maglajska's west, a narrow park under the cover of trees is usually where the pre-match displays of machismo take place and where supporters converge to get the scrapping out of their system. Undoubtedly Red Star's Stadion Rajko Mitić is the finer, more impressive of the two as well as having almost double the capacity of its neighbour. But should it be included in a list of Europe's greatest stadiums on the basis of a few exuberant games each season? The answer is of course no but then Stadion Rajko Mitić is no ordinary stadium. Beneath

and beyond the majestic sight of 58,000 crimson seats, it reveals itself as a subterranean goldmine of Serbian football. Tunnels, murals, deep corridors adorned with 75 years of Red Star artefacts and a plush central lodge known as 5 Zvezdinih Zvezda – five segments each named in honour of a Red Star legend. All this before we even step inside Red Star's astonishing trophy room which firmly drives home the unparalleled success of south-east Europe's most successful club.

Football has been played on the site of Stadion Rajko Mitić since 1927 when Red Star's predecessors, SK Yugoslavia, began developing what was at the time, a modern 15,000-capacity stadium with a pair of rudimentary wooden stands. It would see Yugoslavia's first floodlit match in 1932, an exhibition game against Racing Club Paris, and by the beginning of the Second World War its capacity had been increased to 50,000. Red Star came into existence in 1945 and immediately took up residence, renaming

It is impossible to discuss Stadion Rajko Mitić without mentioning the 73m-long North Tunnel, the claustrophobic route for players making their way from the dressing rooms to the pitch. Resembling a decrepit city underpass, decorated in primitive murals and poorly lit, it passes directly beneath the North Stand where 12,000 bounce above causing it to visibly vibrate. Italian newspaper *La Gazzetta dello Sport* referred to it as 'Dante's Tunnel', comparing the passageway to descending into Hell.

the stadium 'Avala' in recognition of the mountain overlooking the city. The club's popularity soared with huge, fervent crowds spurring on the team to reach a European Cup semi-final in 1957. Less than a year later, on 6 February 1958, Manchester United visited and were held to a 3-3 draw. Their journey home was to result in one of sport's darkest hours when after refuelling in Munich, their chartered British Airways flight 609 crashed on its third attempt to take off, killing 23 including eight of the Busby Babes. By 1959, Red Star had outgrown Avala and played their final game against Novi Sad on 27 December as plans for their new home were drafted.

Original plans were for a 55,000 capacity until members of the Red Star Sport Society's boxing section stepped in to demand that as Belgrade was a rapidly developing city, it should at least be capable of holding 100,000. You don't mess with Serbian pugilists and so with an estimated cost of three million dinars to raise, a scheme was devised involving the selling of coupons known as *ciglice*. Fans bought them, players sold them, including Dragoslav Šekularac, a Red Star great who used his fame to sell an astonishing number. The construction of Stadion Rajko Mitić was a complicated one, fraught with the danger of landslides from excavating the steep hill which descended from Rajka Mitića to Bulevar Oslobodenja in a west to east direction. An estimated 350,000 cubic metres of soil and 15,000 cubic metres of stone was removed from the hill, allowing for the new stadium to be built 12m below its predecessor. Moreover, it allowed the curvature of the stadium to nestle into the land's natural gradient giving it a graceful lopsidedness, accentuated by the later addition of the continuous rolling roof.

It is impossible to discuss Stadion Rajko Mitić without mentioning the 73m-long North Tunnel, the claustrophobic route for players making their way from the dressing rooms to the pitch. Resembling a decrepit city underpass, decorated in primitive murals and poorly lit, it passes directly beneath the North Stand where 12,000 bounce above causing it to visibly vibrate. Italian newspaper *La Gazzetta dello Sport* referred to it as 'Dante's Tunnel', comparing the passageway to descending into Hell. Since 1977 however, players have had to turn left at the end and into a smaller tunnel which brings them out beyond the running track after Spanish player Juanito Gómez, struck on the head by a bottle, returned the middle finger to the crowd, sparking pandemonium. Although violence rarely breaks out inside the stadium nowadays, it is the thrill of the unknown, the palpable tension which permeates the derbies and other high-profile games that sees mums, dads and children alike link arms in unison with the more vociferous elements. It is not for everyone; the choking clouds of coloured smoke, the knees in the back during the scramble for seats, the weapons-grade noise. If not for you, there is always the stadium tour which over an hour takes in every inch of this unique sporting venue.

021

Í Fløtugerði

FUGLAFJØRÐUR // FAROE ISLANDS // ÍF

From Belgrade's 50,000 fans hellbent on wrecking their vocal cords we return to the 'land of maybe', where the 50,000 islanders are outnumbered three to one by the native sheep. In stark contrast, the only noise at Fuglafjørður's little football ground is the primeval thump of a plastic barrel being battered with the handle of an old umbrella.

Amid a crowd dressed almost exclusively in drab thermal waterproofs, the boy banging at his makeshift drum is conspicuous for having turned up wearing a full replica kit of the home side. The fact I am even able to see this, let alone the match taking place, is illustrative of the 'maybe' ; one hour earlier Fuglafjørður had completely disappeared into an impenetrable cloud of rolling sea fog. Now it is lit by a thin watery sunshine.

Even the loneliest places on earth have their very own pockets of isolation. A few miles north of Fuglafjørður at the end of a deep ravine, the lives of the 49 residents of Gjógv are marked by synergism and great endurance. Like many of the islands' outlying communities, they live in perfect harmony with the often hostile environment. With a name which translates as the 'fjord of birds', Fuglafjørður is a veritable metropolis by comparison. With a population of 1,600, the town has a healthy fishing industry, oil depots and the Mentanarhúsið, a cultural centre which since 1999 has been reason enough for tourists en route to Klaksvík to take a detour just after Víkingur's Sarpugerði stadium. Even on clear days only a few will spot that high above the harbourside's bustle, three rusted floodlight pylons mark the spot of one of Europe's most extraordinary football grounds.

Decades before the advent of the artificial pitch, Fuglafjørður's fanatics were battling to piece together enough flat land to lay even an ordinary playing surface. Shielded by seven mountains which slope precipitously into the bay, like many Faroese communities the village has always struggled for horizontal space. Its narrow, crescent-shaped dispersal of housing and industrial clusters is a result of this; expansion along the water's edge is far less tricky than going upwards. However, back in November 1940, a year after the formation of the ÍF club (notably 47 years later than the first Faroese club, TB), members did identify something approaching a level spot at the top of a steep hill leading up from the waterfront. With the help of the municipality, the club began buying up small pieces of the land called *fløtan*. By 1949 they had just enough to mark out Fuglafjørður's first pitch which, even after the domestic football association's demands to widen it in 1979 and again in 2015, remains the smallest of any of the islands' 26 grounds.

To fully appreciate the magnitude of what was accomplished here, a walk along the Tradarvegur road south of the ground exposes the 6m drop created by the building up of the land (by hand) for the pitch to sit level. Nearby, a cairn further reminds us of the foresight, determination and togetherness that went into building what would be christened when opened on 11 November 1956, Í Fløtugerdi: 'the Flat Land'. If the weather is kind, this man-made shelf above the town offers up a truly breathtaking panorama: miles of crystal glass water, declivitous pyramidical mountains, capped with winter snow and flecked with grass-roofed dwellings, and Nón, a hill which the sun always hits at *nónbil* (3pm).

Even on clear days only a few will spot that high above the harbourside's bustle, three rusted floodlight pylons mark the spot of one of Europe's most extraordinary football grounds.

On Eysturoy and its seven western neighbours, the vistas are just a little bit more dramatic, the mountains taller and with endless stretches of water at every turn.

Both ÍF and Í Fløtugerdi have come a long way since those early days. In the season the club won their only Faroese title in 1979, a match against TB drew a crowd larger than the entire population of Fuglafjørður. In all likelihood it was the entire population. More recently, between 2011 and 2015 ÍF competed for three seasons in the Europa League albeit with games against KR Reykjavík, Linfield and MYPA all switched to Tórshavn's two UEFA-regulated stadiums. In March 2021 the original clubhouse that had served since 1981 was replaced by a state-of-the-art, four-storey sports hall in the north-western corner which, financed by the municipality, has quickly become the envy of ÍF's Eysturoy rivals. Pitchside, a television gantry has recently been erected in the centre of the uncovered tribune which, built at a gradient of 1:10, has more in keeping with the steps of a Mayan temple than a football ground. More than most, this one needs its barriers and handrails.

Further north on Iceland's Route 1 ring road, many of its more peripheral football homes can be spotted among landscapes so rugged they appear almost primeval. Similarly, in the Faroe Islands it is virtually impossible for a club's ground not to fall into the category labelled 'spectacular'. But on Eysturoy and its seven western neighbours, the vistas are just a little bit more dramatic, the mountains taller and with endless stretches of water at every turn. Although we are not quite done with the Nordic countries just yet, Í Fløtugerdi is undoubtedly the Faroese number one.

SANDSHIP
HAVSBRÚN
RÓKIN
NORÐOYA SPARIKASSI
FØROYATELE

Vazgen Sargsyan Republican Stadium

YEREVAN // ARMENIA

Ten hours after leaving Tbilisi on the sleeper train, we arrive in Yerevan where we are met by the sight of 12 billowing, multicoloured hot air balloons anchored in Republican Square. Dawn has barely broken but the streets already bristle with a tangible sense of optimism. After three days of *lobiani* and *khachapuri*, two bread-based meals in Georgia, we will later seek out an affordable place to eat. But as post-independence Yerevan has been developed into something akin to a mini Paris, all trendy boutiques and high-end eateries, that could be difficult.

Stepping out beyond the city's centre, however, it becomes apparent that this new Yerevan is merely a screen, shielding tourists from the reality of dilapidated Soviet-era tower blocks and extreme poverty. Although not quite at the level seen in Vanadzor in the north where a third of residents struggle to find money for food and heating, it is certainly an eye-opener.

While the city's magnificent Republican Stadium is our primary concern here, this chapter pertains to two very different football stadiums, one beauty and one beast, both remarkably designed by the same hand. Down on Vardanants Street, number 65 to be precise, the Republican Stadium (Hanrapetakan) has since 1935 been the cradle of Armenian football. Here, where the western hills of Nork-Marash rise up to meet the colossal Armenian Public Television tower, between 1933 and 1935 the first incarnation of the stadium was constructed. Initiated by the Dinamo Sports Club, the long since dissolved former Armenian champions, it was instead arch-enemies Spartak who first took to the field for a match against KBKT Moscow in June 1935. Arranged in a typical oval shape, the foundations had been laid for what in 1953 would be transformed into an ornate, pink-hued coliseum for 20,000 under the auspices of architect and former weightlifter Koryun Hakobyan.

Having expanded the stadium's footprint to 18 rows of terracing, Hakobyan next set to work on topping the curved perimeter with a series of sweeping covered colonnades from which gave access to all parts of the arena. Then came the redesign of the western stand's main entrance and facade to include a veritable glut of bas-reliefs, classical statuettes set within alcoves and decorative flagpole stands from which today's red, blue and orange colours fly. All carried out in the same pink brick which gave Yerevan the sobriquet 'the Pink City', it would be tempting to say that this was Hakobyan's greatest triumph. But in 1967, in preparation for the 50th anniversary of Armenia's Sovietisation in 1970, the 'People's Architect' alongside Gurgen Musheghyan was tasked with designing a brand new stadium.

As early as the 1950s, Soviet politician and revolutionary Anastas Mikoyan had envisioned the Hrazdan Gorge across town as a site for a great natural amphitheatre. The idea was never fully forgotten and with five million rubles allocated for the project, work on the 75,000-capacity Hrazdan Stadium began in the second half of 1969. For their efforts, Hakobyan and Musheghyan were awarded the prestigious Best Construction of the Year award in 1971, and soon afterwards, on 19 May 1971, the stadium hosted its first official match, between Ararat Yerevan and Kairat Almaty in front of 78,000 spectators. During the Soviet era the Hrazdan would host many important matches, not least those of Ararat during 1973 when they became champions of the Soviet Union.

But as a typically bombastic Soviet bowl with monstrously proportioned floodlights the likes of which could never again exist, the stadium soon fell out of favour following Armenia's independence. Nowadays the Hrazdan cuts a sorry sight. With its pitch torn up and concourses left open, many of the city's homeless use the stadium for shelter. A huge market takes place at the weekend, leaving behind all manner of detritus which clings to site. But perhaps saddest of all is the commemoration of the 1973 Ararat team, 19 players and coaches cast in bronze standing proudly behind the Soviet Top League trophy. In May 2020, four were stolen and when we visit in 2023, a rubbish fire is burning at the players' feet.

Back at the Republican Stadium, following the conversion in 2000 to an all-seater with a capacity of 14,403 and having been given a roof a year earlier, fans from as far afield as Wales and Spain have all enjoyed its unique charm as one of Europe's most likeable national stadiums. In tribute to Armenia's president who was shot and killed on 27 October 1999, the stadium was given the name Vazgen Sargsyan two months later. We watch Armenia's new dominant football force, Pyunik, take on city neighbours Alashkert. The crowd is sparse with a few half-hearted pyrotechnic displays sporadically bursting out into the night sky. Admission is free and it is possible to move around the stadium to experience every delightful archway, column or curve as the match goes on below. Much like the city centre itself, the municipality-owned Republican Stadium is impeccably maintained, a gleaming testimonial to modern Yerevan. I am told that fans of the national team especially have a deep-rooted connection to their home which, in light of the on-field progress made with each passing qualifying tournament, is easy to understand why. Although it is hard to forget the sight up on the Hrazdan Gorge and indeed those seen on bus journeys out into the countryside, it must be hoped that Yerevan's great symbol of sporting tradition is used in some way to benefit everyone.

019

Stadio San Nicola

BARI // ITALY // SSC BARI

From the Pompidou Centre in Paris to the Shard in London, Renzo Piano's postmodernist designs have enriched cities across the world. Bold, high-tech and innovative, they represent some of mankind's most iconic architectural achievements. In footballing terms, Bari's Stadio San Nicola, designed by Piano in 1987, goes hand-in-hand with the architectonic extravagance of Italia 90.

The nostalgia that tournament conjures amongst fans 34 years on as I write this remains a powerful one and in its association with the tournament, Stadio San Nicola along with Milan's San Siro and Rome's Stadio Olimpico, remains a stadium adored by fans across the world.

Yet on lists of his greatest works, Piano's only sporting venue is often conspicuous in its absence. Indelible footballing memories were made here; Roger Milla's dance around the corner flag, Salvatore Schillaci's penalty past Peter Shilton securing Italy's bronze medal. The sun blistered that summer in 1990 and Stadio San Nicola looked glorious on TVs around the world. Its legacy seemed assured when the following year, the European Cup Final was held here, at the same time cementing the Italian south's desire for a modicum of equality in the game. But after the razzmatazz came the new reality, domestic football in which club side AS Bari struggled to build a fanbase large enough to utilise the stadium's full potential. Sleepwalking between divisions, AS Bari toiled to fill even half the stadium in Serie A, barely a third in Serie B and on occasion, crowds fell below 5,000. With each passing year, the vivacity of Piano's desert flower began to fade as it fell into steep decline. Cosmetic deterioration maybe, but enough to tarnish the San Nicola's architectural reputation. Desert winds tore away roof membranes, empty banks of seats rotted and much of the high-tech gadgetry such as the pair of Technovision scoreboards, were abandoned. Located on the Achilles heel of Italy's boot, Stadio San Nicola had indeed become Bari's very own Achilles heel.

From the outset, the stadium's exorbitant construction costs had left the working class Barese sore. Coupled with its location out in the arid wilderness, an emotional chill slowly spread between the city's people and stadium culminating with the unaffectionate term *cattedrale nel deserto*, cathedral of the desert (a term comparable with the English white elephant). So far removed from their humble spiritual home of Stadio della Vittoria was it, it is easy to understand why. The Comune di Bari had initially seized the chance of hosting World Cup football and in doing so, satisfyingly denied their Apulian neighbours Lecce the opportunity.

Seen from four miles away on the urban highways leading into Bari, Stadio San Nicola cuts a slightly unnerving figure on the city's horizon.

But by the time of its opening match on 3 June 1990, a Serie A game between Bari and AC Milan, the overall cost of the stadium and infrastructure had soared to £58m (about £140m in today's money). With a capacity of 60,000, still the third largest in Italy, it was an enormous gamble which, with the benefit of three decades of hindsight, commercially at least, has not paid off. Bari is left with a paradox; a stadium of such innovation and importance that is too big to fill and too expensive to maintain.

Seen from four miles away on the urban highways leading into Bari, Stadio San Nicola cuts a slightly unnerving sight on the city's horizon. Its hyperboloid shape has led to it being known as *l'astronave*, the spaceship, and indeed when lit up for evening games, it could be just that. As one approaches from the outer suburb of Carbonara, the landscape remains unchanged from when it was built; a desolate wasteland of abandoned farmsteads, cacti, scrubby brush and fly-tipping. But in this ugly isolation, Stadio San Nicola rises, a gargantuan peony of curving concrete, still proud and still spectacular.

Old entrance gates may be rusted shut and the two narrow towers standing guard at the main entrance unused, but Renzo Piano's vision is still firmly intact. The broad open space around the stadium, the flat radial system of access paths and vast car parks, all designed to create a calming environment, serve to emphasise its monumental architectural impact on the landscape. A curious lop-sidedness in the shape of the roof and consequently, the whole profile of the stadium, is due to each of the 26 upper tiers, or 'petals' being of a slightly different size. A deliberate imperfection which only adds to its appeal. 312 sickle-shaped reinforced concrete sections were constructed to make the petals, the finish textured like aged wood grain. Through 8 metre gaps between the petals, glimpses of the new red and white seating bring colour against the monotone exterior: inside, these voids act as windows on the world, through which the port of Bari and the city can be glimpsed. All is airy and light within; the exterior greys replaced by a riot of colour, a perfect juxtaposition.

Far from abandoning the stadium, there is a resolve within the Comune di Bari to bring it back up to scratch. It may merely be papering over the cracks, but in the summer of 2022 a series of refurbishments took place beginning with the aforementioned new seating. Dotted in red and white to represent the *Gallettis'* (Bantams) colours, they replaced the tired original yellow and green bucket seats and immediately injected some life back into the old girl. Staircases have been repainted too and pledges have been made to replace the Teflon-covered roof membranes. The old scoreboards are due to be replaced with a giant LED screen on the south curve. It has given Stadio San Nicola its first much needed facelift in decades and it looks so much healthier for it. Having been disbanded for a fourth time in 2018, the newly monikered SSC Bari are now back in Series B. Under the ownership of Italian filmmaker Aurelio de Laurentiis, whose portfolio boasts SSC Napoli, the fans are again returning to their new-look stadium. It may not be in the numbers once envisioned, but it is enough to create a matchday atmosphere that Renzo Piano's treasure deserves.

Glentornan Park

DUNLEWEY // IRELAND // DUNLEWEY CELTIC

From Renzo Piano's World Cup masterpiece we travel to the far north-west corner of Ireland for something altogether more tranquil yet similarly detached from its people. Glentornan Park is framed by the mastery of Mother Nature's very own fingertips, nestling on the grassy shores of Dunlewey Lough, virtually camouflaged, a narrow oblong beneath Mount Errigal's shattered gully and scree slopes. With only the whistling, roofless shells of a ghost village and a thousand sheep for company, its all-encompassing solitude gives it a very real shout of being the most beautiful football field in Europe.

North-west Donegal is a place of myth and legend, the Gaeltacht tongue and world-class wilderness. Because of the latter, it is also a place that like Eriskay and Embid has suffered mass emigration over the past century leaving its townlands and outlying villages decimated. In the case of Glentornan, the village is entirely abandoned. The road over the lough from Dunlewey brings footballers and officials to the pitch before coming to an abrupt halt a few metres on among a cluster of ruined stone cottages. In the gardens, jasmine and honeysuckle still grow wild. When Dunlewey Celtic secured the field and were elected into

the Donegal Junior League in 1973, Glentornan had already stood empty for a decade. Life here was vibrant and energetic but also extremely tough. Large families occupied small cottages, employment was virtually non-existent and there was no secondary-level education. I am told of old Johnny Beag, a villager who had owned the first motorcar in Glentornan. Johnny had built the village shop and here folk would gather once a week to read the newspaper through Glentornan's only pair of eyeglasses. Once finished, they would be handed on to the next person. It is a snapshot of 20th-century rural Irish life repeated all over the country.

Glentornan's bustle may have gone with its people but far from having an air of ghostliness it is as beautiful as it is peaceful. 'It's not a bad spot for a game,' says Hugh Cannon, Dunlewey's ex-manager on and off for 22 years, with understatement typical of someone who lives their life surrounded by such natural beauty. He follows up with, 'In the summer, at least.' And there's the rub. Errigal may stand as a bulwark to the Atlantic storms and blizzards but when the colder months arrive, the rain saturates the surrounding peat bogs and lowlands. Good drainage keeps the pitch just about playable but not without the hours of preparation from Hugh's son Mannie, who has taken the baton passed down to him and is now secretary, manager, fundraiser and everything in between. Add to that the recurring challenge of trying to recruit players from the larger townlands of Falcarragh and Gweedore in a land where Gaelic football is king, and the real beauty of this little football club lies in their ability to keep going.

It was on a field in nearby Mín na bPoll in the early 1970s that the foundation stones were laid for what would eventually become Dunlewey Celtic Football Club. Local lads would gather on summer evenings and play until darkness fell, jumpers for goalposts and all that. Around this time, the Donegal League was founded, prompting Dunlewey local Joe McCafferty to seek the assistance of two Gaelic football association colleagues to help find the players a pitch. Both were teachers at Falcarragh Community School and an agreement was reached for Dunlewey to use the school football pitch, where friendly matches were played and a good team assembled. Through a fundraising summer dance in August 1973, the club raised £31 for entry into the Donegal Junior League where despite a few seasons in abeyance due to emigration, they have beaten the odds to compete ever since. The move to Glentornan was made shortly after. A small whitewashed building for changing was built in 1974 and more recently, covered trainers' benches painted with the legend *Ceiltigh Dhún Lúiche*: Dunlewey Celtic.

On grey high streets from Letterkenny to Ballyshannon, a sudden splash of colour can always be spotted. Gaelic football shirts are everywhere. You'd be hard-pressed to find a Manchester United shirt before seeing ten GAA jerseys pass by, hanging on the shoulders of kids returning home from training or fathers entering the pub. Its popularity above association football cannot be underestimated and remains the reason so many junior football clubs across rural Ireland clubs still play out of local schools rather than the established football grounds of their neighbours. The interest is simply not there to justify the construction of purpose-built football grounds. Next to the crystal waters of the lough, a short drive from the Poisoned Glen and the fairy trees believed to be a gateway to the otherworld, Dunlewey do have their own home. It may be modest and visited by less than 30 people each week but in its spectacular isolation, it is a home like no other.

017
BRANDWEG

Oscar Vankesbeeckstadion

MECHELEN // BELGIUM // KRC MECHELEN

One of Belgium's last truly great stadiums is the Oscar Vankesbeeckstadion in Mechelen. Unruly and extrovert, scruffy and antiquated, it's a loveable mongrel of a place where the modernist architectural styles of the 1940s clash and mingle with bombastic 1970s iconography and 21st-century street art.

It wears its heart on its sleeve, much like Racing's loyal and boisterous supporters for whom its imminent demise will surely be hardest felt. Yet solace can be taken from the club's promise that well-loved elements of the stadium, including the iconic main entrance gate and painted motto above the players' tunnel *Waar een wil is een weg* (where there is a will there's a way), will be incorporated into any new stadium built on the site. The pledge was unanimously praised by football supporters up and down the country and we shouldn't be surprised; the Belgians have a deep-seated understanding of the need to preserve their sporting heritage. They may have lost a lot, but they're not going to lose it all.

From high up in the grandstand, aptly referred to by fans as *De Nok* (the Roof), I cast my eyes out beyond the covered terrace and over towards St. Rumbold's Cathedral. The Mechelen skyline has changed dramatically since my last visit in 2011, prefabricated apartments going up everywhere, taller and boxier, elbow to elbow with medieval church spires and dwarfing the red-brick streets below. Yet the reminders of Mechelen's past are everywhere, hewn into the very fabric of the vista. A ghost sign advertising the Gazet van Mechelen painted onto the oxide red brick rear end of a house, distant sawtooth factory roofs and Flemish gables. Inside, the Oscar Vankesbeeck Stadion is a veritable Pandora's Box, crammed with antique pomp and faded dreams. It is a museum without knowing it, one which historians and romantics

By far the most arresting is a 12-foot-high club logo on the fascia, formed in concrete relief and corresponding with the concrete blocks which cover and hide the brickwork of its entire frontage.

flock to from far and wide each season for a taste of football as it used to be. Turning into the ground between the new apartment blocks, it's immediately clear why. Chunky pop art letters, illuminated by night, spell out KRCM on top of the the entrance gate alongside tattered club flags. To the left, the old brick ticket booths are now covered in a 12-foot-high mural of three Racing legends in green and white jerseys, tickets handed over from hatches where by accident or design, their hearts would be. And just beyond, always part-silhouetted before late afternoon matches, the titanic shape of the stadium's centrepiece, the 1948 grandstand which looks every bit as though it has been lifted directly from a Lancastrian football ground circa 1950.

Under the chairmanship of Oscar Vankesbeeck, the stadium was opened for a league match against Cercle Brugge on 2 September 1923. Lawyer and later president of the Mechelen Bar, Vankesbeeck had been one of the founders of the Racing club in 1904 for whom he played. A football man through and through, he was selected as a delegation leader at the 1930 World Cup in Montevideo and became the president of the Belgian FA in 1937 before his untimely death in 1943, a direct result of the torture and deprivation suffered whilst held captive by the Germans during the Second World War. The man's achievements in just 56 short years are now immortalised, not only in name but in another less primitive mural inside the stadium; a moustachioed Vankesbeeck in profile, painted in black and white on a green and white backdrop which supporters affectionately tap as they make their way onto the terraces.

His stadium would have looked a great deal different in 1923, an oval with 21,000 standing places spread over 16 terrace steps on all sides of the field. The original wooden grandstand on the north side, a simple vaulted-roof structure 14m high and 80m long held a further 1,900, was razed to the ground in 1947 in a fire which claimed the entire club archive. Within a year however, its replacement was ready, financed from the proceeds of a benefit match, its design strongly influenced by the grandstand at Brugge's long-lost De Klokke Stadion. As was the fashion in Belgium at the time, its architects squeezed many motifs and insignias into its design whilst just about retaining a balance between fussy and elegant. By far the most arresting is a 12-foot-high club logo on the fascia, formed in concrete relief and corresponding with the concrete blocks which cover and hide the brickwork of its entire frontage. Beneath, the main entrance doors open up into a foyer where above two reception booths, O. Vankesbeeckstadion is boldly engraved in gold upon a marble slab. And below, a more contemporary hand-painted addition: *Welkom in de Hel* in reference to the fans' alternative name for the Stadion, 'De Hel van Mechelen-Noord', and a favourite chant to sing to visitors. A marble staircase sweeps up to the left and then right taking visitors up into a green and gold-hued labyrinthine world of forgotten rooms and dusty offices.

Racing's short-lived halcyon days came in the 1950s, spearheaded by Rik de Saedeleer the club's greatest player and latterly, Belgium's answer to John Motson in the world of television commentary. First Division runners-up in 1951/52, Racing finished bottom six years later and would only return on three further occasions as their neighbours from less than a mile away, KV Mechelen, asserted their grip on the title of the city's most successful club. Dwindling support throughout the 1970s led to the sale of land at either end, the oval becoming a conventional rectangle and the capacity dropping to 13,000. And as the 1980s and 90s drifted by, sections of the stadium were temporarily then permanently closed, most notably the entire western end and various sections of covered and uncovered terracing opposite the grandstand leaving the capacity at just 6,000. The terrace at the eastern end known as 'the good goal' along with the paddock below the stand was appropriated by the younger, more vociferous supporters who as the 21st century rolled in, moved up into the grandstand to be replaced by today's cultish following with their good humour, Peaky Blinders banners and casual clobber.

Few new stadium projects will be as interesting to watch materialise as Racing's will be in the coming years. Juggling the weight of history and the desires of the supporters with the inevitable partners' wishes to incorporate a sports hotel, bowling alley and meeting facilities will undoubtedly be a tightrope. Yet amongst their ranks, Racing may just have an ace up their sleeve. Elected in 2019, current chairman Francois de Keersaecker has followed a similar career trajectory as Vankesbeeck as both lawyer and former chairman of the Belgian FA. More than that however, he is the son-in-law of another former Belgian FA chairman, Louis Wauters. And Wauters? Only the son-in-law of Oscar Vankesbeeck. A hundred years on from where the story began, it brings us full circle.

016

Fritz-Walter-Stadion

KAISERSLAUTERN // GERMANY // FC KAISERSLAUTERN

On the edge of the Pfälzerwald forest, deep in the western state of Rheinland-Pfalz, 1. FC Kaiserslautern have been busy cultivating their own unmistakable identity since 2 June 1900. In the same way Naples, Poznań, Newcastle upon Tyne and other similarly isolated industrial cities have forged some of Europe's more distinctive fanbases, supporters of Kaiserslautern's Red Devils (*Die Roten Teufel*) are regarded as some of the most ardent in all of Germany but at the same time, something of an anomaly.

With a population of just 100,000 and no Bundesliga football since 2011/12, an average crowd of 43,941 came to the Fritz-Walter-Stadion in 2023/24 to watch the team's largely disappointing season in the second tier. In the same division, only Hertha Berlin from a city with a population 36 times larger and Hamburg from a pool of 1.8 million bettered Kaiserslautern's attendances. Meanwhile, in the second divisions of England, Spain and Italy, the Kaiserslautern average topped Leeds United's by almost 10,000 and was double that of Real Zaragoza and Sampdoria. Many pinpoint the origins of this astonishing fanaticism to events in 1954 when two years after the club's second German championship, West Germany called up five Kaiserslautern players to the team which won the World Cup in Switzerland. In 2003, six million cinema-goers watched *The Miracle of Bern*, a portrayal of postwar Germany centred around the events of that final. It was enough to propel Kaiserslautern's tradition back into popular consciousness and introduce legendary brothers Fritz and Ottmar Walter to a whole new generation.

Yet even before the Second World War something was stirring in the city, a sense among the largely working-class demographic that football had been invented for them. Nowadays the Fritz-Walter-Stadion's position on top of 250m-high Betzenberg hill is there for everyone to marvel at. With a profile akin to St James' Park on steroids, it is one of Germany's original city-centre football grounds, a colossus rising up behind the city's main railway station. Kaiserslautern had taken up residency at what was then Sportplatz Betzenberg ('Betze' for short) on 13 May 1920 when 3,500 paid between one and three marks to watch a game against reigning Rhine district champions FC Pfalz Ludwigshafen. After their formation in 1900, the club had played at three grounds: Im Ländel on Friedenstraße; Waldschlösschen, a field behind the restaurant and dance pavilion of the same name; and finally, the Eselsfürth sports field in Barbarossa Park.

But it was at Betze that they built their first grandstand, a wooden structure that on 22 November 1930 was obliterated by a hurricane. Undeterred, Kaiserslautern set about redesigning their home with a new

Allgäuer
Latschen
Kiefer
BETZE SUPPORTERS
Devils Apostles
TOTO
JURI
FÜR
IMMER
K-TOWN
REDS
FRENETIC YOUTH
SEK SV
Generation

As part of Kaiserslautern's preparation for the World Cup, 11 enormous and faintly unnerving concrete players were erected and of course painted in the club's red and white. Under the cover of darkness in August 2019, two players had their heads lopped off and were smeared with blue paint.

grandstand on the north side along with concrete terracing laid at the eastern end and south side. Reopened on 25 September 1932 with 11,000 in attendance, for two decades during which Saarland and Kaiserslautern struggled to shake off the legacy of wartime French occupation, Betze, through the team's on-field exploits, grew to become one of the most feared grounds in western Germany. However, with support for the club reaching fever pitch following two German championships in 1951 and 1953, Betze's shortcomings became painfully obvious. Twice the club were shifted out for spells at Ludwigshafen's Südweststadion while their own ground was expanded to 30,000 and it was here that on 31 May 1956 a remarkable 83,000 gathered for the final game of the season with Karlsruher.

Over the next four decades Betzenberg was developed in a piecemeal fashion and by 1986 it could hold 38,000. A year earlier, on 2 November 1985, Fritz Walter's 65th birthday, the stadium was renamed in honour of its most famous son. Yet the recurring need for the Südweststadion was never far away, most notably in 1972 when 60,000 saw the game against Bayern Munich. Undoubtedly a fine stadium at the time, the Südweststadion was regularly chosen for German internationals and cup finals during this period. But as a second home 65km up the road, it was a fair trek for supporters. And so when on 13 October 2000 Germany was awarded the 2006 World Cup, the city of Kaiserslautern threw its hat into the ring and vowed to build its legions of Red Devils a lasting fortress of their own. Having previously designed Betze's north side grandstand in 1971, local architect Folker Fiebiger was rehired to oversee the project and piece together his earlier visions. Son Karsten, who in 1992 had his 'Rotating Football' sculpture erected on Betzenberg hill, would have been absorbing every aspect of his father's work for he too would go on to great success in the field working on stadiums as far afield as Russia and Ukraine and closer to home, FSV Mainz and FC Metz.

With the Osttribüne opened on 3 April 2004, 47,315 squeezed in to set a new stadium record. Next, the Südtribüne and Westtribüne were expanded, the roof of the latter raised and media towers in the north-west and north-east corners constructed. In September 2005, the 1,200-ton roof of the Sudtribüne was raised by four and a half metres by a team of 30 workers operating 15 hydraulically controlled jacks. When completed, it united Fritz-Walter-Stadion's many disparate components to give it a delightfully unwieldy harmony, one which stood out like a sore thumb when compared with the other perfectly shaped stadiums selected for the 2006 World Cup.

In many ways, the current Fritz-Walter-Stadion is the perfect summation of its club: bold, different and a little off-kilter. Passing under the railway bridge before the great hike up Betzenberg, fans pay homage to the 'Eleven Friends' in the centre of the Löwenburg roundabout. As part of Kaiserslautern's preparation for the World Cup, 11 enormous and faintly unnerving concrete players were erected and of course painted in the club's red and white. Under the cover of darkness in August 2019, two players had their heads lopped off and were smeared with blue paint. With rivals FC Saarbrücken, Karlsruher and Waldhof Mannheim all wearing blue, it is anyone's guess who the guilty parties were. Up on Betzenberg the stadium resembles a space-age landing pad for some unknown entity. An unrefined San Siro, its great appeal is its lack of appeal, all harsh concrete and sharp angles. Inside, the noise especially from the favoured Westtribüne is intimidating just as it is awe-inspiring. Few stadiums in Germany manage to convey the emotion quite like Fritz-Walter-Stadion but then few stadiums have the supporters Kaiserslautern do.

Hásteinsvöllur

HAEMAEY // ICELAND // IBV

My abiding memory of the trip my son Noah and I made to Iceland in 2013 is of David James. Over four June days, the ex-England goalkeeper was never far away; sat alone in the rain in Fylkir's uncovered grandstand, eating half-time cake with supporters in a draughty clubhouse and on the Sunday evening before we left, mooching among the shops on Reykjavík's Laugavegur.

Five years earlier, James had lifted the FA Cup at Wembley yet here he was in Reykjavík in circumstances rather more ordinary. Always among football's more cerebral characters, James, on a rare weekend off from duties at ÍBV, had forsaken the golf course in favour of watching a couple of local matches. Here was a man embracing a new chapter, throwing himself into everyday Icelandic life as he opened up to the *Independent* newspaper about his new home on the Vestmannaeyjar archipelago, 'I've fallen in love with the place. We're all the same here. I don't know everyone, but I've seen everyone.' For me, it took a further ten years to reach the island of Heimaey, four nautical miles off Iceland's southern coast where on our campsite beneath the Elephant Rock, Noah and I too fell in love with the island.

Over the years almost every drop of visual impact Hásteinsvöllur once had has been wrung out in a thousand social media polls and stories showcasing the world's most beautiful football stadiums. Much like Singapore's The Float or Norway's Henningsvær Stadion, Hásteinsvöllur has become so familiar we can almost begin to believe we have been there. Yet of course nothing can ever replace being present in the physical space of somewhere which has lived in our minds. Hásteinsvöllur, whether shrouded in rolling sea haar or lit golden by the Arctic sun, is pure volcanic drama hitherto unseen on my previous visits to Iceland. From cliffs pocked with fish-drying caves, rising up alongside the stadium like a troll-sized slice of chocolate cake, to fields of frozen lava flow and hazy views of mysterious uninhabited islands, Hásteinsvöllur condenses Iceland's raw beauty into one tiny space.

015 // **Hásteinsvöllur**
HAEMAEY // ICELAND // IBV

ÍBV's presence on the north-western edge of Heimaey covers more than just a football stadium, however. Beyond the volcanic cliffs, the natural amphitheatre of the Herjólsdalur valley is home to ÍBV's grass-roofed indoor sports hall and the club's multi-sports divisions. In August each year, Herjólsdalur is taken over by the Þjóðhátíð music festival where on the last evening, the mountainside is set alight with a row of flaming torches the entire length of the valley. Reason enough to return one day. Back on the other side of the cliff, Hásteinsvöllur is primed for matchday. David James's single year between the sticks may be consigned to memory, the tribute Afro wigs now tucked away in sock drawers, but the flags are flying high around the stadium. For a club from a community of just 4,500, by far the smallest in 2023's 'Men's Best Division', to be competing back at the highest level is reason enough for celebration. History tells us that ÍBV have punched above their weight for decades now, lifting the Icelandic title on three occasions, the cup five times and perhaps more impressively, winning seven and drawing nine of their 46 matches in European club competitions. Impressive statistics which have necessitated ongoing improvements to the stadium including 2012's addition of a steel-framed concrete grandstand facing out over the cliffs.

Although ÍBV's modern history is inseparable from Hásteinsvöllur, the club's past is tied to two other football fields on Heimaey. Hásteinsvöllur may have existed for kick-abouts since 1912 but its surface of roughly levelled peat meant it remained unsuitable for competitive football until 1960. During the spring of that year it was expanded to 100m by 66m, sown with grass and soon after ÍBV took up permanent residency. Until then, the club had played on the black crushed lava of Löngulág, a floodlit oval where players would finish matches resembling miners emerging from the pit. Löngulág still exists next to Framhaldsskólinn college, a few hundred yards from Helgafellsvöllur, the old stadium of Heimaey's second club, KFS Vestmannaeyjar. KFS now play on a pitch adjacent to Hásteinsvöllur.

It was to Helgafellsvöllur that ÍBV relocated in 1973 following the catastrophic eruption of the Eldfell volcano. Between January and July of that year, fewer than 500 residents remained on the island. When the evacuated returned, they discovered over one-third of all buildings had either burned or been buried beneath lava and ash and an island that had increased in size by two square kilometres. Stories of how Heimaey harbour was saved through levels of great ingenuity are justifiably legendary, yet the three-year recovery of Hásteinsvöllur, entombed under a blanket of hardened ash, is one less told. In recent years we have become all too familiar with the spectacle of Iceland's raging volcanoes and ash clouds. Yet once the visual drama drops off and the media lose interest, it is likely the last we will hear about the country's latest volcanic episode. This is when the rebuilding of towns and amenities begins, something Icelanders have done with a quiet strength in the face of adversity for over 1,000 years, a strength which filters down through every aspect of islanders' lives. Heimaey may have suffered more than most yet despite its tiny population, has produced a large percentage of the country's most talented footballers including Tryggvi Guðmundsson, who is Icelandic football's all-time top scorer, along with Hermann Hreiðarsson, Guðmundur Torfason and Ásgeir Sigurvinsson. All four began their careers at ÍBV.

A few hours after the match, we are on the ferry back to Landeyjahöfn with the visiting FH team. The setting sun has stained the sky a semi-opaque shade of crimson, through which the shape of Elliðaey rises up alongside us. Images of this tiny speck in the North Atlantic went viral in 2021 when during the Covid-19 pandemic, its single whitewashed cottage at the foot of a steep grassy slope was recognised as the ultimate place to escape to. We are leaving behind one of the more unique landscapes Europe has to offer and almost certainly, Iceland's most beautiful football ground.

History tells us that ÍBV have punched above their weight for decades now, lifting the Icelandic title on three occasions, the cup on five and perhaps more impressively, winning seven and drawing nine of their 46 matches in European club competitions.

Reine Stadion

REINE // NORWAY // REINE IL

It comes as no surprise that one of Europe's most dramatic landscapes gives us another football ground in this list. Our second entry from the Lofoten Islands is a football ground so attractive that even the now world-famous Henningsvær Stadion (100 miles east towards the mainland) pales against its beauty. For what Henningsvær has from the air, Reine Stadion has on the ground. Whichever way you are facing inside the tiny Reine Stadion you have a backdrop of some of Europe's most spectacular scenery.

On an evening in early September, the local team Reine IL take on Svolvær beneath an Arctic sky visibly dancing with colours. Pinks and violets illuminate patches on the towering Reinebringen mountain, the ocean a few feet from the pitch appears almost golden under the setting sun. We are almost at the very end of the archipelago here in the Moskenes municipality. A few miles further west and the island's only main road, the E10, ends abruptly in a car park in the fishing hamlet of Å. The further west we have driven, the more dramatic the mountains have become. The islands are sparser here and linked by elegant curved bridges and tunnels beneath the fjords, the villages strung along the narrowing E10 charming yet weather-beaten.

Despite a population of barely 300, Reine has always been the beating heart of Lofoten's modest yet thriving fishing economy. Months after the *tørrfisk* (the cod which hangs air-drying on racks called *hjell*) have been packed and exported all over the world, the pungent aroma of the fish still hangs heavy in the air. It is said that during the months of May and June when hundreds of thousands of fish are drying around the pitch, teams arriving from other parts of the islands are often so overcome by the smell many are sick on the pitch. A handy advantage

014

for the home side you would think. Reine's story and indeed its football stadium are inseparable from the stockfish. For four generations, the Svederup family have run the village's main fishery, employing many from the community. They own the stadium on which Reine IL play and the company's numerous wooden *hjell* form an immediate backdrop to the football, standing skeletal on three sides like primitive scaffold for the building of Viking longhouses. Beyond, mountains of precipitous, jagged rock, more ancient than much of northern Europe itself, coastal plains and fjords, the distant villages of Hamnøy and Sakrisøy and an endless sea.

As we have already seen in Eriskay and football in Scotland's Western Isles, there is a comparable spirit here in Lofoten in the ability of tiny island communities not just to raise football teams, but to build club infrastructures to serve all ages. The parallels can even be drawn with the club to population ratio on Harris and Lewis which is almost identical to the Lofoten Islands. Twenty-five senior players and 60 juniors are currently signed with Reine, almost one-third of the village. Although the lure of the mainland, its universities and commerce pulls many away,

On the main street, in the window of an art gallery, a display of canvas prints in various shapes and sizes depicting the stadium in its bed of rock. Photographed beneath the aurora borealis, a handwritten note above reads: 'Yes it's real and you are only fifty metres away from it!'

Reine IL have continued to enter competitions continuously since the club's founding in 1939. This has not been without occasional support from other clubs on the islands who often amalgamate temporarily. In 2022, the team from nearby Flakstad found themselves short of players. Reine stepped in and took them under their wing for a season to allow them time to rebuild. It is this kind of camaraderie among the islanders which keeps the game alive.

When the stadium was opened in the 1960s, a crowd larger than Reine's population watched the first senior match. Nowadays, perhaps 50 or 60 villagers will watch games, crowds made up of family and friends, curious hikers or climbers and a mascot dressed as a bright blue lumpfish. In more recent times, a series of modernisations has seen the installation of an artificial pitch, floodlights and an assortment of wooden benches which have been covered with roofs designed to resemble tiny *rorbu*, the distinctive blood-red Norwegian fishing cabins. A two-storey balconied clubhouse and gymnasium stands behind the south-western end of the ground, steps leading down from the first floor bringing the players on to the pitch. Two years after the upgrades in 2004, a violent winter storm wreaked havoc upon the stadium. The ocean carried away large sections of the pitch, washed stone paths away and battered surrounding fencing. When you're this close to nature's wrath, such destruction is taken on the chin. The people of Reine simply salvaged what they could and immediately set out rebuilding.

Back in Henningsvær on a rainswept Wednesday morning, a group of tourists emerge from a campervan, change into favourite football shirts and proceed to have a kick-about on the famous pitch. A drone camera is launched overhead to record the scene for social media. Supporters' group stickers from all over Europe are plastered to signage and floodlight poles, statements of bucket lists being ticked. Down on the high street, the window display of an art gallery is full of canvas prints in various shapes and sizes depicting the stadium in its bed of rock. Photographed beneath the aurora borealis, a handwritten note above reads, 'Yes it's real! And you are only 50 metres away from it!' Yet without regular football, Henningsvær's remarkable feat of engineering plays second fiddle to where the real action is. Lofoten's true footballing miracle is in Reine.

The Oval

BELFAST // NORTHERN IRELAND // GLENTORAN

Sometimes it is the strength of the bond between the football ground, the community and the supporters that elevates a status to something approaching iconic. The Oval's continued existence within the very fabric of east Belfast life has seen it bear silent witness to everything from RMS *Titanic* steelworkers rolling out of shifts to pass through the turnstiles to the intensification of sectarian hostilities during the 1980s. The peacetime of the 21st century has made it easy to look back and gauge just how valuable the Oval's role was in providing a little, fleeting joy from the daily grind for thousands of Glentoran supporters. In Britain, perhaps only stadiums in Glasgow, Liverpool and a few in the industrial north are entwined with the lives of their communities in a similar way. But shaped by both changelessness and homeliness, the Oval's enduring appeal as one of the original bastions of the British game is secure for now.

In Belfast there once bubbled the Glentoran River, one of many streams flowing in and around the developing city which have long since been buried underground and subsequently omitted from maps. If the River Lagan's levels are low enough it is still possible to see the Glentoran outlet at Ravenhill Reach although such is the miserable trickle, you probably wouldn't bother. From this once twisting Gaelic waterway, Glentoran took their name and set up in 1882 at Ormeau Park, the oldest surviving municipal park in Belfast, before switching to King's Field on Bryson Street in the Mountpottinger neighbourhood. Despite a location in the heart of inner east Belfast, that pitch proved a headache for the burgeoning club as it needed draining before each and every match. So after three seasons they again upped sticks and moved in with East End Cricket Club where, from the 'Na Shuler' cricketers, Glentoran adopted their famous red, green and black colours.

As east Belfast's original 'Wanderers', to Musgrave's Park on Templemore Avenue they went. Here in 1890 a rally of support for shipyard owner Gustav Wolff, then standing for election to the Westminster parliament, was held in a gigantic tent on the Glentoran pitch. It is perhaps the first connection between the local football club and shipbuilders Harland & Wolff who 18 years later would present their drawings of the *Titanic* to White Star Line executives. This latest football ground would make way in 1892 for Henry Musgrave's new stove manufacturing foundry, leaving Glentoran to again seek pastures new.

Bounded by Conn's Water to the east, the Belfast to Bangor railway line to the north and the recently built Chelsea and Mersey Streets, a vast wasteland had stood in what would develop into the Strandtown neighbourhood in the shadow of the shipyards. Owned by Sir Daniel Dixon, a prominent developer, factory owner and in 1892, Belfast's first lord

mayor, Dixon signed a long-term lease with Glentoran for a plot of land big enough to house the throngs of supporters who by this stage had become smitten with the club. To paint a sobering picture of the time, Belfast was then a city huddling beneath a filthy, almost permanent blanket of black smog, where in the hot and humid linen mills and foundries tuberculosis was spreading at twice the rate reported in England and Wales. The respite supporters would have found at the Oval cannot be overestimated. Named after its elliptical natural boundary, Glentoran moved in on Christmas Eve 1892 for a match watched by thousands against Scottish club Kilmarnock.

Fast-forward 131 years and I'm standing next to the restored military pillbox atop the Sydenham End's grassy bank. Kilmarnock are again the visitors, the latest in a long line of friendlies with the Glens. The crowd is thin, a fraction of the 4,000 who will gather in a few months' time for the 647th edition of the *Bel Classico* when Linfield visit. To the west, the setting sun casts shadows across the upper slopes of Divis and the Black Mountain. Squat church towers in the distant city appear in silhouette and soaring up just beyond the old 'unreserved' stand and the Sydenham bypass (Northern Ireland's first dual-carriageway when opened in 1959), Samson and Goliath. Just as

Just as the new grandstand had towered above the Mersey Street Primary School playground and surrounding terraced houses when opened on 22 August 1953, Harland & Wolff's colossal twin cranes dominate the skyline.

the new grandstand had towered above the Mersey Street Primary School playground and surrounding terraced houses when opened on 22 August 1953, Harland & Wolff's colossal twin cranes dominate the skyline. They may have been latecomers to the scene when erected in 1969 and 1974 but without them, any number of contemporary Irish TV crime dramas would be worse off.

Until the arrival of the double-decker grandstand in 1953, supporters had just gone 12 years without the luxury of seating such was the state of the Oval after being flattened by Junker bombers in the Belfast Blitz of 1941. Nowadays it is the advertising of a sports betting company and a local pizza parlour that dominate the grandstand's ivy-green frontage but back then, it was adorned with enormous signage tempting supporters with ice-cream, fruit lollies and milk products from nearby Dobsons, an east Belfast company with a dairy in Cregagh. From the Cregagh Estate a few years later came the Best family who introduced a young George to the Oval. Although Glentoran would famously reject Best on the grounds that he was 'far too skinny', his experiences on the impassioned terraces undoubtedly stoked his zeal for the game. Maybe George just needed a few more of those fruit lollies.

Marinated in so much history and dripping with evocative visual reminders at every turn, the Oval has become something of a Holy Grail for enthusiasts seeking the thrill of football past. Many cite it as their very favourite ground, a place to rekindle youthful memories or to find out what all the fuss was about. Most will at some stage stand open-mouthed as planes pass worryingly close to the top of the grandstand on their descent into Belfast City Airport. Over in West Belfast, Cliftonville's Solitude is two years its senior and the oldest football ground in Ireland. Similarly, it is a veritable time capsule and worth anyone's time. But the Oval has it all and then some, a lasting monument to its people and the British game as a whole.

Ibrox

GLASGOW // SCOTLAND // RANGERS

Ibrox is the most complete visual encapsulation of Scottish football past and present. On one hand a monumental time capsule of preserved heritage, on the other a fully functioning modern arena which excels in the 21st century. Fulham's Craven Cottage may offer a softer, more appealing grandeur in keeping with its leafy surrounds but in the diminishing landscape of period British football grounds, Ibrox stands as a dignified giant.

Whether momentous or tragic, there is little Ibrox hasn't witnessed in its 125 years, from six-figure crowds and the fiercest of all rivalries to the 1938 King's speech which became the source material for the film of the same name 72 years later. It is where Britain's greatest-ever club manager Sir Alex Ferguson learned the game on his weekly pilgrimage as a Rangers-mad boy and it is where two of British football's worst disasters occurred. An ever-present through Glasgow's wealthy shipbuilding heyday and on through the mass unemployment and urban decay of the 1970s and 80s, Ibrox has always been a beacon of hope for the city's blue half.

With such a long and often distinguished history it is easy to forget where it all started and indeed, just how nomadic the fledgling Rangers were. Having begun in May 1872 at Flesher's Haugh on Glasgow Green, an open parkland which by 1914 had 14 individual football pitches marked out, Rangers moved to Burnbank Park in the Woodhills areas on 11 September 1875. For a single season only, Burnbank Bank became the club's first regular home. Now covered by the sandstone tenements on Barrington Drive, it was while

CASTORE
BETTER NEVER STOPS
CASTORE
BETTER NEVER STOPS
IBROX
THIS IS OUR
HOME

RANGERS F. C.

With a capacity of 50,987, a far cry from the 118,987 that gathered in 1939, Ibrox is nowadays a tight, boxy arena which, with fans so close to the pitch, is perhaps the most intimidating football ground in Britain.

here that Moses McNeil was capped by Scotland, thus becoming Rangers' first international. Next stop was Kinning Park, former home of the Clydesdale Cricket Club, where Rangers kicked off on 2 September 1876 in front of 1,500 against Vale of Leven. Their stay was brief and although the club had earmarked a new ground in Strathbungo, the idea of having their new, 'rougher' supporter element as neighbours didn't sit well with locals. And so to Ibrox they went in 1887.

Miles from Kelvingrove Park where the seeds of the club had been sown in March 1872, the former Govan suburb of Ibrox was in 1887 little more than open countryside. But with Ibrox train station close by and skilled shipyard workers moving into the area, it represented an excellent new catchment area for the club. The first incarnation of Ibrox Park went up quickly with a 300ft-long wooden grandstand and opposite, a pitch-length uncovered terrace. But by the early 1890s the 15,000 capacity was beginning to prove inadequate for the Rangers support which, by virtue of the club's first league title and first Scottish Cup victory, was expanding exponentially. Perhaps more pertinent was that another club from across the city with whom Rangers had begun to have some serious beef had just left a similarly unsuitable ground and built themselves a fine new 60,000-capacity stadium. When opened in 1892, a journalist reported that Celtic's move 200 yards along Janefield Street was like 'leaving the graveyard to enter paradise'. With that, in December 1899 Rangers moved 200 yards along their own Copland Street and opened their all-new improved Ibrox.

Having caught wind of the planned new stadium, a young up-and-coming local engineer from Glasgow's East End named Archibald Leitch approached the club to offer his services for free. Of course, it is not the first nor last time we will hear of Leitch in these pages, a man whose final resting place in Chiswick Cemetery may be nondescript but whose prewar British stadium designs were among the finest ever built. With a south-side grandstand and a capacity of 80,000 (with 66,000 accommodated on wooden terracing), the latest Ibrox was immediately championed. But just three years later, during a Scotland v England international, 26 fans died and hundreds more were injured when a section of the west terrace collapsed. Although Leitch would face an intense grilling at the subsequent inquiry, his reputation miraculously remained intact. Over the next 20 years Arsenal, Liverpool, Manchester United, Everton, Tottenham Hotspur and Fulham would all call on Leitch's services and despite having settled in London by 1909, his development of his beloved Rangers' Ibrox home was seen through to completion.

Opened on 1 January 1929, his stand on Edmiston Drive is arguably the most recognisable in British football. According to Simon Inglis, it is Leitch's 'greatest work', something that is hard to argue with. Even in the 21st century the frontage of what is now the Bill Struth Main Stand retains a lofty stateliness and an air of the industrial architecture of the day. Two months after its opening, work began on another great 'brick cathedral', London's Battersea Power Station. Leitch's use of Welsh red brick would go on to inform the entire appearance of Ibrox in the intervening years. After giving up its original oval shape in the aftermath of the second Ibrox disaster, when 66 fans lost their lives in a catastrophic crush in 1971, stands built in a similar colour began to be added on the three remaining sides. By 1994 the Bill Struth Main Stand had an extra tier and a new roof which tied the overall internal appearance of the stadium together.

With a capacity of 50,987, a far cry from the 118,987 that gathered in 1939, Ibrox is nowadays a tight, boxy arena which, with fans so close to the pitch, is perhaps the most intimidating football ground in Britain. Most importantly, it is now a safe and comfortable home for Scotland's joint-most successful club. In panelled rooms in the belly of Leitch's grandstand where wood polish permeates the air, those innumerable successes are preserved in glass cabinets crammed with gleaming trophies. Inside and outside, Ibrox is a living, breathing museum from which everyone with an interest in the game can learn.

Estadio Silvestre Carrillo

SANTA CRUZ DE LA PALMA // SPAIN // CD MENSAJERO

In Werner Herzog's 1982 film *Fitzcarraldo*, the titular character played by Klaus Kinski forces a group of Amazonian tribesmen to haul a dismantled steamship up and over a mountain and onto a parallel river system. The incongruity of that scene, a 320-ton boat marooned halfway up a slope, is seared into celluloid legend, symbolic of the victory of the weightlessness of dreams over the heaviness of reality. Such themes can be applied to Estadio Silvestre Carrillo, not least its visual impact on the landscape.

This football stadium on the tiny island of La Palma, illogically wedged into the far end of a steep tropical ravine and elongated to ships proportions due to the lack of space, is as preposterous as it is striking. Walking up Avenida del Puente from Santa Cruz de la Palma, the island's capital, it looms into view like a stranded ocean liner tossed out of the ocean by a tsunami, a vision in red and white against the verdant greenery of the valley's cacti, tabaiba and dragon blood trees. Upon visiting for the first time, I am sure I wasn't alone with my first thought being 'this just shouldn't be here'. Estadio Silvestre Carrillo's existence is certainly a result of La Palma's mountainous topography where flat land is at a premium, but building it in such a challenging spot is indeed a victory for a few dreamers overcoming the heaviness of reality.

Despite CD Mensajero's paradisal location, their story is as volcanic and unpredictable as the island itself. A century of feuding with cross-valley rivals SD Tenisca continues to this day, a result of unresolved claims over which club are La Palma's oldest. Tenisca refute Mensajero's claims of being founded in 1916, vehemently arguing that Mensajero came into existence as a result of their own players forming a breakaway club. To the outsider, this may be seen as trivial, a petty grievance, but on a remote island 300km off the coast of the African continent, rich in its passion for the game, such accolades are worth fighting for. In 1983 this is exactly what the two clubs did. Often referred to as the most violent game in the history of Spanish football, the derby at Estadio Silvestre Carrillo descended into such on-field brutality it made the Battle of Santiago look like an under-9s game in comparison. Grainy video footage of the game shows a barbarous carnival of upper cuts, high kicks and headbutts amongst which the referee picks himself up off the dirt pitch multiple times.

The move from the old pitch adjacent to the black sands of Bajamar beach, shared with Tenisca, and up into the valleys north of Santa Cruz had been driven by the club's first president Silvestre Carrillo in a bid to escape the fierce Atlantic winds.

It led to 48-game sanctions and 25,000-peseta fines for those involved. Estadio Silvestre Carrillo's location in Barranco de los Dolores, known locally as the Ravine of Sorrows, seems perfectly apt.

Six years earlier, on 17 December 1977, Mensajero played their opening game at their new stadium. The move from the old pitch adjacent to the black sands of Bajamar beach, shared with Tenisca, and up into the valleys north of Santa Cruz had been driven by the club's first president Silvestre Carrillo in a bid to escape the fierce Atlantic winds. A plot of land, overgrown with ancient orchards and littered with rockslide debris was purchased by Carrillo and he tasked his players, fans and friends to clear the site. As we have seen in previous chapters, where there is great will and many hands it is possible to create something special although it took almost three years for the first incarnation of Estadio Silvestre Carrillo to be realised.

In 1999 the stadium was remodelled with further excavation of the north and east sides to allow new larger terraces to be built. At the eastern end, six storeys of office space were tucked underneath the new terrace, the pitch on top, and it is these which give the stadium the illusion from the outside of one much larger than its capacity of 6,000.

It is impossible to tell the story of Mensajero without introducing Pepe Pérez Rodríguez here, a lifelong Mensa supporter and a man with a van. Pepe's truck was used almost exclusively to move those rocks from the site and once football began at the new ground, Pepe took to watching his team from a cave, known as 'La Cueva de Pepe' high up on the southern face of the ravine. From here Pepe was able to gather a few friends, have a drink and ruminate whilst overseeing every game Mensajero played from a plastic garden chair directly above the pitch. Following his death in 2014, the club placed a banner at the entrance to the cave in honour of their greatest, if not most eccentric, supporter. To this day, the club's supporters' group Peña de la Bocana sing a ditty in tribute to the immovable Pepe: 'Going up the ravine, through the ravine of Dolores, there is a soccer field that belongs to one of the best teams.'

In 1999 the stadium was remodelled with further excavation of the north and east sides to allow new larger terraces to be built. At the eastern end, six storeys of office space were tucked underneath the new terrace, the pitch on top, and it is these which give the stadium the

illusion from the outside of one much larger than its capacity of 6,000. As the road tapers out at the opposite end, the pitch sits at street level demonstrating the sharp gradient of the land it sits upon. The changing rooms, club offices and TV platforms are all built up hard against the southern face of the ravine meaning Estadio Silvestre Carrillo is very much a three-sided football ground. Small as it is however, Mensajero have played 12 seasons in the third tier of the Spanish league system here, regularly welcoming visitors from upwards of 2,000km from the mainland. Atlético Madrid and Real Zaragoza have played here in the Copa del Rey, highlighting Mensajero's recent history as one of continual overachieving and success. For the Canarias archipelago's football giants CD Tenerife and UD Las Palmas, success at national level is expected. Yet for Mensajero and their crowds of barely 1,000, to compete at this level is nothing short of remarkable.

During the months of September and October 2021, the western flanks of La Palma's Cumbre Vieja volcano were decimated by syrupy roiling lava flows rolling east to west. In its path, entire villages were engulfed, one particular video showing the football stadium of La Laguna being swallowed beneath the flow. On the opposite side of the volcanic ridge however, and less than 20km from the crater, Mensajero continued their season at Estadio Silvestre Carrillo unaffected against Villanovense and Antequera from the mainland. For Mensajero are fighters, continually punching above their weight and all within a stadium that is perfectly ship-shape.

010
Craven Cottage
LONDON // ENGLAND // FULHAM
London's Original Football Club
Fulham v Brentford

Fulham's new addition to their grand old lady carries with it a level of sophistication hitherto unseen at the humble British football ground. When fully opened, the Riverside Stand will contain a pair of restaurants staffed with Michelin-starred chefs while three of the topmost floors will be given over to a 'Sky Deck' (complete with an open air swimming pool) that will offer unparalleled views across London and beyond. What is certain is that the eye-watering prices will be divisive among the Fulham fanbase. It will undoubtedly be a game-changer in the corporate world of the Premier League, but for those lifelong supporters recently spotted holding placards reading 'please don't price us out' in response to an 18 per cent increase in ticket prices, such unaffordable luxury may not be so welcome.

Before we are able to fully scrutinise the new Riverside Stand's impact on club and stadium, however, we must rest assured that lead architect Philip Johnson has given full respect to Craven Cottage's historic character. Working with a palette of light-grey brick to reflect Fulham's club colours, its integration has been carefully coordinated so as not to detract from its classic components. Archibald Leitch's Grade II-listed Johnny Haynes Stand may now find itself faced with a partner twice its height but by swerving any temptation for something bolder, the hard lines and slim subtlety skilfully complement the early 20th-century elegance. Most importantly it will increase Craven Cottage's capacity by 5,000 to 29,600, which although small by Premier League standards, will ensure Fulham's home of almost 130 years will be fit for many years to come.

When opened on 10 October 1896, Craven Cottage was fringed by market gardens and accessed by farm tracks off Fulham Palace Road.

It is a far cry from the days when stripped to the waist after a game, players would wash from zinc bowls placed on a bench outside the dressing rooms having first scraped away an accumulation of grime. When opened on 10 October 1896, Craven Cottage was fringed by market gardens and accessed by farm tracks off Fulham Palace Road. The site had lain abandoned and overgrown since the original cottage built in 1780 for the Countess of Craven had been destroyed by fire eight years earlier. Before the godfather of stadium architecture was brought in to oversee the development of the site, a

Following an aborted attempt to merge Fulham with Arsenal to create a 'London superclub' in the early 20th century and after 1933's plans to demolish the ground in favour of a new 80,000-capacity stadium were scuppered by the Great Depression, Craven Cottage ticked along as the home of one of the capital's footballing underdogs.

hastily constructed grandstand known as the 'Rabbit Hutch' by fans and the 'Orange Box Stand' by the press had stood on Stevenage Road. Perhaps only Wrexham's Racecourse Ground can lay claim to having had a more peculiar stand in English football, the 'Pigeon Loft' a repurposed balcony from a nearby cinema erected high above the Town End terracing. The 'Rabbit Hutch' was to all intents and purposes four separate wooden stands each capable of holding 300 with a gabled corrugated iron roof above each. It didn't last long and was condemned having been deemed dangerous by London County Council after just 18 months of service.

With this, landowners and club directors Sir Henry Norris and W.G. Allen (who at the time were busy developing much of the housing we see now around Craven Cottage) sought to secure the services of Archibald Leitch. Fresh from his Ibrox Park commission in Glasgow and having previously designed numerous factories in the city, of which only the Sentinel Works in Polmadie remains, Leitch was a man in demand. Indeed, it is said that while the construction of the Johnny Haynes Stand was in full swing, he would regularly nip across to Stamford Bridge to oversee his firm's work on Chelsea's new ground. Working with the same distinguishing red brick that had given Ibrox its character, for a sum of £15,000 (a record at the time) Leitch gave Fulham a new grandstand and pavilion which over the next 100 years would become recognised as two of the finest examples of his work in the field of football stadium architecture.

Until 1933 the pavilion operated without electricity but still functioned as a one-bedroom flat for the Craven Cottage caretaker. By the mid-1920s club captain Alec Chaplin had moved in with his wife and four children. On one occasion in 1926, from their bedroom on the second floor, Chaplin overheard the club directors below voting to sack then manager Andy Ducat. The pavilion continued to serve as Fulham's offices and hospitality area until the club moved operations to Motspur Park in the 1990s. Although I have never been inside myself, I am reliably told that the manager's office in particular was little bigger than a broom cupboard. More than any other structure on the site, it is Leitch's pavilion that is most cherished. Some would go so far as to say it is the single most iconic structure in English football following the loss of Wembley's twin towers. Certainly it is the most romantic.

Following an aborted attempt to merge Fulham with Arsenal to create a 'London

superclub' in the early 20th century and after 1933's plans to demolish the ground in favour of a new 80,000-capacity stadium were scuppered by the Great Depression, Craven Cottage ticked along as the home of one of the capital's footballing underdogs. They were the last club in the old English First Division to erect floodlights and it took until 1972 and the sale of Alan Mullery to Tottenham Hotspur to cover the Hammersmith End. Indeed, when I first stood on Craven Cottage's then uncovered Putney End terrace in 1996 it had the unvalued appearance typical of a club languishing in the third tier of the English game: scruffy, outdated and in need of some serious attention.

What has taken place here since 1998's renovation of Leitch's Johnny Haynes Stand facade is nothing short of miraculous. A two-year stint across Hammersmith at QPR's Loftus Road in the early 2000s gave Fulham time to consider their options. They spent £8m on the refurbishment of Craven Cottage which when completed in 2004 brought it in line with Premier League requirements. Twenty years on with the club now a prominent member of English football's elite, Craven Cottage manages to blend the opulence of the modern game with the almost twee charm of its beginnings. It is a standalone example of what can be achieved when history is honoured. Put simply, Craven Cottage is the most beautiful football ground in England's professional game.

009

Stadion Kantrida

RIJEKA // CROATIA // NK OPATIJA

Hunkering down in a hollow beneath the city, Stadion Kantrida has now been kissed by sea breezes and dusted by sand for over a century. With only the tops of the floodlights, monstrously huge at road height, giving any indication of what lies below, seeing Kantrida from the Istarska road for the first time is awe-inspiring, even for those with no interest in football.

Peering down over a 3ft wall and a sheer vertical rock face, Kantrida reveals itself as a vivid patch of green in a landscape a thousand shades of blue. Ringed by an oxblood running track, without its athletics meets it would likely not have made it this far. Beyond, the Adriatic Sea rolls off towards the horizon, mostly serene but at times savage and squalling, distant islands piercing the blue. Kantrida's lone grandstand stands framed by water on the southern edge, its facade given a nautical touch with balconies and staircases painted sea blue giving it the appearance of an old-world cruise liner. Flanked by simple curves of open seating, everything is carefully designed to blend with the vista right down to 1975's floodlight columns which mimic ship masts, guarding Kantrida from approaching seafaring enemies. Ingeniously, their opposite numbers have been erected upon horizontal pads carved into the vertiginous rock face. Barely one metre above sea level, Kantrida has become one of the most recognisable football stadiums in Europe. It is testament to what can be achieved when sheer will and bloody-mindedness prevails among a few dreamers to overcome nature's obstacles.

Although the construction of a football stadium in a quarry is not unknown, particularly in Croatia where in Pula and Žurkovo much smaller grounds were carved out of abandoned mines, Kantrida's uniqueness lies in its topography of sea, rock and urbanisation. The fact that international and European club football have regularly been played here makes it even more remarkable. Its story begins early one summer's morning in 1912. Five long-distance runners from the Sušacka Victoria club, out training on the coastal road between Rijeka and Volosko, found themselves resting on a wall high above the Kantrida quarry. Looking down upon a vast saucerful of stone, the athletes joked about the possibility of turning it into a football field. A seed had been sown and returning the next day with a litre of wine, they descended into the quarry and discovered to their surprise that the earth beneath piled stone was entirely flat. Yesterday's laughable idea of building a football pitch in a pit of stone, just yards away from the water of the Adriatic Sea, suddenly didn't seem quite as funny.

Whether or not Tona Margan and his friends saw the location's visual appeal or just its practical use is purely conjecture but their will to move mountains in the quest for a sports field away from the little pitch in Pioppi became all the motivation the young athletes needed. The very same evening the group learned that the Kantrida quarry (which had been used for stone extraction in the building of the port of Rijeka and its breakwaters) was no longer used. Talks soon began with its owners, the Istrian Municipality of Kastav, who rented the site to Hungarian quarrying company Schwarz & Gregerson. Within weeks, permission had been granted to lease the site to the students of Victoria and funds raised to develop Kantrida.

By December, Margan, his friends and the entire Victoria football team were arriving at dawn every Sunday, leaving long after darkness fell to clear the site. Six hundred carts of stone were moved and many larger stones buried nearby. Centre-half Forenpocher

By 1 June 1913, Kantrida was ready for its grand opening match between Victoria and the Gradanski club of Zagreb, then one of the finest teams in the Croatia-Slavonia football championship.

With the city's promise that the club would be reinstated at a new, state-of-the-art Kantrida stadium in a few years, the future looked bright for both club and ground. However, by 2016 the project had stalled as planning permission for various accompanying developments such as a hotel and shopping centre could not be obtained.

procured beams for goalposts while reserve goalkeeper Blasich wove nets with a leftover rope used to tie parcels. A calligrapher among the team's ranks created a beautiful sign which was erected at the entrance to the ground. A grass pitch was still some decades off but the football rolled true across earth. By 1 June 1913, Kantrida was ready for its grand opening match between Victoria and the Građanski club of Zagreb, then one of the finest teams in the Croatia-Slavonia football championship. Within the space of a year, the little joke among a few ambitious friends had resulted in a playing field that over the next 100 years would play host to Juventus and Real Madrid, Dino Zoff, Joe Jordan and Luka Modrić.

Kantrida remains an indispensable part of the visual identity of Rijeka. Through 100 years of changes to the old quarry, the industrial, social and cultural development of the city can be traced. It goes some way to explaining why the people of Rijeka are so emotionally connected to the place. In July 2015, with Kantrida deemed unsuitable for modern football, HNK Rijeka bade an emotional farewell and decamped to a hastily constructed stadium built on land in Rujevica. With the city's promise that the club would be reinstated at a new, state-of-the-art Kantrida stadium in a few years, the future looked bright for both club and ground. However, by 2016 the project had stalled as planning permission for various accompanying developments such as a hotel and shopping centre could not be obtained. Although the stadium itself had been given the green light, investors had made it clear that the commercial part was crucial to the entire project's feasibility and an impasse was reached, much to the anger of the supporters. The clamour to return to their spiritual home, not least from the Rijeka Armada Ultras faction grew and in 2018, the Armada brought their team back home for a friendly against NK Maribor which attracted a crowd of over

10,000. Finally in 2019 a memorandum of understanding was signed between Stadion Kantrida LLC and Chinese construction company SCEGC regarding the construction of a new stadium on the existing site.

While the wait for HNK Rijeka to return home continues and Kantrida rusts and peels in the sea air, third division side NK Opatija have taken up residence at the stadium. It's a far cry from the days when 22,000 would squeeze in with many more climbing the cliff for a perch with a view (the capacity was slashed to 10,500 in 1999). On matchdays the Istarska road is still lined with casual viewers but instead of thousands of Armada belting out the Rijeka hymn down below, the only sounds are of the referee's whistle and the occasional thwack as a ball bounces off the rocks. For the sake of this iconic football stadium, we can only hope the spirit of Tona Margan and friends lives on within those looking to bring back professional football to Kantrida.

008

Stadio Renato Dall'Ara

BOLOGNA // ITALY // BOLOGNA 1909

It is possible to walk the 3km from Bologna's city centre to Stadio Renata Dall'Ara almost entirely under the cover of the city's famous porticos. As the capital of Italy's third-rainiest region, therefore, there is the very real prospect of getting wetter inside than out by virtue of the fact Renato Dall'Ara is still two-thirds uncovered.

Writing this a week on from Bologna's highest Serie A finish in over 50 years, however, this may soon change. Although strategies to bring the old girl in line with the modern game have been floated regularly over the years, this time there is a feeling among the Bolognese that finally something is about to happen. The designs presented in 2023 look sublime, a sympathetic but bold connecting of old and new which if it comes off will transform Stadio Dall'Ara into an even finer specimen than it already is. Italian football's old friend bureaucracy will almost certainly make an appearance before any shovel is lifted but with the Champions League back in *La Dotta* for the first time since 1964/65, the time is right.

For a stadium that has been so entrenched in the lives of the football-loving people of Bologna, it has served its time and served it well. But ask any fan of the *Rossoblù* if they would prefer a move away and to a man, woman and child they will tell you their football team is nothing without Stadio Dall'Ara. The stadium's relationship with the municipality is one that works too; tucked out of sight in the far south-west of the city it already sits in a most agreeable location. Like so many of its contemporaries built under Mussolini's fascist dictatorship, it was another known as Stadio Littoriale (see Chapter 94) when opened on 29 May 1927 for an international between Italy and Spain. Architect Giulio Ulisse Arata and engineer Umberto Costanzini had been awarded the contract to design the stadium shortly after Bologna's first of seven Serie A titles. With Arata fresh from a commission to redesign the recovery of Bologna's historic centre after the First World War, his intimate working knowledge of the city would inform every aspect of the stadium.

As the world's original city of towers, the continued presence of Arata's Marathon Tower neatly knits together Bologna's past and present. Between the 12th and 13th centuries an estimated 80 to 100 slender stone towers (some more than 90m tall) crowded and leaned precariously above the city centre. Dante referred to the Garisenda tower in *Inferno*, 'From underneath its leaning side, and then a cloud passes over and it seems to lean the more.' Including Garisenda, fewer than 20 remain but of those that do, it is the thicker-bodied gateway towers that most resemble Stadio Dall'Ara's Marathon Tower.

Straddling the Portico di San Luca (the world's longest covered walkway), it is itself a gateway into the east stand and until 1943 it was festooned with fascistic ornamentation: framed by a tall arch on the second level, a gaudy bronze statue of Mussolini on horseback stood facing out over the pitch. When the end came for Il Duce, it was melted down and used to cast likenesses of two partisans who fought to depose him. While we should not forget that both stadium and tower were among the first built under Mussolini's rule to serve as a symbol of the regime's power, it is still a hugely impressive focal point. When eventually the lid goes on Stadio Dall'Ara, its design indicates there will be a shallow dip on the eastern side allowing the tower to still be seen from inside.

By the early 1980s both Bologna and their stadium were in a bad place. For the first time in the club's history, at the end of 1981/82 they were relegated out of Serie A, something even Roberto Mancini couldn't stop with his nine goals that season. It was an unthinkable ignominy for such a powerhouse of the Italian game but a year later it got a whole lot worse when they slid into Serie C. Meanwhile, Stadio Dall'Ara was in such poor condition it was feared that without financial support needed for repairs it would have to be closed. The lifeline came in 1987. With the *Rossoblù* back in Serie B, Bologna was selected as a host city for the 1990 World Cup. The cost of the stadium soared beyond the government's grant but by the time the tournament came around, Stadio Dall'Ara had a whole new second tier and space for an additional 9,000. For supporters of England the stadium will forever be remembered as the one where David Platt scored 'that goal'. Conversely, it is also the stadium England supporters would like to forget as the one where San Marino scored 'that goal'.

Those who have visited both would agree that Stadio Dall'Ara and nearby Florence's Stadio Artemio Franchi were cut from a similar

As the world's original city of towers, the continued presence of Arata's Marathon Tower neatly knits together Bologna's past and present.

cloth. Designed under the same political influence and opened four years apart, there is fundamentally not a great difference between the pair in terms of size, layout and both having a powerful identity. I have discovered through conversations with Italians, however, that although both have countless devotees, fans not specific to either club tend to strongly like one but not the other. The inference is that the devil is in the details: Giulio Ulisse Arata's chunky classicism executed in the same warm brick tones that permeates so much of Bologna versus Pier Luigi Nervi's slimline geometry rendered in cool reinforced concrete. Both are earmarked for imminent redevelopment and it will be interesting to see who gets there first.

For Stadio Dall'Ara the plan is for a stylish new roof of transparent polycarbonate panels below which the removal of the track would see stands brought in tighter to the pitch. Outside, stripped of the clumsy steel web erected to support 1990's extra tier, the delightful two-storey red-brick frontage with its abundance of arched windows and doors would at last be given room to breathe again. With such an impeccable record in Italian football marked by only the briefest of misfires, Bologna deserves a stadium this good. Moreover, for a century of unwavering world-class support their fans have earned it.

For the most part Union were a club consigned to the history books, the average Belgian supporter likely even unaware of their continued existence in the depths of the country's league system.

Stade Joseph Marien

BRUSSELS // BELGIUM // ROYALE UNION SAINT-GILLOISE

For the majority of Bruxellois, the name Royale Union Saint-Gilloise would have conjured little recognition a decade ago. Perhaps only in the amber glow of a quiet backstreet *estaminet* would you have caught a conversation among octogenarians, recalling with hushed reverence names such as Daring, Racing, Léopold Football Club and Union, Brussels' original pioneers of the game. For the most part Union were a club consigned to the history books, the average Belgian supporter likely even unaware of their continued existence in the depths of the country's league system. Before we get to what locals are calling 'the fairytale', we need to wind back the clock to when industrial Brussels was booming and daring was indeed the order of day.

With the Belgian game still in its infancy and before its many delightful intricacies were mapped out, Union had already won seven league titles by 1914. Taking on the mantle from Racing Club and FC Liégeois (with five and three titles respectively in the first eight years of competition), Union would dominate for the next ten years from a cramped pitch on Rue de Forest. Brussels at the time was experiencing rapid economic growth and a widening middle class whose interest in football was fast approaching fever pitch. The popularity of its trailblazers was such that their football grounds had within a few short years become unfit for purpose, leaving most scrabbling for land on which to build larger, more comfortable homes to accommodate their newfound audiences.

Union themselves were in 1909 offered 2.5 uncultivated hectares of Parc Duden by the Donation Royale in Forest, a then burgeoning commune of brewing, printing and mechanical engineering a mile south of Saint-Gilles. The Donation had been founded in 1900 for the purpose of giving back to the nation land and buildings acquired by King Leopold II during his lifetime. A 30-year lease was agreed with the club but with the catch that any installations built on the site would be returned to the administration at the end without any compensation. Thankfully that situation never arose following an agreement spearheaded by club president Joseph Marien in 1923 to pay the Donation a portion of gate receipts in return for a new long-term lease. The construction of the stadium (then known as Stade de la Butte from its location at the bottom of the park which itself is the city's highest point) began in 1915 and continued through the First World War. Opened on 14 September 1919 for a gala match with AC Milan, it was an instant hit with supporters but it still had a long way to go before becoming the beautiful stadium we now recognise as the pinnacle of Belgium's 1920s sporting pomp.

Since 1761, the word 'grandstand' has been used to describe seating for spectators at an outdoor event. At the turn of the 20th century, however, its usage as a verb to characterise someone or something 'showing off' entered European vocabulary from its origins in American baseball slang. Albert Callewaert's design for Union's new main stand was, and to this day still is, a grandstanding grandstand. With the bricky opulence of Leitch's 1905 Stevenage Road stand at Craven Cottage and art deco stylings of Highbury's East Stand, it remains one of football's most flamboyant surviving period pieces. Callewaert's first proposal for the stadium's remodelling in 1921 had been rejected in favour of maintaining the existing stands while modestly increasing the site's capacity. Undeterred, however, the 33-year-

In a style symbolic of architectural renewal, one that throws off the fussy shackles of art nouveau and those recalling the atrocities of the Great War, Union's Stade Joseph Marien featuring Callewaert's masterpiece was opened on 29 August 1926.

old architect went back to Marien in February 1922 with a new, more architecturally exciting design that immediately piqued the interest of the club. It wouldn't come cheap (600,000 francs) and before any work could even begin Union found themselves embroiled in a struggle to hold on to the site, which had fallen under the threat of being expropriated for the building of a new hotel. This was averted when Marien signed the aforementioned long-term lease, allowing demolition of the old stadium to begin.

In a style symbolic of architectural renewal, one that throws off the fussy shackles of art nouveau and those recalling the atrocities of the Great War, Union's Stade Joseph Marien featuring Callewaert's masterpiece was opened on 29 August 1926. Renowned Brussels sculptor Oscar de Clerck had created seven panels depicting in a semi-cubist style scenes of football and athletics, the two sports that Union had thoroughly mastered. Embedded above the seven main windows on the grandstand's facade, the display serves as a precursor to the reliefs on the 1937 Palais de Chaillot opposite the Eiffel Tower, one of the art deco movement's most celebrated buildings. Above each are seven 'USG' motifs then an array of decorative rooftop finials, every panel, relief, ornament and window frame built in concrete and set within recessed brickwork of varying patterns which curve subtly at each end of the stand. After almost a century of Brussels smog, the exterior has aged to resemble the facade of a prewar factory.

Inside, even the most recent modernisations that were needed for 'the fairytale' to happen here cannot disguise Stade Joseph Marien's age and unsuitability going forwards. Huge swathes of steep terracing (buried under decades-old trees and bushes when I first visited for a third-tier game in front of 700 in 2007) have either been patched up or given seats but with Union's astonishing return to the big time in 2021, it is very much an anomaly on the map of European stadiums hosting top-level football and one the club desperately wish to move out of. Three successive seasons of Champions League football have led to virtually all games at the now 9,400-capacity stadium selling out. A new hipster fanbase has arrived, Gazelles, bucket hats and handlebar moustaches replacing the Homburgs, overcoats and walrus moustaches that were seen here when Union were last this good. Renovation remains impossible with Parc Duden's status as a protected green space and Stade Joseph Marien classified as an important heritage site. Wherever the future takes Union, it is reassuring to learn that they plan to move their ladies' and youth teams into the old ground when a new stadium is built. For a club that resonates with historic significance and a home of such vintage, it sounds like the perfect end to the latest chapter of the fairytale.

Stadion Gospin Dolac

IMOTSKI // CROATIA // NK IMOTSKI

Across the past two and a half decades, so many superlatives have been laid at the feet of Our Lady of Angels stadium that it's difficult to imagine an online top ten of the world's most unique football stadiums without it. Imotski has become a byword for the beautiful ground, a bucket-list topper, a window into a world where the formulaic ground of western Europe is turned on its head. Like many in this book, we owe its existence to the vision of a single romantic and the sweat of the local townsfolk.

I remember when I first set eyes upon Stadion Gospin Dolac. It was early 1997, the world wide web was a novelty and I was half-heartedly answering complaints in a call centre while simultaneously working out which of Alta Vista or Google got the best results. A search for Zvonimir Boban, then captain of the Croatia national team, led me to his birthplace and from there to the town's football team. A postage stamp-sized image appeared and clicking on it, I was transported through a revolving door and into another realm. Without realising, this is what I had been looking for. In a year that Bolton, Derby and Stoke would add to the UK's growing list of unremarkable new stadiums, here was a ground like no other. One hewn into an Elvish otherworld, backdropped by distant craggy summits and 1,000-year-old Illyrian fortress, a lake of opaque turquoise formed in a sinkhole behind. Variations of the image have since become well-known among lovers of the game but they still provoke a similar response.

It took 14 more years for me to visit and I have since gone back a further two times. Each time biblical rains have come down, clattering the terracing like keys on that old computer. Rivendell mists have rolled in, shrouding Imotski in an eerie veil. Three times I have retreated to a nearby bar in the town square, wringing wet. And still Gospin Dolac, if not quite the greatest ground in Europe, remains my favourite. Without it, this book would likely not exist.

In a town where everything is either uphill or down, Imotski's footballing history between 1927 and 1954 is one of steep dead-ends. Prewar pioneers of the game Zagorac and NK ISK had forged a fierce rivalry and with it, a wave of enthusiasm for football grew among locals. Yet as in Positano across the Adriatic, Imotksi's arch-nemesis was its topography; the near vertical terrain stifled the game's development as

down on the coast in Split, football boomtime arrived. Matches were played in the stony meadows of Perinuša and Konjevodama far below the town or at 'Plac', a rough earth pitch which stood where the marketplace is today. Things improved slightly in the early 1950s when a new mini-football field next to the town's gymnasium was built, a pitch where Boban would hone his skills. But it was with the return of Fulgencije Fudo Vučemilovic to Imotski in 1954 that the first seeds were sown for a new stadium in town.

Fudo, a charismatic chameleon with no lack of talent, had been a Croatian pop singer who reinvented himself in Brazil and Argentina as a successful football coach under the moniker Aldo Valentini. Witnessing the development of the game in South America first-hand, upon visits home he would speak unabashedly of the need for a stadium in Imotski. On 4 August 1954 over drinks with friends in Imotski's City Cafe, Fudo first laid out his idea in the typically casual manner of the Imot folk. 'We shall build a stadium beneath the Topana Fortress,' adding, 'One day, it will become a real wonder of the world.' Yugoslavia's breakaway from Moscow influence after the Tito-Stalin split a few years earlier had left its people emboldened, open to ideas and with Fudo's respected status in the town, the idea stuck. The fact it took 34 years for Stadion Gospin Dolac to be fully realised only serves to emphasise the people of Imotski's unwavering feeling for such an outlandish concept.

The site beneath Topana Fortress was Jelavića dolac, one of the three enormous karst sinkholes on the eastern fringes of Imotski created by the collapse of ancient cave systems. Whereas Crveno jezero and Modro jezero (the Red and Blue Lakes) were formed, shaped and flooded over centuries by underground waters from Herzegovina,

Jelavića dolac remained dry, its depth much less than its neighbours. A photograph taken long before the stadium shows a precipitous hillside falling away from Topana fortress to a point 28 metres lower than where the pitch sits now, the upper land crisscrossed with paths and trails. Although the land was privately owned by the Elavići family, it was a place much loved by Imotski's young sweethearts who would descend and shortcut their way through it from town to the Blue Lake to swim and picnic.

While Fuđo's dream lived on in the imagination of the town's sports enthusiasts, nothing happened for over two decades and Imotski remained devoid of a decent football team and stadium with the Zagorac and NK ISK clubs having folded after the Second World War. It took the building of a dam and reservoir in the nearby village of Ričice in 1976 to reignite the dream. Fuđo's merry band of devotees jumped in, begging and bartering for truckloads of earth, borrowing heavy machinery for a few hours as the Jelavića dolac sinkhole slowly began to be filled in. It is estimated that tens of thousands of cubic metres of earth were poured into its centre as the height was raised and levelled. A large portion of the land was owned by the family of Mate Parlov, a Yugoslavian boxer who had won a gold medal at the Munich Olympics in 1972 and latterly became the first professional world champion from a communist country. Parlov's family further encouraged the project and use of the land and through such stories of sporting partnership coupled with the Croat people's collective desire to overcome obstacles, we can trace a line of how an independent Croatia became the sporting anomaly we now know, a country of barely four million achieving sporting greatness.

Fudo's merry band of devotees jumped in, begging and bartering for truckloads of earth, borrowing heavy machinery for a few hours as the Jelavića dolac sinkhole slowly began to be filled in.

With the site now renamed Gospin Dolac after the small church next to the fortress, work ground to a halt in the mid-1970s, the kitty empty, until the Association for Physical Culture took over the work together with the local government in 1980. By 1988, the stadium was ready for its finishing flourishes and it is estimated that half the townsfolk of Imotski, both young and old, came together to lay the pitch, paint and install signage and construct pathways which would pave the way for the likes of Luka Modrić, Ante Rebić and Eden Hazard to play football here. Gospin Dolac still needed a football team, however, and as Croatia declared independence in 1991, NK Imotski were founded and proceeded to climb through the regional leagues to reach the second division by 2006.

Yet the story doesn't quite end here. With Gospin Dolac's online star in the ascendency, in 2015 a young architect named Ivo Žarko from the University of Zagreb wrote a thesis for his diploma course which added a new layer of fantasy that sparked media excitement. In it, Žarko reimagined Gospin Dolac as a sleek 21st-century stadium; a single circular roof acting as a deck or open plaza where people would meet before descending into the stadium. Beneath, 5,000 seats were arranged in a more conventional shape along with a new pavilion behind the southern goal. Fascinating as the designs were, however, the reality is that in 2024, NK Imotski are playing regional football again in front of a few hundred supporters and such a stadium would be an unnecessary extravagance, not least an unaffordable one. In the immediate future, the new management of NK Imotski and the town's sporting enthusiasts will continue to come together at the close of each season to undertake more modest cosmetic tasks. Going forwards, with the cooperation of the City of Imotski, the owner of the stadium, plans include the installation of floodlights, new club rooms and another small tribune. Fuđo envisioned an arena where nature, history and sport united without detriment to the landscape. Once these final pieces are complete, we can consider Fudo's modern wonder of the world fully realised.

Estádio Municipal de Braga

BRAGA // PORTUGAL // SPORTING BRAGA

They say less is more, a principle that architect Eduardo Souto de Moura and engineer Rui Furtado fully embraced when they set about designing Estádio Municipal, Braga's new stadium for the 2004 European Championship. Very few grounds have been able to retain the visual impact they once had upon completion. Fewer still have managed to connect so successfully to the natural environment and those that have are all featured within these pages. By swerving trends and approaching their commission in a 'skin and bones' manner, the pair achieved such greatness in 2004 that seeing Estádio Municipal for the first, second and countless times thereafter still packs the same heavyweight punch 20 years on. Its €108.1m cost (including €20m to explode 1.7 million cubic metres of rock from the quarry it nestles in) represents a bargain for a stadium that jolted a generation of designers into reconsidering sport's relationship with nature.

Each approach to the Municipal is an entirely different experience, one airy and one grounded. Both are valuable in giving a feel for the singular topography of the area while offering opposing perspectives from which to begin to appreciate the enormous scale of the work that was undertaken here. From Bairro das Andorinhas, so high is the start of descent down into the stadium from the top of Monte Castro that the first sighting one has is the very top of the stand roofs. Flights of open staircases lead on to a path carved into the

From Bairro das Andorinhas, so high is the start of descent down into the stadium from the top of Monte Castro that the first sighting one has is the very top of the stand roofs.

quarry face which at a more gentle gradient carries spectators to ground level. Watching the stadium filling up from here, through gaps between two enormous rainwater-collecting gargoyles and the 30m-long LED scoreboard (the largest in Europe when built), can be quite a sight. Conversely, arriving from Dume it is the vision of the East Stand that greets supporters, reclining back among the weeping willows of the Cávado valley like a colossal concrete deckchair. Both views will have stopped thousands in their tracks and until a stadium of similar structural peculiarity comes along they will continue to do so.

Estádio Municipal's real magic, however, lies in its finer details, those above and below which are often overlooked or simply not visible. The West Stand's proximity to the quarry face means matchday access can only be made through the East Stand via a vast subterranean hypostyle beneath the pitch. If you've ever visited a cave system, coming up in the bowels of the West Stand on its series of escalators and steps is exactly like that; damp walls of rock, the occasional stalagmite, a crepuscular light and 5,504 concrete anchors bolting the structure to the rock face while simultaneously preventing landslides. As the stand rises with the same backwards tilt of that opposite, each section is supported by a new level of the rock face until near the summit, a concourse and car park on the top of the 50m quarry further supports the building from the rear.

With no quarry to lean on opposite, the East Stand instead maintains balance through its deep foundations and the thickness of its 16 upright ribs. Four tiered concourses run the length of the stand, each threaded through 16 circular portholes between which seven balconies look out over the incoming crowd. Any precariousness in the tilt is offset by Souto de

2928

Moura's palette of raw concrete and steel which gives it an encouraging solidity. If there were still any doubts, the 68,202m of steel cable strung high above the pitch from each roof adds further support. Inspiration for the slightly inclined roofs came from the suspended bridges of ancient Peru and replaced Souto de Moura's early plans for a continuous concrete slab above the pitch similar to that of his Portuguese Pavilion in Lisbon.

Souto de Moura said of his work in 2004, 'There is no ecological architecture, or intelligent architecture, or sustainable architecture – there is only good architecture.' Most football fans, including myself, will not be versed in the intricacies of architecture but all will recognise a good ground from a bad one. Souto de Moura's simplification of the art in both his words and style is something everyone can get behind: simple but different, a good piece of architecture regularly hailed as one of the world's greatest stadiums.

On the flipside, some continue to bemoan the Estádio Municipal's two-sidedness, citing the absence of stands at either end as disadvantageous in creating an atmosphere. Try telling that to Sporting fans, however, when Porto or the Champions League arrive in town. The *Arsenalistas* have learned that the harder they sing, the louder the noise bounces back off the rock face, an employing of the natural environment that would undoubtedly delight Souto de Moura. But despite being a noisy bunch, filling even a third of the stadium for lower-key matches has been a persistent worry for the club. Since 2004 the average Sporting league attendance has only three times surpassed 15,000, half the stadium's capacity. While far from the experiences suffered by Beira-Mar or Leiria in their Euro 2004 legacy homes, it still carries an element of disappointment in that such a groundbreaking arena is so rarely used to its full potential. And although less needy for international football than those stadiums, the Estádio Municipal has still only hosted four Portugal matches since 2004 and those against largely minor opposition.

Meanwhile, 270km south of Lisbon between the Atlantic beaches and golf resorts of Portugal's southern coast, Faro/Loulé's Estádio Algarve – built for the same competition – has racked up a total of 13 internationals. For a region not traditionally associated with the game, the continued favouring of Faro/Loulé as host for Portugal internationals is a curious one especially when you consider the two towns' combined population is 60,000 fewer than Braga. Still, with tickets for Sporting matches always readily available, at least those keen to experience the splendour of the Estádio Municipal first hand are able to do so. Every home match sees a host of new visitors taken under its spell. Groups travelling from far and wide, some with tag-along friends with only the faintest interest in football or architecture, are all similarly bowled over by *a Pedreira* (the Quarry). Good architecture has the ability to do that.

Pancho Aréna

FELCSÚT // HUNGARY // PUSKÁS AKADÉMIA

The story behind Hungary's Pancho Aréna is one of the strangest and most controversial in modern European club football. On the surface the stadium is an architectural triumph, a football venue heaven-sent with its myriad of ecclesiastical flourishes and rural quiet calm. Yet from inception to completion, it was the subject of deafening public outrage, a nationwide hatred from supporters' groups, and not least the murky rumblings of governmental corruption. With the dust finally settling a decade on from its opening, only now can we really begin to assess its architectural merit and place in the great pantheon of European stadiums.

At the turn of the millennium, Hungary's club football stadiums were largely decrepit relics of an era belonging to the Mighty Magyars; to Puskás, Hidegkuti, Kocsis and Bozsik. With the exception of Ujpest whose 2002 rebuilding of their Szusza Ferenc Stadion represented the first ripples of change, cracked terracing wrapped around communist-era bowls across the country from Szombathely in the west to Debrecen in the east. Even Budapest's national Népstadion, once capable of holding 104,000, was frozen in a state of stasis. For the football nostalgist, it was an evocative landscape, similar to that in Poland, Bulgaria and large swathes of Russia. All was about to change, however, with the arrival of Viktor Orbán as prime minister in 1998. Hungary's bid to host the 2004 European Championship may have been lost to Portugal, initially leaving Orbán's radical programme of rebuilding in the balance, but by the time of his second term in 2010, it picked up apace.

Between 2010 and 2020, the Hungarian government spent over £700m on stadium reconstruction and infrastructure designed to fulfil the country's sporting needs for the next 60 years. In line with this, the national team woke from their doldrums, twice reaching the European Championship finals in 2016 and 2020. It appeared that Hungary had finally caught up with neighbours Austria both on and off the pitch. Barely any traces of those famous Magyar venues remain, their names buried beneath prefabricated structures and the weight of sponsorship deals. Ferencváros demolished their Flórián Albert Stadion, rebuilding it as the Groupama Aréna. Just up the road, MTK's Nándor Hidegkuti Stadion would now be known as the Marshall Arena. In an era of mass stadium rebuilding, no other country had blitzed through its old sporting landscape quite like Hungary.

Out in Fejér County, in his childhood village of Felcsút, Orbán was planning a new sporting temple of his very own. For here in this rural backwater is where his true loyalties lay: his amateur football team Felcsút FC, for whom he played as a striker until 2005. His summer residence upon whose land the stadium would be built. And the model village which by 2009 was the richest Hungarian settlement by capita. Dismissed by many as a vanity project, an unnecessary spending of funds in a village of barely 1,700 people, controversy beset Orbán's folly from the start. Costing five times the figure allocated to rebuild the stadium of Debrecen, Hungary's most successful 21st-century club, the Pancho Aréna was built at a cost of 3.8bn HUF (approximately £7.9m).

004 // Pancho Aréna
FELCSÚT // HUNGARY // PUSKÁS AKADÉMIA

Back in September 2006, alongside his beloved Felcsút team, Orbán had opened a football academy in the village. Operating similar to a boarding school, it would eventually evolve into the Puskás Akadémia, with the working notion that it would provide players for nearby top-flight club Videoton (now Fehérvár FC). By 2009, Puskás Akadémia, having absorbed Felcsút and their position in the league, were running as the reserve side of Videoton; soon after, they terminated the Videoton cooperation deal and won promotion to Hungary's top flight.

During these few short years, only a handful of players ever made the jump from academy to Videoton while any connections between the academy and the great Ferenc Puskás, who died in late 2006, were spurious to say the least. Supporter groups were vociferous in their loathing of Puskás Akadémia, not least those from Budapest Honvéd who felt cheated by the transfer of the name of their club's greatest player to Felcsút. And then, to top it all, Orbán opened the Pancho Aréna for the team in April 2014, naming it Pancho in reference to the Galloping Major's nickname at Real Madrid. His grandiose pet project to establish his village club as one of Hungary's top teams was complete and within the next decade, Akadémia would become one of the best teams in Hungary; runners-up in 2020/21 and regulars in European club competitions.

We are left with a stadium like no other; a luxury, futuristic sporting venue which wouldn't look out of place on a tour of Gaudí's buildings in Barcelona. Orbán was keen for his stadium to embrace the organic architecture trend of the late 20th century, a movement in stark opposition to the brutal uniformity of old. He employed Imre Makovecz, chief proponent of the movement, who like Frank Lloyd Wright or Rudolf Steiner 100 years earlier was adept at incorporating elements of ancient myth, crafts and folk traditions into his designs. Makovecz's buildings are spread throughout Hungary, many in similarly rural communities. They serve as cultural centres, churches, schools and camping complexes. The Pancho Aréna may well be his greatest achievement.

Standing in absolute harmony with the surrounding fields and horse paddocks, the Pancho Aréna utilises 1,000 tonnes of wood in its roof construction, its crowning glory. Splayed up and outwards from concrete piers, the timber spreads like tree branches to support the roof. Similar to the fanned ribs seen in cathedral vaults, they give the stadium the unique feel of being inside a church which is further enhanced with colourful backlighting during night matches. The roof alone took seven months to construct and is topped with thousands of small, slightly metallic slate tiles. From outside the tiles allow its undulating and low-hanging nature to roll in unison with the surrounding landscape while giving it a shimmering, reflective finish. The base of the stadium is carefully considered too, circular portals within the concrete piers giving the spectator walkways an Escher-like never-ending appearance. It is a staggeringly

Standing in absolute harmony with the surrounding fields and horse paddocks, the Pancho Aréna utilises 1,000 tonnes of wood in its roof construction, its crowning glory.

inventive place, every angle offering a new and surprising perspective.

While it is undeniable that the Pancho Aréna would be better located in a major city where it could be truly appreciated, Orbán's single-mindedness has given Hungary a venue which bucks the modern trend of bland, cost-cutting prefabricated stadiums. Its capacity of just under 4,000 is more than enough for Puskás Akadémia who average under 2,000 each game. It is likely the future of the stadium will be in hosting youth internationals and prestige friendlies for which it is perfectly proportioned. By granting such events to a stadium that simply screams to be seen, it may just begin to justify all that fuss.

003

Stockholms Stadion

STOCKHOLM // SWEDEN // FC STOCKHOLM INTERNAZIONALE

On a Monday evening in late 2022, I went to watch Djurgårdens clinch the Allsvenskan runners-up spot with a win away at Norrköping. Häcken had won the title just 24 hours before and I expected only a despondent few from Stockholm would make the journey. In the 50th minute of the game, 3,000 travelling fans abruptly unleashed a spectacular pyrotechnic display which would result in the game being suspended; dozens of fireworks, black and blue smoke bombs and crimson flares filled the stadium with a thick, acrid fog while the drummers played on. It took almost 15 minutes to clear before play could resume. This was a fanbase expressing themselves in a most visually arresting way, embracing modern football and its visual potential to represent their club.

003 // Stockholms Stadion

STOCKHOLM // SWEDEN // FC STOCKHOLM INTERNAZIONALE

The city's efforts are uncompromising; when a fire destroyed a section of the West Stand in 1954, rather than rebuild in more fire-resistant materials, large amounts of timber from the same source as the original wood were ordered in.

I thought back to my two previous visits to Stockholms Stadion to watch Djurgårdens in the period just before they left to join bitter rivals Hammarby at the new Stockholmsarenan in 2013. In stark contrast, those matches were sedate affairs, fans quietly looking on as if in reverence to their environs, a tangible respectfulness as if too much bouncing on the open terrace could invoke the wrath of the Stadion's old gods – the grave, moustachioed athletes of the past whose statues stand all around. It appeared that Djurgårdens' move in the spirit of progress had breathed a new energy into the club, as European football returned and a league title in 2019 replaced years of middling tedium and the threat of relegation.

And yet, with Djurgårdens' future brighter than it has been in decades, a deep-rooted desire to return to the Stadion – where they played from 1936 – persists. Stockholmers' fiercely traditionalist values are certainly a factor as is a desire among the pan-Stockholm support to return the club to the city centre; it was from Kungliga Djurgården island in central Stockholm that the club took its name. Djurgårdens' offices remain tucked away in wood-panelled rooms within a stately building attached to one of the two castellated towers. In an administrative sense at least, they are still here. In a country refusing to bow to the modern football demands of VAR and goal-line technology, it is a mindset which is at once admirable and refreshing. But whatever the root of Djurgårdens' homesickness, top-flight football and all its trappings of comfort and safety could never realistically be held at the Stadion again. The world's oldest Olympic stadium still in use has barely changed in well over 100 years; its lofty architectural status in the city's consciousness guarantees it will remain this way for the next 100. High-profile athletics meetings continue and therefore Stockholms Stadion still serves the purpose it was built for. The only football played here now is of the third-tier variety with Stockholm Internazionale playing in front of barely 500 people. Among those, a fair portion come simply to feel themselves back inside the stadium.

This collective feeling of pride Stockholmers have for the Stadion cannot be overstated. It regularly features in tourist lists of the city's top architectural attractions alongside Kungliga slottet (Royal Palace) or Stadhuset (City Hall) and within its design, elements of both can be found. Its towers are closely

Its towers are closely related to Stadhuset klocktornet; built one year earlier, its mock-medieval design echoes nearby Gripsholm Castle.

related to Stadhuset klocktornet; built one year earlier, its mock-medieval design echoes nearby Gripsholm Castle. With a growing reputation as one of Sweden's brightest young architects having designed Solliden Palace for the Swedish royal family in 1906, Torben Grut was commissioned to design the Stadion for the 1912 Olympic Games. Young Grut must have been bursting with ideas as the result was a wildly eccentric fairytale; a fortress of arches, tunnels, towers and fantastical motifs.

A copper-roofed canopy, built for King Gustav V and dignitaries in 1912, stands in the centre of the main stand, resembling an oriental pagoda, its golden finials still gleaming. Behind this and back down the steps through the King's entrance, a period-glass telephone kiosk stands, perfectly preserved. Look up from here and there's the copper clock face, keeping perfect time of course, and above it at the summit of the tower, one of two sets of neatly integrated rooftop floodlights. A small concession to modernity. Numerous sets of wrought-iron turnstiles, a pair of turreted gatehouses, arched wooden doorways leading this way and that, a golden crown marking the King's personal gate. Details great and small are everywhere: it would be possible to visit the place 50 times and still discover something pleasingly new on your 51st trip.

With a nod to ancient Greek and Roman amphitheatres, Grut designed the stadium in a horseshoe shape. Like much of Stockholm, it was built using distinctive violet grey Helsingborg brick, making it immediately compatible with its surroundings. Its capacity was always limited – just 22,000 at the time of its grand opening, making it one of the smallest Olympic stadiums ever built. For the Games, a temporary grandstand was erected at the northern end and taken down soon afterwards; in 1958, as football crowds grew, another stand went up here, this time a two-tiered cantilever built from materials sympathetic with the rest of the stadium. The upper tier of this stand was taken down during a series of refurbishments in 2011 and a beautiful arcade of 18 arches built in its place. Now an open terrace sandwiched between the two towers, this is where the Djurgårdens Ultras would gather.

Grut's masterpiece remains the best preserved prewar stadium in Europe, quite probably beyond. Stockholm Municipality's conservation of the stadium is exemplary with a team of maintenance staff permanently on-site, dusting down Nordic symbols embedded in the brickwork, polishing granite busts of long-forgotten athletes and touching up the paintwork on the wooden totem pole roof supports. Even the ivy climbing the main entrance gate is immaculately pruned. The city's efforts are uncompromising; when a fire destroyed a section of the West Stand in 1954, rather than rebuild in more fire-resistant materials, large amounts of timber from the same source as the original wood were ordered in. In 1967, another fire, this time in the East Stand – the same conservational solution.

There is nothing quite like Stockholms Stadion anywhere else. Stadium designers have occasionally flirted with the inclusion of elements of ancient castles at Rotterdam's Het Kasteel and Bristol Municipal Stadium in Tennessee. In Qatar, Al-Shamal Sport Club was built in 2008 to resemble Al Zubara Fort, a historic Qatari military fortress. Such idiosyncratic designs can be a welcome distraction in a world of often uniform modernity. For the nostalgic, Grut's fantasy stadium is the grandfather of them all and is a must-see.

Mestalla

VALENCIA // SPAIN // VALENCIA CF

Valencia's great expansion of the Mestalla between 1997 and 2001 proved to be one of the single most significant stadium upgrades ever undertaken on European shores. It may not have achieved a capacity comparable with Spain's very largest stadiums, and it certainly did not garner plaudits from the world of architecture. Moreover, as time has gone on it has failed to quell continued calls for a replacement (which currently stands in semi-abandonment 3km west). But in the eyes of the humble football fan, the Mestalla did become perhaps the greatest source of wonder in the entire landscape of European football stadiums. Maybe only our final entry and La Bombonera in Buenos Aires hold more weight when it comes to the much overused term 'iconic'.

When club president Paco Roig pressed ahead with his plans for a third tier on top of an already steep-sided bowl, Valencia's home since 1923 was transformed into an implausibly precipitous arena, one which has gone on to frighten the life out of visiting teams and fans alike for over two decades. Surrounding the Mestalla is an almost cultish devotion, disciples from Dublin to Dubrovnik all having stories in the bank of their own experiences in reaching the fabled top rows. Although the Nou Mestalla project has recently been rekindled and earmarked as a potential World Cup venue when Spain co-hosts the tournament in 2030 (and how the nation deserves to), the old girl is likely to be with us for a few years yet. As such, it should not be missed by anyone with even a passing interest in the game.

Back on 20 May 1923, the nascent Valencia opened their new 17,000-capacity Mestalla enclosure with a match against Levante who by ten years are the city's more senior club. This wasn't, however, the club's first home. Between their formation in 1919 and 1923, Valencia had set up on a field behind the Alameda Cavalry

002

AMSTEL
1999
2002
2004
ESTO ES
SKODA
Coca-Cola
TM
divina
seguros
MAIL BOXES ETC.
E-Commerce

barracks on Calle Finlandia, wedged between the headquarters of the Civil Guard and the Estacion de Aragon. El Camp de l'Algirós was rented to Valencia by plot owner Eugenio Miquel for 100 pesetas a month. A donation of 25,000 pesetas from club director Gonzalo Medina (which had been intended for his wedding) was used to erect a fence around the site allowing for Valencia to charge their own entry which for a game on 7 December 1919 against Castalia FC, was 37.5 pesetas. However, with 2,500 members signed up by 1921, the capacity of 8,000 at Algirós and the restrictively narrow pitch (just 47m wide) quickly became a sticking point.

Just two streets and 150m north of Algirós, close to the Mestalla drainage river and bounded by acres of uncultivated land, the club paid 316,000 pesetas for the plot upon which their temple would be built. Club member Francisco Almenar Quinzá was given the task of designing the first incarnation of the Mestalla which by 14 June 1925 was deemed fit to stage an international between Spain and Italy. Further prestige was to come when by virtue of its neutrality and location equidistant between Barcelona and Madrid, the Mestalla was selected to host three Copa del Rey finals before the outbreak of the Second World War. However, devastated during the Spanish Civil War and hastily reconstructed for its postwar opening on 18 June 1939, it was never going to be sufficient for a club who were about to embark on their first golden era with three La Liga titles between 1942 and 1948. In 1950 club president Luis Casanova Giner decided it was time to go large. Very large. In doing so, the Mestalla began to take on the distinctive appearance we see today.

Casanova brought in architect Salvador Pascual Gimeno to oversee the stadium's complete overhaul. Two towering new stands went up at the north and south ends and then in 1954, perhaps recognising the competition in Barcelona where work was just starting on Camp Nou, Gimeno began construction on a new grandstand. Even today, looking down upon Gimeno's colossal, now rusted cantilever roof from the Mestalla's third tiers, the daring scale of the structure is unmistakable, not least because without any supporting columns it appears to hover in space. When the Valencian public first laid eyes on it on 27 December 1955, they would surely have been filled with a mixture of both wonder and terror. Alongside, two art deco-styled media towers were added level with the stand's second tier. Development continued until the end of the decade when floodlights were switched on for an Inter-Cities Fairs Cup match against Reims in 1959.

Known as Estadio Luis Casanova between 1969 and 1994, the Mestalla's next momentous revamp began in 1978 in readiness for the World Cup of 1982 where Spain would play each of their three group games at the stadium. Squeezed by the multiple apartment blocks that had shot up in the intervening 50 years and an annexe of the town hall, the Mestalla had nowhere to go other than up (as it would under Paco Roig two decades later) or down. Architects Salvador and Manuel Pascual boldly went down, excavating an estimated 3m below the existing pitch level to create a whole new tier with 20 rows of seating. The capacity remained at 50,000 but fans were delighted with the stadium's new total of 33,053 seats.

At the turn of the millennium, Valencia became a household name across Europe, runners-up in the 2000/01 Champions League Final, two-times La Liga champions and UEFA Cup winners in 2003/04. Roig's third tier had gone on and the club quite reasonably believed they were about to frequently challenge the Barcelona and Madrid stranglehold. For this to happen, a new stadium was needed and in 2006 plans for a 75,000-capacity venue in the city's north-western Benicalap suburb were unveiled. Although fans were up in arms over the imminent loss of their beloved home, work on the €344m Nou Mestalla began on 1 August 2007 but as if in protest, the team was about to have its worst season on the pitch in almost 20 years. With no Champions League football, worse was to follow when in 2008 four construction workers died after scaffolding on one of the ten main towers collapsed. Valencia's debt spiralled to over €500m and by 2009, the half-built shell of the Nou Mestalla was abandoned.

And so, as perennial mid-tablers, Valencia plod on at their home which in 2024 reached its centenary. Besides the gargantuan height of its stands, the Mestalla's enduring appeal lies in its ability to transport fans back to a time when the idea of supporter comfort was a toilet floor not overflowing with urine. Although we have thankfully made progress from that, it is European football's greatest symbol of an era when people went to a ground just to watch the match, without all the distractions of the 21st-century game we have come to expect. There is no sentimentality in this. Valencia's Mestalla is simply the ultimate footballing throwback and a great one at that.

Valencia's great expansion of the Mestalla between 1997 and 2001 proved to be one of the single most significant stadium upgrades ever undertaken on European shores.

Stadio Giuseppe Meazza

MILAN // ITALY // AC MILAN & INTERNAZIONALE

While every entrant, absence and numerical placing in this top 100 is of course open to debate, I suspect our number one will satisfy most readers. For over 30 years Milan's Stadio Giuseppe Meazza has evolved in the collective imagination of supporters to become arguably the most iconic stadium of all. When in September 2022 the San Siro was handed its death sentence, the shockwaves were felt from Tokyo to Tbilisi. The news triggered an outpouring of emotion hitherto unseen for the loss of a football stadium and as the countdown began, so did the frenzied scramble for match tickets.

However, just shy of a year later common sense prevailed when the Lombardy Commission for Cultural Heritage slapped a label of 'cultural significance' on *La Scala*. Ticket prices reverted back to as little as €5 and both the Municipality of Milan and its two clubs were forced back to the drawing board. While the San Siro as a football stadium is not out of the woods yet, its selection as the host venue for the opening ceremony of the Milano Cortina 2026 Winter Olympic Games bodes well. And while both Inter and AC Milan are still both keen on their new stadium projects in Rozzano and San Donato respectively, it is hoped that after seeing the visualisations of the renovated stadium both will change their minds.

Everyone will have their own favourite memories of the San Siro. For me, West Germany's Lothar Matthäus setting alight the Italia '90 World Cup, prompting TV cameras to pan across its enormous scale, is one. More than just memories, however, the San Siro in 1990 represents the end of an old world and the beginning of a new, a goodbye to the muddled, tragedy-blighted 1980s and hello to a new era of the Taylor Report, television revenue and the beginning of the game's stratospheric rise in popularity. AC Milan with their Dutch Holy Trinity, Paolo Maldini and the £13m world-record transfer of Gianluigi Lentini (which the Vatican described as 'an offence to the dignity of work'), were busy ripping up the rulebook and tearing up the European game. Soon after, they would kick-start an unceasing movement that would see hundreds of scouting missions descend on Africa in search of the next George Weah. Meanwhile, in bedrooms up and down the United Kingdom, the fascination with the Italian game escalated wildly when the *Football Italia* show hit television screens in 1992. Paul Gascoigne left for Lazio and David Platt had signed for Bari in the summer of 1991. Always at the centre of it all seemed to be the San Siro, unlovely yet so glamorous in the way some may imagine their favourite band's backstage to be.

001 // Stadio Giuseppe Meazza
MILAN // ITALY // AC MILAN & INTERNAZIONALE

In 1955, three years after Rome's Stadio Olimpico was reconstructed and rechristened briefly as Stadio dei Centomila, Milan opened the turnstiles to their own remodelled San Siro. They too had envisaged their stadium as being roomy enough to hold 100,000 which itself was a downsizing from the original plans drafted in 1947 (the year Inter departed the dear old Arena Civica to move in). Then it was planned to transform the San Siro into a whopping 150,000-capacity stadium spread across three tiers. In the end a more realistic target of 82,000 was achieved but it was the new layout which really caught the imagination. Nineteen helical ramps had been wrapped around the exterior walls to take spectators on a journey around the stadium and up to their chosen spot in the second tier. Innovative and attractive, the stadium now had the template for its next big change when the World Cup came calling in 1990.

By 1987 it had been renamed in honour of the great Giuseppe Meazza, a player the International Federation of Football History & Statistics in conjunction with FIFA selected as one of the 25 best on its list, World Players of the 20th Century. Yet by this stage it was a dilapidated shadow of its former self and with or without Italia '90, it was in dire need of renovation. FIFA's requirement for the tournament was for stadiums to be all-seated and for hosting the opening ceremony, a minimum capacity of 80,000. This left San Siro short by 13,000 seats and so in order to keep pace with Rome (which had been given the final), Milan set in motion its astonishing plan to take the arena up into the heavens.

It is said that a building is a stage. This one had become the world's stage and its very favourite. If you're going to go big and funds are available, you may as well go monumental.

Before the world's eyes turned on Milan, Italians had tuned in on television in their millions to watch the four load-bearing girders being lowered on to four new cylindrical corner towers. Another 4,000 watched from the ground, captivated by the suspense of the operation for over four hours. Of all San Siro's components it is the enormous red girders that are most recognisable. Visible from the city centre 8km away, the aesthetic value they bring to the otherwise colourless exterior is immeasurable. If four hulking lumps of steel can have iconic status it is these. The proximity of the adjacent racecourse dictated that the stadium's eastern side was left at two tiers which with a little luck gave San Siro another of its plentiful idiosyncrasies: an enormous frame through which on a clear day it is just possible to spot the distant statue of Madonnina perched atop Milan's Duomo cathedral.

001 // Stadio Giuseppe Meazza
MILAN // ITALY // AC MILAN & INTERNAZIONALE

12

001 // Stadio Giuseppe Meazza

MILAN // ITALY // AC MILAN & INTERNAZIONALE

Of all San Siro's components it is the enormous red girders that are most recognisable. Visible from the city centre 8km away, the aesthetic value they bring to the otherwise colourless exterior is immeasurable.

That World Cup would become one of the most-watched events in television history with an estimated 26 billion non-unique viewers. Opening the tournament on 8 June 1990, the San Siro pitch was briefly transformed into a virtual catwalk as Milan delivered an extravaganza of fashion, football and global unity. On the same pitch a few hours later, African football finally arrived when Cameroon beat Diego Maradona's Argentina.

It is said that a building is a stage. This one had become the world's stage and its very favourite. If you're going to go big and funds are available, you may as well go monumental. Oversize it, challenge the status quo and if needs must, irk the purists. Four thousand tonnes of raw steel and a small town's worth of bare concrete? Don't clad it, show it off! Fortune favours the brave and in the next few years we will find out whether Milan is brave enough to keep alive Europe's greatest football ground.

Reference books

100 Jahre Ellenfeld-Stadion: Vom Borussia-Sportplatz zum Erinnerungsort, Tobias Fuchs and Jens Kelm, 2012

100 Jahre Fußball in Tiefenort: 1913–2013, Ralf Magdeburg, 2013

All Played Out: The Full Story of Italia '90, P.C.W. Davies, Random House, 1991

Behind the Curtain - Travels in Eastern European Football, Jonathan Wilson, Orion, 2006

Betzenberg: 100 Jahre zwischen Himmel und Hölle, Dominic Bold, *Die Werkstatt GmbH, 2020*

British Football's Greatest Grounds: One Hundred Must-see Football Venues, Mike Bayly, Pitch Publishing, 2020

Building the Yellow Wall, Uli Hesse, W&N, 2019

C'era una volta a San Siro: Vita, calci e miracoli, Gianfelice Facchetti, Edizione Piemme, 2021

Eibar the Brave: The Extraordinary Rise of La Liga's Smallest Team Euan McTear, Pitch Publishing, 2015

Engineering Archie: Archibald Leitch - Football Ground Designer, Simon Inglis, Historic England, 2005

European Fields, Hans van der Meer, StiedlMACK, 2006

Football League Grounds for a Change, Dave Twydell, 1991

Fotbalové stadiony v České republice, Tomáš Habrcetl, Eurogreen, 2001

From Partition to Solidarity: The First 100 years of Polish Football, Ryan Hubbard, 2019

Generazione Wunderteam: The Rise and Fall of Austria's Wonder Team, Jo Araf, Pitch Publishing, 2021

Great Yarmouth's Sporting Heritage: The Early Years, David Tubby, 2013

Gümüşhane, Bünyamin Aygün, İskenderiye Yayınları, 2009

Histoire d'un Grand Club: L'Union Saint-Gilloise, Emmanuel Leroy, 1998

Icelandic Football: In the Land of Fire 2018, Marc Boal, 2018

Inside the Hermit Kingdom: Football Stories from Stalinist Albania, Phil Harrison, Pitch Publishing, 2024

Kantrida Bijelih Snova, Marinko Lazzarich, Adamić, 2008

Lifted Over the Turnstiles: Scotland's Football Grounds in the Black & White Era, Steve Finan, D.C. Thomson & Co. Ltd, 2018

Magical Magyars: The Rise and Fall of the World's Once Greatest Football Team, David Bailey, Pitch Publishing, 2019

Morbo: The Story of Spanish Football, Phil Ball, WSC Books, 2011

Offside, Jurgen Vantomme, Lannoo, 2015

Olympiastadion Berlin und Olympisches Dorf Elstal, Martin Kaule, Christoph Links Verlag, 2014

Played in Glasgow: Charting the heritage of a city at play, Ged O'Brien, Historic Scotland, 2010

Played In Germany - A Footballing Journey Through a Nation's Soul, Kit Holden, Duckworth, 2024

Sampdoria: La grande storia della tifoseria blucerchiata, Francesca Galleano, Editrice ZONA, 2023

Storia del Calcio a Tricarico e Vicende Della Società AS Tricarico, Giuseppe Selvaggi, RCE, 2020

Tapas en Verde Y Blanco: Conoce las 150 Tapas de los mejores Futbolistas del la Historia del Real Betis Balompie, José Antonio Campos Martín, 2017

The Balkans, Mark Mazower, Phoenix, 2002

The Faroes: The Faraway Islands, Anthony Jackson, Robert Hale, 1991

The Football Grounds of Europe, Simon Inglis, Collins Willow, 1990

The Football Grounds of England and Wales, Simon Inglis, Collins Willow, 1983

The Game, Stuart Roy Clarke, The Bluecoat Press, 2018

The Land of Maybe: A Faroe Islands Year, Tim Ecott, Short Books, 2021

The People's Game: Football, State and Society in East Germany, Alan McDougall, Cambridge University Press, 2016

There's A Green Sward Called the Oval, Sam Robinson, 2016

Tor! The Story of German Football, Uli Hesse, Polaris, 2022

Últimes vesprades a Mestalla - Segona Part, Editorial Samaruc, 2016

Va-Va Voom - The Modern History of French Football, Tom Williams, Bloomsbury, 2024

Photo credits

Thanks

So many people from across Europe have volunteered both time and knowledge to help bring the stories of these football grounds to life. From librarians and local archive staff to club historians and countless supporters wanting to share a lifetime of memories, without your invaluable input this project would not have been possible let alone half as interesting as it was to undertake:

Ágúst Örlaugur Magnússon
Alex White
Alexander Krassimirov
Alistair Joyce
Andy Potts
Arli Kokalari
Arno Bucher
Barbara Smith
Bas Tukker
Bob Foulkes
Bogdan Chiritescu
Brian Livie
Cam Waterhouse
Cristina Nascimento
Daniel Hager
Dave Harry
Davit Tchintcharauli
Dimitar Shopov
Eliza Spruntule
Emanuel Roşu
Ertürk Yakut
Fabian Pertschy
Fabio Betulli
Ferenc Szabó
Franco Segarra
George Kourelis
Georges Rouah
Giovanni Minieri
Göran Janson
Graham Kenworthy
Han Balk
Haraldur Pálsson
Heiko and Astrid Adler
Herma Hinnen
Ilia Ivanov
Jacques Davier
James Rendall
Jan Erik Simonsen
Jason Dickinson
João Melo
Joris van de Wier
Jovan Kliska
Jens Kelm
Jens-Uwe Hanssen
Jim Proudfoot
Jiří Fišara
Jock Gardiner
Justin Walley
Julian King
Konstantin Kapchin
Leonardo Aleotti
Les Chappell
Lidija Vrhovac
Luis María Garcés
Luka Kolovrat
Luka Lagvilava
Maarten Verdoodt
Mannie Cannon
Marc Boal
Marc Verlinden
Mark Donnelly
Marcin Fastyn
Massimo Moscardi
Matthias Löffler
Michael Siegesmund
Moni Georgiev
Niall McGilp
Nick Davis
Nils Ek
Njörður Sigurðsson
Noud Leermakers
Patrick Reddering
Pedro Pajuelo
Peter Miles
Petur Simonsen
Prof. Paolo Giacomel
Robert Guruian
Ronny Edvardsen
Sam Robinson
Slaven Bošnjak
Sóley Guðmundsdóttir
Steinar Green Hansen
Stephen MacDonald
Taneli Okkonen
Terje Mollestad
Thanos Michael
Thomas Glöy
Thomas Holland
Thomas Waerness
Tomáš Komara
Unnar Magnusson
Vito Sacco
Yves van Ackeleyen

On a personal note I would also like to thank those who went that extra mile and those whose ongoing support and encouragement got this book over the line without the need for VAR:

David Kuipers, Jano Zatiashvili, Les Leedham (RIP), Mike Bayly, Phil Harrison and Simon Inglis.

And finally, thanks and love to my biggest supporters who between them have been dragged from Armenia to the Arctic Circle: Hannah, Noah and Elle.